ALL-AMERICAN

Low-Fat
and No-Fat
Meals in Minutes

**300 Delicious Recipes and
Menus for Special Occasions or
Every Day—In 30 Minutes or Less**

SECOND EDITION

M.J. SMITH, RD

★ ★ ★

CHRONIMED
PUBLISHING

All-American Low-Fat and No-Fat Meals in Minutes, Second Edition
© 1990, 1997 by M.J. Smith.

Library of Congress Cataloging-in-Publication Data

All-American low-fat and no-fat meals in minutes, second edition/ M.J. Smith

      p.   cm.

Includes index.

ISBN 1-56561-101-2: $14.95

Edited by: Jolene Steffer
Cover Design: Terry Dugan Design
Text Design & Production: David Enyeart
Art/Production Manager: Claire Lewis

Printed in the United States of America

Published by
Chronimed Publishing
P.O. Box 59032
Minneapolis, MN 55459-9686

10   9   8   7   6   5   4   3   2

Table of Contents

★ ★ ★

Foreword. v

Acknowledgments vii

Author Biography. viii

The All-American Low-Fat Diet 1

Lowering Blood Cholesterol 5

Weight Loss—Why Calories Still Count 17

How to Take Fat Out of the American Diet. 25

If You Have Diabetes 71

Spring & Summer

A Month of Low-Fat Dinner Menus 76

A Week of Breakfast and Lunch Menus. 78

Special Occasion Menus for Spring and Summer. 80

Appetizers and Beverages. 83

Breads. 94

Salads 103

Main-Dish Salads and Casseroles 125

Poultry and Fish 157

Red Meats. 174

Vegetables and Starches 184

Desserts 199

Fall & Winter

A Month of Low-Fat Dinner Menus 226

A Week of Breakfast and Lunch Menus. 228

Special Occasion Menus for Fall and Winter. 230

Appetizers and Beverages. 234

Soups and Stews 252

Breads. 266

Main-Dish Salads and Casseroles 290

Salads 306

Poultry, Fish and Game. 317

Red Meats. 342

Vegetables and Starches 356

Desserts 371

References. 397

Index 399

Foreword

Overheard in the dietitian's office..."I'm wondering how many of these low-fat potato chips I can eat." "Can you give me two weeks worth of low-fat low-calorie menus?" "Does alcohol have any fat grams?" "How many grams of saturated fat can I eat and still control my cholesterol?" "Losing weight is important to me, but my family loves good food."

The low-fat diet revolution is in full swing, and people have more questions than ever before. This book was written to help people answer all kinds of questions about dietary fat and to translate the low-fat lifestyle into interesting menus and good food. Even if you don't have a weight or cholesterol problem, a low-fat diet is nutrition insurance—one of the best prescriptions for good health.

For fifteen years I have been helping people modify their family's favorite casseroles and plan birthday parties without butter creme frosting. Each of the more than 300 recipes in this book has been thoughtfully developed using common ingredients, and most require less than 30 minutes of hands-on preparation. My family and friends have served as official taste testers, and they have enjoyed the job. I am the first to admit that fat-free cream cheese doesn't pass muster in the "mouthfeel" department, and you'll see that I've used small amounts of the 50 percent reduced-fat stuff to protect taste.

This cookbook is unique because, beyond the winning menus and tasty recipes, you can use this book as an all-in-one nutrition reference. Look up the fat grams in eggs, the saturated fat in ground beef, or the type of kitchen gadget recommended for low-fat steaming. Find out the benefits of the Mediterranean Diet Pyramid, learn about the science of low-fat food flavor, or find out how dietitians evaluate the new fat substitutes.

Low-fat eating is not going out of style any time soon. The diet strategy tops the list of nutrition tips from cancer, coronary, and government health experts alike. Even fine restaurants are becoming a low-fat playground where chefs practice new ways to extract honest flavor with lean cooking techniques such as roasting and smoking, and coating foods with herb crusts. This book represents a world-class collection of recipes and topics to refine your appreciation for the feel-good, taste-good quality of a low-fat diet.

M.J. Smith, M.A., R.D., L.D.
Registered Dietitian

Notice:
Consult your Health Care Professional

Readers are advised to seek the guidance of a licensed physician or health care professional before making any changes in prescribed health care regimens, as each individual case or need may vary. This book is intended for informational purposes only and is not for use as an alternative to appropriate medical care. While every effort has been made to ensure that the information is the most current available, new research findings, being released with increasing frequency, may invalidate some research.

Acknowledgments

★ ★ ★

Thanks to my mother, Mary Agnes Budweg Rewoldt, for teaching me how to cook; to my husband, Dr. Andrew Smith; and to my friends for their research and review of this book. It is dedicated to the hundreds of clients who have shared questions and frustrations and who have made my work fun.

Author Biography

★ ★ ★

M.J. Smith, M.A., R.D., L.D. is a dietitian and cookbook author residing in Guttenberg, Iowa.

The first edition of *All-American Low-Fat Meals in Minutes,* Ms. Smith's first cookbook, ushered in '90s style low-fat cooking. Her subsequent titles include: *60 Days of Low-Fat, Low-Cost Meals in Minutes; 366 Low-Fat Brand-Name Recipes in Minutes; The Miracle Foods Cookbook; Year-Round Low-Fat & No-Fat Holiday Meals in Minutes;* and *Around the World Low-Fat and No-Fat Meals in Minutes.*

Ms. Smith continues to test recipes and evaluate food products, perfecting the low-fat food style for all-American taste with the help of her clients, friends, and family. Readers can correspond with her via her website, All American Low Fat Kitchen, at http://agmall.com/lowfatkitchen.

She lives in a rural Mississippi River community with her husband, Dr. Andrew Smith, a family physician, and her two children, Frederic and Elizabeth. Her time away from the kitchen is spent as a leader/teacher in Stephen's Ministry, a Christian program for caring for one another, within her Lutheran church.

Her favorite all-American foods are barbecued chicken, sweet and sour cucumbers, and fresh raspberry pie.

The All-American Low-Fat Diet

★ ★ ★

Nearly everyone is trying to control fat. Whether you're a power walker, a gourmet cook, or a meat and potatoes type, chances are you're working toward reducing your fat intake. Low-fat diets have been in vogue since the late 1980s when health experts advised them for weight loss, cholesterol control, and cancer risk reduction. Now there's a new wrinkle in the low-fat story: In a two-year study published in the *New England Journal of Medicine,* researchers found that skin cancer patients following diets with no more than 20 percent of calories from fat developed 70 percent fewer precancerous lesions than a similar group whose diet remained about 36 percent fat. So whether you're taking care of your skin, your heart, or your waistline, a low-fat eating style is health insurance that tastes good!

But what about taste? How can low-fat food really taste good? The science of taste is being appreciated more and more as dietitians focus on what clients perceive as pleasurable food. Taste refers to our ability to perceive four qualities: salt, sugar, sour, and bitter. These are chemical messages in foods that come in contact with taste receptors on our tongue's taste buds. Our ability to perceive a taste occurs when the chemical message is translated into a nervous signal that travels to our brain via the cranial nerve. The concept of taste and flavor are very similar, and we cannot perceive flavor without smelling the food. Odor chemicals are translated into nervous signals at the olfactory bulb (located behind the bridge of the nose) and reach the brain via the cranial nerve. We experience smells through the nostrils, but also through our mouths. This second release of odor happens when we put a food in our mouth and chew it. Chewing releases odorants in the food and creates pressure that pumps the odorants up through the oral cavity to the olfactory receptors in the nose. We know that both genetics and conditioning influence our preference for particular flavors. As a cookbook author, I have worked to perfect recipes that have intense pleasant flavors; and though palates and preferences vary widely, these recipes combine color, texture, presentation, and aroma that promote enjoyable nourishment.

As a dietitian, I have found that staying with a low-fat eating style is easier if the family cook has a slingshot full of low-fat tricks to ensure delicious food for the whole gang. It seems we start healthy food habits so easily on Monday morning, but somehow by Wednesday night, the fat has crept back in. I would challenge readers to write down the family's *Top 10 Menus*. It might be pizza, spaghetti, tacos, chicken, meat loaf, lasagna, egg casserole, or pancakes; then just look up how many of them are in this book.

But before you get to the recipes, this book will tell you how a low-fat diet fits with the *Dietary Guidelines for Americans* and the American Cancer Society's *Ten Steps to Reduce Cancer Risk*. Next comes the theory and prescription for lowering cholesterol and losing weight. You will also better understand the differences in the types of fat, food labels, and food pyramids; and learn how to find low-fat foods and snacks at the fast food restaurant, supermarket, or wherever.

Have fun becoming an expert at answering all of the questions about fat in the American diet.

What do the Dietary Guidelines for Americans say about fat?

Issued jointly by the U.S. Department of Agriculture and Health and Human Services, the fourth edition of the Dietary Guidelines for Americans was released in 1995 and advises:

1. **Eat a variety of foods.**
2. **Balance the food you eat with physical activity**
   —maintain or improve your weight.

3. **Choose a diet with plenty of grain products, vegetables, and fruits.**
4. **Choose a diet low in fat, saturated fat, and cholesterol.**
   This guideline emphasizes that no more than 30 percent of total calories come from fat. However, it does not apply to infants and toddlers below the age of 2 years. After 2 years of age, the guideline recommends that children gradually adopt a diet that, by about 5 years of age, contains no more than 30 percent of calories from fat.
5. **Choose a diet moderate in sugars.**
6. **Choose a diet moderate in salt and sodium.**
7. **If you drink alcoholic beverages, do so in moderation.**
   Moderate consumption is defined as a maximum of one drink per day for women and two drinks per day for men. These are the same levels that research has shown to be protective against coronary heart disease.

American Cancer Society Advises Low-Fat Diet in Ten Steps to Reduce Cancer Risk

1. **Eat more cabbage-family vegetables;** these appear to protect from colorectal, stomach, and respiratory cancers.
2. **Add more high-fiber foods to protect against colon cancer.**
3. **Choose foods with vitamin A** for protection against cancers of the esophagus, larynx, and lung.
4. **Do the same with vitamin C,** which protects against esophagus and stomach cancers.
5. **Control your weight,** as obesity is linked to cancers of the uterus, gallbladder, breast, and colon.
6. **Trim fat from your diet** to decrease risk of breast, colon, and prostate cancer. Let's face it, besides clogging up our arteries, many high-fat foods are dense and filling. They don't leave much room for vegetables, grains, and fruits—the prime sources of fiber and vitamins that protect us from cancer.
7. **Subtract salt-cured, smoked, and nitrite-cured foods from the diet.**

8. Stop cigarette smoking.
9. Go easy on alcohol.
10. Respect the sun's rays.

The Food Guide Pyramid Limits Fat

The Food Guide Pyramid is a simple picture for making low-fat food choices. The pyramid calls for eating a variety of foods to get the nutrients you need while eating the right amount of calories to maintain a healthy weight. Each of the food groups provides some, but not all, of the nutrients you need. Foods in one group cannot replace another. Americans are encouraged to consume more servings from the base of the Pyramid, working toward a very sparing intake of fats and oils. This small tip of the pyramid includes salad dressings, oils, cream, butter, margarine, candies, and sweet desserts. Fatty and sweet foods are a concentrated source of calories. In addition, very small amounts of fats and oils can meet our need for linoleic acid (an essential fatty acid) and vitamin E.

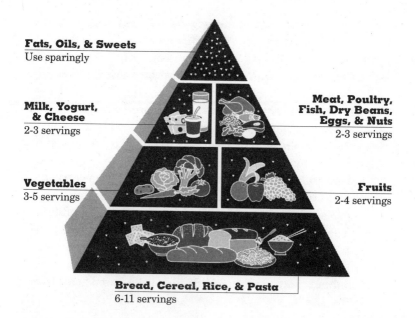

Fats, Oils, & Sweets
Use sparingly

Milk, Yogurt, & Cheese
2-3 servings

Meat, Poultry, Fish, Dry Beans, Eggs, & Nuts
2-3 servings

Vegetables
3-5 servings

Fruits
2-4 servings

Bread, Cereal, Rice, & Pasta
6-11 servings

Lowering Blood Cholesterol

★ ★ ★

Reducing blood cholesterol is a first defense in reducing heart disease, America's leading cause of death. Nutrition scientists began studying fat and cholesterol in food 20 years ago when high levels of cholesterol were found in the blood of men who had heart disease. For the past two decades, Americans have tried to make sense of their own blood cholesterol levels and adopt diet strategies to keep them at desirable levels. As a practicing dietitian, I have been through the fish oil craze, the oat bran revolution, and the French paradox along with my clients striving to reduce blood cholesterol. But through it all, a low saturated fat diet has come through as the primary diet remedy for keeping blood cholesterol levels in check. Let's review some basics.

Cholesterol, a fatty, waxy, soapy substance that circulates in the blood, is a necessary part of mammal physiology. It's a precursor, or beginning form, of many hormones. It's also involved in the formation of bile acids, which are needed for digestion. Cholesterol is widely distributed through the body and is an essential component of all cell membranes. It only becomes a problem when our livers begin producing too much of it from saturated fat in foods that we eat.

Too much cholesterol in the blood leads to clogging of arteries and veins, a disease known as atherosclerosis. This clogging process starts when cholesterol becomes too concentrated in the blood and starts precipitating out. It's much like trying to stir a cup of salt into a cup of water. The salt is too concentrated and ends up collecting at the bottom of the glass.

When cholesterol is too concentrated in the blood, it is deposited on the sides of arteries and veins. Minerals, such as calcium, are then attracted to the affected areas. These minerals form a hard "plaque" that narrows the blood vessel, reduces its flexibility, and slows blood flow. Heart attack and stroke can follow.

Physicians use the following range to define blood cholesterol risks:

Less than 200 mg/dl is desirable or low risk
(mg/dl refers to milligrams of cholesterol present in
1 deciliter of blood)
200 to 240 mg/dl is borderline high risk
More than 240 mg/dl is high risk

If your blood cholesterol is over 200 mg/dl, a diet low in saturated fat and cholesterol is the first recommended treatment. In addition, your physician will look at your lipid profile. This is a laboratory test that examines the types of cholesterol that make up the total.

High density lipoprotein cholesterol, commonly known as HDL, is protective. That is, levels above the normal range are associated with low cardiac risk. HDL carries cholesterol away from body tissues and back to the liver so it can be eliminated from the body. If your HDL cholesterol is above 35 mg/dl, that is desirable. There is no magic dietary bullet to raise HDL, but a sustained program of aerobic exercise will help.

Low density lipoprotein cholesterol, commonly known as LDL, is dangerous. LDL cholesterol levels above normal are associated with increased risk of heart disease. LDL cholesterol carries cholesterol from the liver to other tissues and forms deposits on the blood vessel walls. If you do not have coronary artery disease and your LDL cholesterol is above 160 milligrams/dl, that is worrisome. If you have coronary artery disease and your LDL is above 130 mg/dl, that is equally worrisome.

My patients remember the difference between the two types of cholesterol by thinking of HDL as the "happy" kind, and LDL as the "lousy" kind.

A common way to evaluate your lipid profile is to use the ratio of total cholesterol to HDL cholesterol. The American Heart

Association recommends that the ratio be 5.1 or lower, with the optimum ratio being 3.5. The ratio is obtained by dividing the HDL cholesterol level into the total cholesterol.

For example, if my total cholesterol is 200 mg/dl and my HDL cholesterol is 45 mg/dl, the ratio is 4.4. Ask your physician about your lipid profile and your ratio of total cholesterol to HDL.

The primary treatment for high blood cholesterol is a diet low in saturated fat. Saturated fat is the raw material for cholesterol manufacturing in the liver. It is different from cholesterol in foods. The cholesterol you eat in foods was once manufactured by an animal and stored in the animal's fatty tissue. For example, chickens manufacture cholesterol and store it in the yolk of eggs. Cows store cholesterol in the fat next to their muscle tissue. When you eat these animal foods, you eat that stored animal cholesterol.

However, a far more important factor is that your body produces its own cholesterol in the liver from saturated fats that you eat. Even if you ate no cholesterol from animals, your body could make it out of the saturated fat found in fatty animal products and the tropical plant oils used in processed and fast foods.

Doubly troublesome saturated fat and cholesterol are found in many of the same foods. We find them in eggs, whole-milk products, and fatty meats. In addition, saturated fat is found in the tropical plant oils used in commercial baking and frying. To reduce the amount of circulating cholesterol, avoid these foods:

Visible or marbled fat in beef, veal, lamb, and pork
Poultry skin and fat
Butter, cream, and whole milk
Products made from cream and whole milk, such as
   cheese and ice cream
Solid shortening
Coconut oil
Cocoa butter
Palm and palm kernel oil
Hydrogenated fats and oils (These oils are changed from
   their natural liquid form to become more solid.)

The American Heart Association advises that no more than 10 percent of total calories come from saturated sources. Instead, polyunsaturated and monounsaturated fats should be used.

This translates to a saturated fat limit of 12 to 15 grams a day for adults working to lower their blood cholesterol. The following list shows the amount of saturated fat in common foods.

Pocket Guide to Saturated Fat Grams

FOOD	SERVING SIZE	SATURATED FAT (G)
Fruits	1/2 cup	0
Avocado	1 medium	5
Potato, plain	1 medium	0
Hash browns	1 patty	4
French fries, baked	10 pieces	2
Vegetables, plain	1/2 cup	0
Whole milk	1 cup	5
2% milk	1 cup	3
1% milk	1 cup	2
Skim milk	1 cup	0
2% low-fat yogurt	1 cup	3
Nonfat yogurt	1 cup	0
Creamy cottage cheese	1 cup	3
Low-fat cottage cheese	1 cup	2
Cheddar cheese	1 ounce	6
Part-skim mozzarella	1 ounce	4
American cheese	1 ounce	4
Ice cream	1/2 cup	9
Fat-free ice milk	1/2 cup	0
Trimmed beef arm roast	3 ounces	6
Trimmed pork rib	3 ounces	6
90% lean ground beef	3 ounces	4
Hot dog	1	6
Skinless chicken breast	3 ounces	1
Halibut fillet, broiled	3 ounces	0
Crab legs, steamed	2 medium	0
Large egg	1	2

FOOD	SERVING SIZE	SATURATED FAT (G)
Butter	1 teaspoon	2
Stick margarine	1 teaspoon	1
Diet margarine	1 teaspoon	<1
Canola oil	1 teaspoon	<1
Coconut oil	1 teaspoon	4
Mayonnaise	1 teaspoon	1
Sour cream	1 tablespoon	2
Light cream	1 tablespoon	1
Cream cheese	1 ounce	6
Chocolate bar	1.5 ounces	5-7
Taco chips	1 ounce	2
Caramel popcorn	3 cups	12
Microwave popcorn	3 cups	2
Potato chips	1 ounce	2
Fast Foods		
Biscuit	1	3
Sausage/egg biscuit	1	11
Beef cheese burrito	1	8
Chicken fillet sandwich	1	5
1/4 lb. cheeseburger	1	14
Canadian bacon pizza	1/4 of 12"	4-8
Supreme pizza	1/4 of 12"	14
Milk shake	1	4

Check the label of your favorite foods for saturated fat grams.
Record them below:

_____

_____

_____

_____

_____

_____

Adults working to lower cholesterol: limit saturated fat to 12
to 15 grams/day.

If you are serious about reducing cholesterol, consider keeping a food diary of saturated fat intake, like the one shown below. For help with portion sizes of foods, see the following section.

Counting Saturated Fat Grams

Food Intake Record

Date ___Monday___

FOOD/BEVERAGE	SATURATED FAT (G)
1 raisin bagel	0
1 teaspoon tub margarine	1
8 ounces orange juice	0
1/2 cup tuna	0
1 teaspoon fat-free mayonnaise	0
8 Wheat Thins	1
1 tomato	0
2 slices Canadian bacon pizza	8
1 cup skim milk	0
2 slices watermelon	0
	10 grams

Limit: 12/day

Estimating Portion Sizes

Reducing your cholesterol level by tracking saturated fat means being diligent with your food diary and measuring food accurately. Use the following information to help you:

Meats:

1/4 cup of ground meat = 1 ounce

1 regular slice of lunch meat or 3 thin slices = 1 ounce

1 piece of cooked meat, the size of a deck of cards = 3 ounces

1/2 chicken breast = 3 ounces

1 shrimp = 0.5 ounces

1 chicken drumstick = 2 ounces

Three Types of Fat

Saturated fat intake and its link to the heart has been our focus so far. However, there are two other friendlier types of fat that we eat. The three types are defined by the fatty acids present. These fatty acids have distinctive chemical makeups and are presented below:

SATURATED FAT

Physical Properties: Solid at room temperature. **Sources:** Lard, palm kernel oil, palm oil, cocoa butter, shortenings, stick margarines, fat in red meat, fat in dairy foods such as butter, fat in whole or 2% milk. **Health Link:** Avoid or limit to 12-15 grams/day, linked to prostate and colon cancer

POLYUNSATURATED FAT

Physical Properties: Liquid at room temperature. **Sources:** Corn oil, safflower oil, sunflower oil, cottonseed oil, liquid margarine. **Health Link:** Type of fat preferred in cholesterol-lowering diets; use prudently to control total fat.

MONOUNSATURATED FAT

Physical Properties: Liquid at room temperature. **Sources:** Olive oil, canola oil, almonds, hazelnuts. **Health Link:** Type of fat preferred in cholesterol-lowering diets; use prudently to control total fat; contains protective antioxidants

Most foods contain a combination of the three types. The following chart compares common oils with regard to the type of fat present.

Comparing Dietary Fats

Dietary Fat	Cholesterol (mg/tbsp)	Sat. fat fat	Polyunsat. fat	Monounsat. fat	Linoleic Acid
Canola oil	0	6%	22%	10%	62%
Safflower oil	0	10%	77%	trace	13%
Sunflower oil	0	11%	69%	20%	
Corn oil	0	13%	61%	1%	25%
Olive oil	0	14%	8%	1%	77%
Soybean oil	0	15%	54%	7%	24%
Peanut oil	0	18%	33%	49%	
Margarine	0	19%	30%	2%	49%
Cottonseed oil	0	27%	54%	19%	
Veg. shortening	0	28%	26%	2%	44%
Chicken fat	11	31%	21%	1%	47%
Lard	12	41%	11%	1%	47%
Meat shortening	9	45%	6%	1%	48%
Beef fat	14	52%	3%	1%	44%
Butter (fat)	33	66%	2%	2%	30%

Trans-Fatty Acids or Phantom Fats

There is an additional type of fat that just doesn't fit neatly into the three broad categories just mentioned. This fourth type is known as trans fat and is present in many vegetable shortenings and margarines.

Fried foods and baked goods usually are made with hydrogenated vegetable shortening and behave similarly to saturated fats. Hydrogenation is a process that pumps hydrogen into liquid oils making it more solid and increasing its shelf life. But there is evidence that hydrogenation increases the saturation profile of a favorable fat and in the process raises blood cholesterol.

Food labels clearly reveal the saturated fat in processed foods, but so far the same labels ignore trans fats. This discrepancy in labeling is the reason that hydrogenated fats containing trans-fatty acids are becoming known as the "phantom fat."

Trans fat is being studied by the USDA and may someday be

tucked neatly into the saturated fat category for all practical purposes. In the meantime, it is best to avoid hydrogenated shortenings, oils, and margarines. This processing of liquid oil creates an undefined risk.

The P/S Ratio

Another way of evaluating the types of fat found in food involves the polyunsaturated-to-saturated (P/S) fat ratio. To illustrate, we can look at the following nutrient information that would appear on a label from Mazola Light Corn Oil Spread.

Nutrition Facts

Serving Size 1 Tablespoon
Servings Per Container (1 lb.) 32

	Amount Per Serving
Calories	170
Protein	1 g
Carbohydrate	0 g
Fat	6 g
Polyunsaturated Fat	2 g
Saturated Fat	1 g

Notice the P/S ratio in this food is 2-to-1. This is preferred. If the ratio is less than 2-to-1, the food has more saturated fat than desirable.

What About the Cholesterol Content of Foods?

The cholesterol found in animal foods has received less attention in the past year as a University of Washington study found little danger in consuming cholesterol (specifically from eggs) as long as saturated fat intake is very low. However, the American Heart Association recommends eating no more than 300 milligrams of cholesterol daily, and the bottom line is that most foods high in saturated fat are also sources of cholesterol.

Cholesterol Content of Food

FOOD SOURCE	SERVING SIZE	CHOLESTEROL (MG)
Whole milk	1 cup	33
2% milk	1 cup	18
Skim milk	1 cup	5
Low-fat yogurt	1 cup	14
Nonfat yogurt	1 cup	4
Creamy cottage cheese	1 cup	31
Low-fat cottage cheese	1 cup	19
Cheddar cheese	1 ounce	30
Part-skim mozzarella cheese	1 ounce	15
American cheese	1 ounce	27
Ice cream	1/2 cup	30
Ice milk	1/2 cup	9
Lean cooked beef arm roast	2 ounces	77
Lean cooked pork rib	3 ounces	67
Lean cooked skinless chicken	3 ounces	75
Halibut fillet, broiled	3 ounces	48
Crab legs, steamed	2 medium	96
Large egg	1	213
Butter	1 teaspoon	10
Mayonnaise	1 teaspoon	3
Sour cream	1 tablespoon	5
Light cream	1 tablespoon	10
Cream cheese	1 ounce	31

The Mediterranean Diet

The Mediterranean Diet is a slightly different slant on the low-fat eating style. Breads, pasta, rice, couscous, polenta, bulgur, and other grains make up the base of the dietary scheme. Mediterraneans consume double the quantity of fruits and vegetables of Americans, so these foods receive special emphasis—just above the base. Meat is eaten sparingly and olive oil is the preferred source of fat. Mediterranean people generally experience lower incidence of heart disease, stroke, certain cancers, and diabetes. The link between their low-fat, antioxidant-rich diet and relatively low rate of chronic disease continues to be studied.

The Mediterranean Diet Pyramid

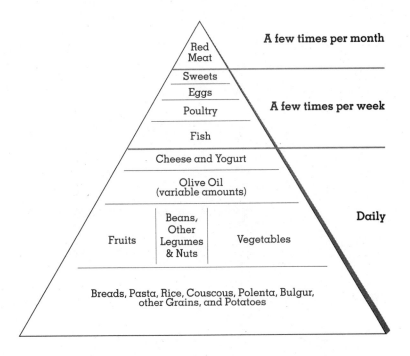

A few times per month

Red Meat

Sweets

Eggs

Poultry — A few times per week

Fish

Cheese and Yogurt

Olive Oil (variable amounts)

Fruits | Beans, Other Legumes & Nuts | Vegetables — Daily

Breads, Pasta, Rice, Couscous, Polenta, Bulgur, other Grains, and Potatoes

Regular physical activity

Wine in moderation

The Traditional Healthy Mediterranean Diet Pyramid was jointly developed by Oldways Preservation & Exchange Trust, World Health Organization (WHO) European Regional Office, and WHO/FAO Collaborating Center in Nutritional Epidemiology at Harvard School of Public Health.

Weight Loss—
Why Calories Still Count
★ ★ ★

For years, calorie restriction was the one-way ticket for weight loss. Fatty foods were a major player in the restriction as they are concentrated sources of calories. Then in the 1980s, nutrition research slammed fat as the number one dietary villain, and Americans scoured food labels and recipes for fat gram counts instead of calories. These 1980s obesity studies indicated that we use fat calories differently from carbohydrate or protein calories.

The body tends to use calories from fats more efficiently than those from carbohydrate and protein. For every 100 calories of carbohydrate we eat, we may burn up 25 just processing (or metabolizing) that food energy. On the other hand, we only use about 5 of every 100 calories in processing fat. In times of famine or the stress of a serious illness, this "fat efficiency" is desirable. But for many Americans, the body's efficient storage of dietary fat results in extra pounds, larger sizes, and serious health risk.

Counting fat grams to lose weight became very popular in the 1990s as this research was publicized and interpreted by dietitians. Many people had success with low-fat diets, because restricting fat grams automatically reduced calorie intake. However, we learned that calories still counted. And dieters who used the fat gram counting prescription to binge on fat-free, high-carbohydrate foods like bagels, brownies, and pasta ended up very frustrated with little or no weight loss success.

The late '90s focus is strict and authoritative weight loss dieting with lots of structure. When I have a patient interested in gradual weight loss, fat gram counting is an easy way to get started, but it will work only as long as the client keeps food records where calories can also be monitored. Fat-free, high-calorie foods like regular soft drinks, licorice, and fat-free desserts must be strictly limited.

But fat gram counting is not the single answer. There are five required strategies for successful weight loss.

Weight Loss Strategy 1: Fat gram counting

For women to lose weight, limit fat to an average of 25 to 30 grams daily. This averaging may reflect an intake of 20 fat grams on Thursday, but 35 grams on Saturday.

For men to lose weight, limit fat to an average of 35 to 40 grams daily.

Counting fat grams works because you will notice the zero fat gram count in fruits and vegetables parallels a very low calorie content. On the other hand, fat grams are high in margarine and oil (5 grams per teaspoon) and calories are packed in as well.

Pocket Guide to Fat Grams

The following guide can be used for estimating intake of fat. Numbers reflect averages for the food group.

FOOD	FAT (GRAMS)
Nonfat non-caloric beverages, 1-cup serving	0
coffee, decaf, fat-free broth, tea, mineral water, flavored water, and sugar-free soft drinks Nonfat non-sugar fruit juices, tomato and vegetable juice; calorie-containing beverages including soft drinks, beer, wine, wine coolers, mixed drinks, cocktails, and fruit drinks	
All fruits, 1/2-cup serving	0
(except avocado, 30 grams in each)	
Lean vegetables, 1-cup serving, including asparagus,	0
beets, broccoli, carrots, cauliflower, celery, cabbage, cucumber, eggplant, green or yellow beans, jicama, lettuce, mushrooms, onions, peas, radishes, Brussels sprouts, kohlrabi, leeks, okra, pea pods, spinach, sauerkraut, zucchini, yellow squash, and water chestnuts	

Food	Fat (grams)
Starchy vegetables, 1/2-cup serving, including	0
potatoes, corn, squash, baked beans, lima	
beans, sweet potatoes, and yams	

Dairy Products

Food	Fat (grams)
2% milk, 1 cup	5
1% milk, 1 cup	3
Skim or nonfat milk, 1 cup	1
Low-fat cottage cheese, 1/2 cup	3
Nonfat cottage cheese, 1/2 cup	1
2% low-fat yogurt, 1 cup	5
Fat-free yogurt, 1 cup	0
American cheese, 1 oz.	9
Swiss cheese, 1 oz.	8
Light American cheese, 1 oz.	2
Light-Line cheddar cheese, 1 oz.	2
Fat-free cheese, 1 oz.	0
Ice cream, 1/2 cup	7
Sherbet, 1/2 cup.	0
Ice milk or frozen yogurt, 1/2 cup	3
Sorbet, 1/2 cup.	0

Grains, Cereals, and Legumes

Food	Fat (grams)
Any cereal without nuts, 1/2 cup	1
Rice, pasta, couscous, cracked wheat, 1/2 cup	1
Bread (1 slice) or pita bread, 1/2	1
Bun, English muffin, bagel, 1/2	1
Cooked beans, peas, legumes, 1/2 cup	1
Soda crackers or Ry-Krisps, 4	1
Pretzels or breadsticks, 1 oz.	1
Molasses cookie, 1	1
Angel food cake, 1 slice	1
Vanilla wafers, 2	1

Meats, 1-ounce cooked serving

Food	Fat (grams)
Skinless white poultry	1
Skinless dark poultry	2
Fish, any white fish or tuna	1

FOOD	FAT (GRAMS)
Lean trimmed beef, including chuck, flank, rib-eye, round, lean ground beef, top loin, T-bone	4
Lean trimmed pork, including chop, loin, or shoulder or very lean ham	4
Canadian bacon	2
Egg, 1 whole	5
Nonfat egg substitute, 1/4 cup	0

Fats, Oils, Condiments, and Seasonings

FOOD	FAT (GRAMS)
Reduced-fat margarine, 1 tsp.	2
Soft tub margarine or vegetable oil, 1 tsp.	5
Mayonnaise or peanut butter, 2 tsp.	5
Cream cheese, 1 Tbsp.	5
Nonfat cream cheese, 1 Tbsp.	0
Sour cream, 2 Tbsp.	5
Nonfat sour cream, 2 Tbsp.	0
Fat-free salad dressing, 1 Tbsp.	0
Seeds or nuts, 1 Tbsp.	5
Nonstick cooking spray	0
Ketchup, mustard, salsa, soy sauce, lemon juice, horseradish, soy sauce, pickles	0
Herbs and spices	0

Snack Foods

FOOD	FAT (GRAMS)
Regular potato or corn chips, 1 oz.	10
Light chips, 1 oz.	6
Baked chips, 1 oz.	1
Air-popped corn, 3 cups	0

Add your favorite foods:

_____

_____

_____

_____

_____

My fat allowance is ___ grams daily.

Detailed daily food records with fat gram counts must be kept as shown below. Reviewing the information about portion sizes found on page 10 is a first step in food recording. As clients keep food records, I carefully monitor calories. In most cases, calories come in below 1500 for women and below 2000 for men. Gradual weight loss occurs and long-term habit changes are underway as the person learns a new low-fat eating style. However, when calories from high-sugar or high-alcohol foods and beverages

Date __Monday__	
Food/Amount	Fat Grams
2/3 cup low-fat granola	6
1 cup skim milk	0
1 small apple	0
6 ounces grilled chicken	6
1 bun 1	
mustard, pickles	0
10 French fries	10
1 peach	0
Casserole:	
1 cup bow-tie pasta	2
2 ounces fat-free ham	0
1/2 cup peas	0
fat-free mushroom soup	0
green salad	0
fat-free dressing	0
1 cup skim milk	0
1/2 cup fat-free chocolate ice milk	0
	25 grams

My fat allowance is **25 grams daily**

creep in and the totals go over 1500 for women, or over 2000 for men, then daily calorie counting must be added to the regimen.

To count grams of fat from processed and prepared foods, you may need a food counter book. I recommend Corrine Netzer's *The Complete Book of Food Counts*. It is available for less than $10 from Dell Readers' Service, Box DR, 1540 Broadway, New York, NY 10036. Ask for ISBN number 0-440-21271-5. This book lists plain foods as well as name-brand processed and prepared foods in common serving sizes.

I have included a nutrition analysis and fat gram count for all the menus and recipes in this book.

Weight Loss Strategy 2

Build daily menus and weekly shopping lists around the fruit, vegetable, grain, lean protein, and skim-milk food groups. These are the nutrient-rich, low-calorie food groups that protect us from heart disease and cancer. Fiber is the best friend for those weary of weight control. Fiber moderates digestion much like protein does and we get a longer stronger signal that we are full when our diet is rich in fiber. Include these high fiber foods daily:

Bran cereals
Whole grains like whole wheat bread and brown rice
Fresh fruits like strawberries, pineapple, and apples
Fresh vegetables like broccoli, cauliflower, and carrots
Dried beans, peas, and legumes

Weight Loss Strategy 3

Include a low-fat protein source at each of five daily feedings. Five feedings may sound like too much, but smaller amounts of food eaten more often delivers food fuel to the body at a consistent moderate rate, leveling out hunger and satiety. Breakfast is mandatory. Eating breakfast makes it improbable that you're going to binge by mid-morning. There is some thought that foods eaten in the morning are metabolized, or burned up, more rapidly than foods eaten in the afternoon. Five small feedings are needed because a low-fat dieter experiences true hunger more quickly than before. Fat is the satiety agent in the diet, so the frequent smaller meals ensure that you won't get a headache from being truly hungry and that you will be eating when you're going to need it for activity. The secret here is the word "planned." Snacks must contain some protein and be planned. That may translate into keeping fat-free, sugar-free yogurt in the fridge at all times or taking a low-fat cereal and skim milk to the office. Check out the section entitled "A Low-Fat Snack for Every Taste Bud" on page 48 to help you get started. Protein-containing snacks are highlighted.

Weight Loss Strategy 4

Avoid saturated fats; choose mono- and polyunsaturated fats instead. This means reading labels for the best fat profile. A low-fat eating style naturally must be continued to maintain a slender body, and avoiding saturated fat keeps your heart healthy.

Weight Loss Strategy 5

Exercise and fluids are mandatory. That is, to lose pounds and maintain a healthy weight over the long term, some regular form of exercise is necessary. The reason is simple. By elevating your heart rate during exercise, such as brisk walking, biking, swimming, dancing, or jogging, you burn calories faster. And that faster burn continues for one to three hours after you've stopped exercising. Also, exercise helps build and maintain muscle, and muscle uses more calories for energy than fat does. It makes sense to eat when you're going to work it off. Too many people save most of their fat allowance for the evening meal. Unless you take a brisk walk or perform some type of exercise in the evening, it's unlikely that those calories will be used for work. Instead, try to eat at least half your fat allowance before 2 p.m.

After years of promoting aerobic exercise, dietitians now recognize the value of any and all physical activities. Exercise in all its forms promotes weight loss, along with control of blood cholesterol, blood glucose, and blood pressure. In addition, it reduces stress, builds and maintains muscle mass, improves circulation, and increases bone density. Choose from any of these activities to boost calorie burning:

Caloric Expenditure of Common Activities

ACTIVITY	CALORIES BURNED / 30 MINUTES
Light housework, strolling (1 mph)	60-90
Golfing with a cart, gardening, walking (2 mph)	90-120
Moderate housework, bowling, cycling (6 mph)	
Golfing (pull cart), walking (3 mph)	120-150
Doubles tennis, cycling (8 mph)	150-180
Brisk walking (4 mph), cycling (10 mph)	180-210
Singles tennis, walking fast (5 mph)	210-240

Boosting fluid intake goes hand in hand with exercise and activity. The body's metabolic machinery is oiled with water! Being slightly dehydrated seems to be the fluid status of the average American. The next time you are feeling totally without zip, with dry eyes and cotton mouth, water is the remedy to reach for. Keep a water bottle on your kitchen counter, or on your desk at work, or in the cup holder in the car. Aim for at least 12 cups (that's just three of those quart bottles) of water daily in addition to the fluid you take in from juice, coffee, tea, and sugar-free soft drinks.

How to Take Fat Out of the American Diet
★ ★ ★

This chapter explores low-fat terms (How Many of Your Calories Come from Fat?) and answers common questions about the low-fat diet (Finding Fat on the Food Label and Getting to Know Fat Replacements).

How Many of Your Calories Come from Fat?

This is a question and concept that has been put forth by major health organizations in advising Americans to reduce total fat intake as it is related to calories. Currently, fat makes up about 35 percent of the total calories the average American eats. Major health groups have recommended reducing this number to 25 to 30 percent. How do we arrive at these percentages?

Calories come from carbohydrates, protein, fat, and alcohol.

1 gram of carbohydrate has 4 calories

1 gram of protein has 4 calories

1 gram of fat has 9 calories

1 gram of alcohol has 7 calories

We can use a food example to show what this means.

One slice of French bread has 15 grams of carbohydrate and 2 grams of protein. One teaspoon of margarine has 5 grams of fat. From the slice of bread, we get 68 calories, and from the margarine we get 45 calories.

And now for the important part. Zero percent of the calories in French bread are from fat. One hundred percent of the calories in margarine are from fat. When we combine the bread with the margarine, we take in a total of 113 calories. Forty percent of these calories now come from fat.

Here's an example of a dinner menu.

Menu à la Fat

6 ounces prime rib
1 baked potato
1 teaspoon margarine
1/2 cup cauliflower au gratin
1 cup fresh greens with 2 tablespoons salad dressing
1 cup strawberries
1/2 cup ice cream
coffee

Total calories: 987
Carbohydrate: 50 gm., or 200 calories, 20 percent of total
Protein: 46 gm., or 184 calories, 19 percent of total
Fat: 67 gm., or 603 calories, 61 percent of total

Menu à la Lean

3 ounces sirloin
1 baked potato
1 tablespoon yogurt with chives for potato
1 cup steamed cauliflower
1 cup fresh greens with 1 tablespoon no-oil dressing
1 cup strawberries
1/2 cup ice milk
coffee

Total calories: 424
Carbohydrate: 55 gm., or 220 calories, 52 percent of total
Protein: 24 gm., or 96 calories, 23 percent of total
Fat: 12 gm., or 108 calories, 25 percent of total

Notice the simple changes that were made to reduce the fat from 61 percent to 25 percent of the total calories. The 6-ounce prime rib was changed to a 3-ounce sirloin. Yogurt and chives were used to dress up the potato instead of margarine. The cheese sauce was left off the cauliflower. The salad dressing was made with no oil, and ice milk took the place of ice cream.

The menus and recipes in this book are designed in a similar fashion—to keep the percentage of calories from fat at 30 percent or less and the percentage of calories from saturated fat at no more than 10 percent.

The Low-Fat List

We have talked about avoiding saturated fat to lower blood cholesterol and counting fat grams to lose weight. What if you are looking for a simpler approach? Some of my patients have asked for a straight-forward yes-or-no way to control total and saturated fat. It involves the liberal consumption of lean foods (fruits, vegetables, grains, and skim-milk products), portion control of lean meats and unsaturated fats and oils, and avoiding saturated fats. To review, the saturated fats are those visible on or marbled in red meat; poultry skin; butter, cream, and whole milk; products made from cream and whole milk; solid shortening, coconut oil, cocoa butter, palm and palm kernel oil, and hydrogenated fats.

This back-to-the-basics plan is what I call the Low-Fat List, and it's very easy to understand—very black and white. Once you're familiar with the list, and more importantly the more you follow it, you're home free.

This Low-Fat List is similar to the American Heart Association Diet, an Eating Plan for Healthy Americans.

Low-Fat List

EAT	AVOID
Fruits and Vegetables	
All in liberal amounts, except those noted	Olives, avocado, and coconut Palm, coconut, and palm kernel oils
Milk Products	
Skim and 1% milk	Whole and 2% milk, cream
Any food made from skim or 1% milk	cheese with more than 2 grams of fat per ounce
Cheese with 2 grams or less of fat per ounce	Nondairy creamers Regular and low-fat cottage
Nonfat cottage cheese	cheese and yogurt
Nonfat yogurt	

EAT	AVOID
Breads and Cereals	
Plain breads and rolls	Egg-, butter-, or cheese-rich
Low-fat crackers	breads
Pretzels, breadsticks	Party crackers
Popcorn	Potato and snack chips
Cereals	Mixes for cakes,
Rice and pasta	breads, or cookies
Starchy vegetables	Rice and pasta mixes
Broth or skim-milk	with added fat
based soups	Chunky soups

Meat, Fish, Poultry, Proteins—Limit meat to 3 ounces per meal (portion size = deck of cards)

Skinless chicken and	All poultry skin
turkey	Duck, goose
Trimmed red meats	Prime red meats
90% lean ground beef	Regular ground beef
Packaged sandwich	Pastrami, ribs
meats with 1 gram or less	Rib-eye cuts, hot dogs
of fat per ounce	Sausage, bacon
Most fish	Luncheon meats
Dried beans, peas, legumes	Bratwurst
Egg whites	Organ meats
Wild game	

Fats and Oils—Limit intake of the following oils to 1 or 2 tsp. per meal

Canola or Rapeseed	All solid fats and shortenings
Safflower	Butter
Corn	Bacon fat
Soybean	Ham hocks
Cottonseed	Meat fat
Sesame	Chocolate
Olive	Margarines not made
Coconut	from approved sources
Soft tub or squeeze	Coconut oil
margarines made	Palm oil
from those oils	Palm kernel oil

Eat	Avoid
Salad dressing made from those oils	
Oil-free salad dressings	
Fat-free salad dressings	
Peanut butter	
Seeds and nuts in 1 tablespoon servings	

Getting to Know Fat Replacements

As the American public has accepted the mission to lower their fat intake, food manufacturers have researched fat replacement options. A potato chip lover can chop a whopping 10 grams of fat from a one-ounce bag of the fat-free product. Any and all of the fat replacements may be healthy if consumed within the context of the Dietary Guidelines for Americans or the Food Guide Pyramid. The danger comes when nutrient-poor, fat-reduced foods such as cookies and chips replace nutrient-rich fresh fruits, vegetables, lean meat, dairy, and whole grain foods. And don't forget, calories still count from these fat-reduced foods.

Guide to Fat Replacements

CARBOHYDRATE-BASED REPLACEMENTS

Includes: dextrins, modified food starches, polydextrose, fibers and gums. **Properties:** heat stable and can be used in baking; do not melt and cannot be used for frying.

Product name:	Used in:
Maltrin	margarine, frozen dessert, salad dressing, snacks
N-Oil	frozen desserts, dressings, spreads, sour cream
Paselli SA2	dips, dressings, sauces, ice cream, frosting, baked goods
Oatrim	dips, dressings, ice cream, baked goods
STA-SLIM 143	salad dressing, processed meats, spreads, dips, frozen desserts, baked goods, frostings, soups

PRODUCT NAME:	USED IN:
Polydestrose	baked goods and mixes, chewing gum, salad dressing, frozen dessert, gelatins, puddings, candy, confections and frostings
Avicel	salad dressings, frozen desserts
Gums	salad dressings

PROTEIN-BASED REPLACEMENTS

Includes: modified protein texturizers. **Properties:** protein is heated and blended to simulate the texture of fat. Not an effective conductor of heat, so is not used in frying

PRODUCT NAME:	USED IN:
Simplesse	cheese, mayonnaise, sour cream, salad dressings, yogurt

FAT-BASED REPLACEMENTS

Includes: monoglyceride and diglyceride emulsifiers. **Properties:** used to replace or reduce shortenings in baked goods; may be used in frying. Found in baked goods, cake mixes, cookies, icings, candy, snacks such as potato chips, and fried foods.

PRODUCT NAME:	USED IN:
N-Flate	shortening replacement in cakes and cookies
Dur-Lo	shortening replacement in mixes, cookies, icings, and vegetable dairy products
Caprenin	cocoa butter replacement in candy
Olestra	frying oil substitute used in savory snacks

Products under review by FDA: DDM, EPG, TATCA, Raffinose polyester

Z-Trim is a no-calorie fat substitute from oat and corn hulls invented by a government scientist. This insoluble fiber is under patent review and may soon be added to brownies, ice cream, ground meat, yogurt, and cheese.

A Low-Fat Shopping List for Your Kitchen

If the idea of controlling fat is new for you, it may be time to make a clean sweep in the kitchen. Throw out or give away the pesky foods that sabotage your best efforts.

What are the known troublemakers? The list might be endless. Chocolate and fatty candies, jars of nuts that tempt you, ice cream you scoop from your freezer, high-fat chips, most microwave popcorn, and those home-baked cakes, cookies, and bars that you're saving for a special occasion.

If you use a solid shortening, give it away or put it away because it is a saturated fat. If you have loads of frozen sausages, bacon, bratwurst, hot dogs, or bologna, give them away. If you have tuna packed in oil, rinse it well in hot water before using it.

Whipped toppings are generally high in saturated fat. Try to eliminate them from your life. Check out the boxed foods and mixes you have on hand. Many packaged side dishes, such as potatoes and rice, call for margarine in preparation. You can get by with a quarter of the amount called for.

Look at your salad dressings. Are they high in fat? If so, throw them away and buy the reduced-calorie, fat-free, or no-oil brands.

Look at the label on your margarine. Is it made from liquid oil? If not, use it up and find a liquid oil soft tub margarine on your next shopping trip.

How much cheese is in the refrigerator? Is it made from skim milk? If not, invite the neighbors over and serve cheese. It is silly to think you can have these nasty foods around and not eat them. If you're serious about a low-fat diet, plan your next shopping trip from foods on this list!

Brand names of the most popular low-fat foods are listed.

Deli Case

Lean roast beef
Turkey and chicken breast
Part-skim mozzarella
Breadsticks
Hard rolls
Pita and sandwich pockets
Gelatin with fruit
Copper penny salad
Corn relish
Diet tossed salad
Baked beans
Barbecued beef
Chili
Chop suey
Cheese pizza
Fruit tray
Soups: Vegetable beef, bean, vegetable chowder, and chicken noodle

Ham and turkey ham
Part-skim farmer's cheese
Lorraine reduced-fat cheese
Submarine buns
Rye, French, and Italian bread
Triple bean salad
Cranberry-orange relish
Pickled cauliflower
Diet chef's salad
Dressing with chicken meat
Chicken to go, with no skin
Spaghetti
Beef stew
Almond chicken
Vegetable relish tray
Deluxe meat tray

Bread and Bakery

Wheat or white breads, rolls, buns
Matzo
Croutons, Wasa bread

Bagels
Pita bread
Angel food cake
Breadsticks and English muffins

Meat, Fish, and Poultry

Sirloin sandwich steak
Lean beef cuts
    Minute steaks
    90% lean ground beef
    Ground chuck

    Sirloin steaks
    Ground round
    Eye of round

Top round
Top loin
Tenderloin
Lean pork cuts
　Pork loin chop
　Pork rump roast
All fresh fish except mackerel
Crab legs and lobster tail
Rabbit
All chicken (remove skin)
　Tyson skinless chicken
　Louis Rich white chicken
Butterball fat-free turkey and
　chicken products
Turkey breast
Louis Rich turkey ham
Oscar Mayer free turkey
　breast or smoked turkey
Louis Rich ground turkey
Oscar Mayer free hot dogs
Carving Board fat-free meats
Canadian bacon
95% lean ham
Any 97% lean sliced ham,
　turkey, or roast beef

Round tip
Flank

Pork sirloin cutlet
Plain catfish
Raw shrimp
All unbreaded fish fillets

Land O Frost chicken

Whole turkey
Healthy Choice meats
Beef or turkey burgers
Louis Rich turkey breast
Louis Rich turkey sausage
Healthy Choice low-fat
　sausage
Louis Rich frankfurters
Hillshire Farm deli select
　meats
Oscar Mayer free ham

Produce Section

All fresh fruits
Mori Nu Lite tofu
Potatoes and other tubers
Dried Fruits:
　Prunes
　Apple chips

All fresh vegetables except
　avocados

Bordeau dates

Salad Dressings and Condiments
Limit serving to 1 tablespoon:

Miracle Whip light dressing

Hellman's low-fat mayonnaise dressing

Weight Watchers Salad Celebrations dressings

Kraft fat-free dressings

Hidden Valley Ranch fat-free dressing

Seven Seas Free, ranch

Girard's fat-free dressings

Estee packaged dressing mixes

Smart Temptations French Honey Dijon

Hellman's low-fat tartar sauce

Bacon bits

Flavored vinegars

Mustard and ketchup

Chili sauce

Picante sauce

Steak sauce

Worcestershire sauce

Weight Watchers light mayonnaise

Kraft Deliciously Right salad dressings

Newman's Own Light Italian

Henri's Less Oil Dressing

Hidden Valley Ranch coleslaw dressing

Wishbone fat-free

Marie's fat-free dressings

Good Seasons fat-free dressings

Cooking wines

Vinegars

Pickles

Kraft barbecue sauce

Enchilada sauce

Salsa

Horseradish

Mrs. Dash steak sauce

Canned and Bottled Foods

Jam

Fruit butters

Peter Pan Smart Choice peanut butter spread

Jelly

Honey

Canned Fruits and Vegetables

Any canned fruit

All canned vegetables

Tomato paste

All fruit juices

Tomato sauce

Pork and beans

All canned beans
All vegetable juices

Old El Paso fat-free refried
beans

Chinese and Mexican Foods

Soy sauce
Oyster sauce
Salsa
Chow mein noodles
Taco sauce
Garbanzo beans

Teriyaki sauce
Picante sauce
Water chestnuts
La Choy classic dinners
Taco shells
Taco seasoning

Canned meats

White chunky chicken
Any tuna packed in water
Sardines in water or tomato
sauce

Premium white chicken
Salmon
Herring, clams, and oysters

Pasta, Grains, and Legumes

All eggless pasta
No-Yolks pasta
Dried beans, peas, lentils
Couscous
Minute rice

Creamette yolk-free pasta
Whole-wheat eggless pasta
Dried bean soup mix
Barley
Long grain and wild rice

Pasta sauces

Tomato sauce and paste
Contadina light chunky
tomato sauce
Healthy Choice sauces
Weight Watchers Smart
Options pasta sauce

Ragu light pasta sauce
DiGiorno light chunky tomato
sauce with basil
Hunt's light spaghetti sauce
Pritikin sauces

Prego extra chunky garden
combination sauce

Packaged Dinners and Side Dishes

Most rice, pasta, and potato packaged dinners call for 1/4 cup
margarine. Trim fat by using 1 tablespoon margarine with 3
tablespoons broth, beer, wine, milk, or water.

Rice a Roni	Suzi Wan rice dishes
Country Inn dishes (add no fat)	Lipton rice and sauce
Uncle Ben's rice	Near East dishes
Franco-American spaghetti (no meat)	Cheese pizza mixes

Entrée Sauces

Campbell's Simmer Chef golden honey mustard sauce	Campbell's Simmer Chef oriental sauce
Campbell's Simmer zesty tomato mexicali sauce	Green Giant Create a Meals sweet and sour meal starters
Hunt's Ready tomato sauce	Ragu Chicken Tonight light simmer sauce
Uncle Ben's Cooking Sauce sweet and sour	
Gravies	
Franco-American gravy	Heinz fat-free gravy
Heinz Home-Style gravy	Pepperidge Farm gravies

Frozen Foods

Plain frozen vegetables	International vegetables
Birdseye Custom Cuisine	Chow mein vegetables
Microwave vegetables	Pict Sweet Express
Pasta Accents	Healthy Choice dinners

Le Menu Lite Style:
  Turkey divan
  Chicken cacciatore
  Herb-roasted chicken
Weight Watchers:
  Chicken fajitas
Louis Kemp fat free
  Crab Delights
  Scallop Delights

Lean Cuisine:
  Chicken Marsala
  Glazed chicken w/ vegetables
Turkey breast

London broil

Lobster Delights

All fruit juices and drinks

Pillsbury microwave pancakes
Belgian Chef waffles
Kellogg's Special K waffles
Tombstone or Totino's pizza:
  Cheese and Canadian bacon
English muffins and bagels
Aunt Jemima pancakes
Aunt Jemima low-fat waffles
Microwave super pretzels
Whole fruits
Rhodes bread dough
Ice milk
Frozen low-fat and fat-free yogurts including:
  Ben and Jerry's
  Breyers
  Dannon
  Healthy Choice
  Sealtest
  TCBY
  Cool Whip Free
Kemps Juice Koolers
Jell-O Pops
Sugar-free Fudgesicles
  Bordens
  Columbo
  Edy's
  Kemps
  Weight Watchers
  Yoplait
  Sherbet and sorbet
  Crystal Light bars
  Kemps Lite Fudge Jr's
  Kemp's Lite assorted pops

Refrigerated and Dairy Products

Fruit juices and drinks
Vegetable juices
Fleischmann's
Morningstar Farms
Whole fruit products
Egg substitutes including
Healthy Choice
Second Nature

Table Ready

English muffins

Bagels

Dairy Products

Skim and 1% milk

Swiss Valley Light 1/2% milk

Light sour cream

Fat-free sour cream

Bird's Eye no-fat veggie dip

Nonfat or 1% cottage cheese

Ricotta part-skim and
fat-free cheese

All 1% or nonfat yogurt

Butter Buds

Margarine and spreads with 1 gram
or less saturated fat per tablespoon:
Blue Bonnet lower-fat margarine
Fleischmann's lower-fat margarine
I Can't Believe It's Not Butter 40% vegetable oil spread
I Can't Believe It's Not Butter spray
Imperial diet reduced-calorie margarine
Parkay Light 40% vegetable oil spread
Promise 40% vegetable oil spread
Weight Watchers light margarine
Lorraine reduced-fat cheese

Original

Jalapeño

Chive and onion

Alpine Lace fat-free cheeses

Borden fat-free cheeses

Healthy Choice fat-free cheeses

Kraft Healthy Favorites
fat-free cheeses

Kraft Philadelphia Free fat-
free cream cheese

Laughing Cow light cheese

Kraft Velveeta light cheese

Smart Beat fat-free cheese

Mootown Snackers string cheese

Weight Watchers cheeses

Light and Natural Kraft cheese

Fresh fettuccini and angel
pasta hair

Corn and flour tortillas

Staples, Seasonings, Baking and Dessert Items

All flours and cornmeal

Bread machine mixes

All spices and salt

Seasoning mixes

Molly McButter
Mrs. Dash crispy coating
Pam no-stick cooking
    spray
Weight Watchers cooking
    spray

Mrs. Dash
    Garlic and herb
    Onion and herb
    Salt-free
    Extra spicy
    Lemon pepper
    Original

Sugar and substitutes

All gelatin products
Angel food and chiffon
    cake mixes
Betty Crocker low-fat muffin
    mixes
Pie fillings
Cocoa
Jelly, jam, and honey
Carnation cocoa mix
Evaporated skim milk
Carnation Coffee-Mate fat-free
    non-dairy creamer

Pudding mixes
Betty Crocker light cake mix
Low-fat and fat-free brownie
    mixes
Royal light cheesecake
Canned pumpkin
Yeast
Maple and corn syrups
Instant dry milk
All coffee and tea
Farm Rich fat-free
    non-dairy creamer

Breakfast cereals and products

Carnation instant breakfast
Fruit Wrinkles and Rollups
Barbara's Bakery Nature's
    Choice fat-free cereal bars
Barbara's Bakery Nature's
    Choice fat-free granola bars
Oatmeal and all oat cereals
    except Cracklin' Oat Bran
Cream of Wheat
Maltomeal and grits
All bran cereals (no nuts)

Shark Bites and Fun Fruits
Nature Valley Bar
Health Valley fat-free bars
Ultra Slim Fast breakfast
    bars
Quaker Chewy granola bar
Quaker whole wheat
Oat bran
Maltex, Ralston, Maypo
All types of muesli (no nuts)
All corn and rice cereals

Grape Nuts
Puffed rice and wheat

All wheat cereals
Hungry Jack pancake and
waffle mix (made with
skim milk)

Cookies and Candy

Archway fat-free cookies
Famous Amos fat-free brownies
and bars
Keebler Fruitastic fruit bars
Nabisco fat-free Newtons
SnackWell's fat-free cookies
R.W. Frookies fat-free cookies
and brownies
Ultra Slim-Fast cookies
Weight Watchers Smart
Snackers
Animal crackers
Twizler's licorice
Spicettes and Orangettes

Entenmann's fat-free choles-
terol-free cookies
Health Valley fat-free brownies
Little Debbie fat-free straw-
berry fruit cookies
Pepperidge Farm fat-free
blondies and brownies
Sunshine fat-free bars and
cookies
Keebler Elfin Delights
Vanilla Wafers
Sweet Escapes Hershey Bars
Perky's candy and hard candies

Crackers and Soups

Knorr and Lipton soup mixes
Soup Starters and bouillon
Campbell's broth soups
Campbell's Healthy Request
ready to serve and
condensed soups
Hilton's chowder
Graham crackers
Wheatables
Wasa extra crisp
Finn Crisp
Old London melba

Mrs. Grass soup mixes
Progresso broth and vege-
table soups
Health Valley soups
Healthy Choice soups
Pritikin soups
Soda and oyster crackers
Thin Bits
Jacobsen's toast
Ak-Mak original crackers
Health Valley fat-free crackers
Ry-Krisp

Devon Melba crackers and melba

Snacks and Soda

Orville Redenbacher's gourmet light popcorn

Louise's fat-free caramel popcorn

Orville Redenbacher's Smart popcorn

Any whole popping corn

Rice cakes

Guiltless Gourmet baked chips

Louise's 95% fat-free tortilla chips

Dorito's light chips

Northern Lights tortilla chips

All sodas and bottled waters

Estee caramel popcorn

Fiddle Faddle fat-free caramel popcorn

Weight Watchers Smart Snackers

Confetti popcorn

Fat-free pretzels

Health Valley Cheddar Lites

Louise's fat-free potato chips

Lay's baked potato chips

Tostitos baked tortilla chips

Weight Watchers Smart Snackers

Beer, wine, and spirits as directed by your doctor

Kitchen Gadgets that Cut the Fat

Metal or plastic strainer—to drain ground beef
No-stick skillet—to minimize need for oil
No-stick loaf and muffin pans—for baked goods
No-stick baking sheet—for baking fish
No-stick saucepan—for sauces and soups
Cutting board—for slicing vegetables and trimming meats
Grater—for grating carrots and part-skim cheeses
Perforated meat loaf pan—to let the fat drain away
Microwave casserole dishes—for freezing and thawing
Salad bowl with cover—for salads that keep
Steamer—for bright tender-crisp vegetables
Wire whisk—to make smooth sauces from skim milk
Salad spinner—to wash and store fresh greens
Wooden spoons—for no-stick surfaces
Pastry brush—for light coats of oil or margarine

Egg separator—to use just the whites
Electric mini-chopper—for chopping vegetables
Hand-held salsa maker—for chopping vegetables
Roasting pan with grate or rack—to keep meat out of fat
Broth separator—for defatting broth
Pepper mill—for fresh ground taste
Measuring cups and spoons
Spatula
Slotted spoon
Ladle
Pasta portioner
Kitchen scissors
Kitchen scale
Mortar and pestle—for grinding herbs and spices to perfection
Microwave popcorn popper—for fat-free corn in 3 minutes
Perforated nonstick pie pan—for crisp pie crusts from low-fat
    ingredients
Pastry cutter
Tupperware Micro-Steamer—for super baked potatoes from
    the microwave
Scoop colander—to scoop and drain pasta quickly

More expensive:

Bread machine—for low-fat sweet treats
Grill Express—indoor 2-sided grill speeds cooking time on lean
    meat
Simac II Gelataio SC—electronic ice milk and sorbet maker
LeCreuset Jumbo Reversible Grill—for nonfat pancakes and
    French toast
Cast iron stovetop wok—does double duty for stews and soups
Calphalon Grill Pan—ridged nonstick grill pan

Check your favorite kitchen store or request catalogs from the
following mail order suppliers of fine quality kitchen gadgets:
    Colonial Garden Kitchens - 1-800-245-3399

Chef's Catalog - 1-800-338-3232
Wooden Spoon - 1-800-431-2207
Community Kitchens - 1-800-535-9901
Williams Sonoma -1-800-541-2233
King Arthur Flour and Baking Supplies - 1-800-827-6836
Crate and Barrel - 1-800-323-5461

Fast-Food, Restaurant, and Carry-out Dining

You know that feeling. You're on your way home from work or a meeting or shopping and you have nothing started for dinner. A quick stop at a fast-food restaurant is tempting. But how can you use these foods without blowing your fat allowance?

Here are the dietitian's choices from fast-food restaurants:

Sandwich Shop

Fresh sliced veggies in a pita with lowfat dressing
Cup of minestrone soup
Turkey breast sandwich with mustard, lettuce, and
    tomato with fresh fruit

Be assertive: Order two extra slices of bread with the big deli sandwich. Remove half the filling, wrap in foil or napkins, and refrigerate it for a second meal the next day.

Rotisserie Chicken

Chicken breast without the skin
Steamed vegetables
Mashed sweet potatoes
Tossed salad
Fruit salad

Be assertive: Select plain rolls without butter or margarine instead of cornbread or biscuits.

Hamburger Joint

Single hamburgers without cheese
Grilled chicken breast sandwich without the sauce
Grilled chicken salad
Garden salad
Lowfat or nonfat yogurt
Fat-free muffin
Cereal
Lowfat milk

Be assertive: Order orange juice for your fruit choice or bring a piece of fresh fruit to round out your meal. Keep salads healthy with lowfat dressings.

Salad Bars

Broth-based soup
Fresh bread or breadsticks
Fresh greens
Chopped fresh veggies
Beans
Lowfat dressing
Fresh fruit salad

Be assertive: Avoid white creamy dressing and oil-drenched bean and pasta salads

Asian Take-Out

Wonton soup
Pho (Vietnamese noodle soup)
Hot and sour soup
Steamed vegetable dumplings
Vegetable mixtures over steamed rice or noodles

Be assertive: Request vegetables be steamed or stir-fried with as little oil as possible.

Pizza Places

Choose flavorful, lowfat toppings such as peppers, onions, tomatoes, spinach, broccoli, or mushrooms
Be assertive: Ask for your pizza with less cheese.

Mexican Food

Bean tostada or baked bean burrito
Chicken fajita
Veggie taco
Refried beans
Rice

Be assertive: Ask for just half the cheese, but extra tomatoes and lettuce on your tacos and burritos. Request fat-free sour cream.

Check the Fat with your Coat and Hat at Fine Dining Establishments:

Does your favorite restaurant:
Offer skim milk?
Offer reduced-fat margarine?
Offer baked or broiled fish, turkey, or poultry products?
Offer salad dressing, sauce, and gravy on the side?
Offer egg substitutes?
Offer fat-free sour cream?
Prepare without added margarine or oil?
Offer steamed, poached, or grilled meat, fish, or poultry?
Trim visible fat from meat?
Prepare vegetables without added fat?
Remove poultry skin before cooking?
Offer 4- to 6-ounce portions of meat, poultry, and fish?

Offer reduced portions to all age groups?
Offer fresh fruit for dessert?
Serve sherbet, sorbet, or low-fat frozen yogurt?
Serve reduced-fat cakes or pies?
Offer bagels or English muffins for breakfast?

Avoid restaurant menu items described by these terms (they're full of fat by a different name):

au beurre	flaky
batter-dipped	croquette
alfredo	hollandaise
au gratin	fritters
breaded	bernaise
creamy	crispy
carbonara	parmigiana
tempura	

Sorting Out the Salad Bar

Don't get trapped in all that fat at the salad bar. Use this sample menu as a guide for designing a carry-out main-dish salad:

3 cups assorted fresh vegetables including lettuce, carrots, broccoli, cauliflower, celery, pepper, mushrooms, onions, and tomatoes
Top with 1/4 cup sliced lean turkey
1/4 cup shredded mozzarella cheese
1 ounce alfalfa sprouts
1 scoop of croutons
1 scoop of chow mein noodles
Drizzle 2 tablespoons reduced-calorie creamy dressing over all.

Calories: 390 Fat: 16 gm.
Sodium: 1068 mg.
Cholesterol: n/a

For exchange diets, count: 2 lean meat,
1 starch, 3 vegetable, 3 fat

Dressing Up Carry-Out Foods

Tease your family or guests with glamorized low-fat foods from your favorite deli.

Bean Salad

To 3 cups of drained bean salad add:
> 1 cup chopped mock crab and 1 teaspoon grated lemon peel. Garnish with a twisted sliced of lemon.
>
> 1 cup sliced artichoke hearts packed in water. Garnish the top with a sprig of fresh parsley.
>
> 1 cup chopped lean ham and 1/4 teaspoon garlic powder. Serve on a bed of greens garnished with carrot curls.
>
> 1 cup finely chopped celery.

Cabbage Salad

Choose a salad with a sugar-and-vinegar type dressing, then drain well. To 3 cups of drained salad, add:
> 1 teaspoon dill weed. Garnish with sprigs of fresh dill.
>
> 1/2 cup chopped red bell pepper, then garnish with red and green pepper rings.
>
> 1 cup chopped fresh pineapple. Serve in a scooped out pineapple shell.
>
> 1 cup chopped fresh orange sections and 1 teaspoon finely grated orange peel, then garnish with a twisted section of orange.
>
> 1 1/2 teaspoons caraway seeds. Serve in a flat bowl lined with cabbage or spinach leaves.

Carrot Salad

To 3 cups of drained carrot salad, add:
> 1/2 cup chopped dates or raisins, then serve on a lettuce leaf.
>
> 1 cup seeded and chopped fresh tomatoes. Garnish with

cherry tomatoes.

1 tablespoon fresh basil or 1 teaspoon dried basil. Garnish with a sprinkle of Parmesan cheese.

Cucumber Salad

Choose one with a clear or vinaigrette dressing. Drain and add to 3 cups of salad:

1 teaspoon fennel. Garnish with a sprig of fresh mint.

1 cup chopped fresh orange. Garnish with an orange wedge.

Pasta Salad

Choose one with a clear or vinaigrette dressing. Drain and add to 3 cups of salad:

1 cup salad shrimp and 1 tablespoon white wine. Garnish with coarsely grated pepper.

1 cup chopped lean roast beef and 1 tablespoon red wine. Garnish with radish roses.

A Low-Fat Snack for Every Taste Bud

A low-fat diet promotes a "grazing" (or frequent feeding) style of eating. This is because the fatty component in foods takes longer to be digested than carbohydrate and protein. The traditional high-fat meal promotes a feeling of fullness. As we reduce the fat in our meals, we experience true hunger between times. Frequent eating does not have to be a problem. You can respond to true hunger between meals with a sensible snack. A good choice of snack is one that is low in fat, yet satisfies your hunger and provides some vitamins, minerals, or protein. It is essential to keep a variety of sensible snacks on hand at home. Consider this following extensive list of snacks for every taste. Some of the snacks listed contain large amounts of regular sugar (see Sweet) and are not indicated for persons with diabetes. Other snacks are high in sodium (see Crunchy), and are not meant for persons with high blood pressure.

Snacks containing at least 4 grams of protein are highlighted. These are more likely to stick with you until the next meal.

Crunchy Snacks

	Calories	Fat (g)	Sodium (mg)
Apple, 1 whole	81	<1	0
Asparagus, 1 cup raw pieces	30	<1	2
Wheat toast, 1 slice with 1 teaspoon jam	80	1	140
Breadsticks, 1 ounce	86	<1	444
Broccoli, 1 cup florets	46	<1	16
Carrots, 1 raw	31	<1	25
Cauliflower, 1 cup florets	24	<1	35
Celery, 1 stalk	6	1	90
Graham crackers, 3 squares	80	1	90
Finn Crisp crackers, 4	80	0	28
Ideal Crisp bread, 4	68	0	158
Kavli Norwegian thick crackers,	2	70	64
Melba rounds, 5 pieces	50	1	n/a
Oyster crackers, 24	72	1	264
Wasa crackers, 1 piece	44	0	66
Saltines, 6	72	1	252
Kohlrabi, 1 cup	38	<1	28
Green pepper, 1 cup of slices	24	<1	4
Dill pickle, 1 large	6	0	300
Popcorn popped in oil, 3 cups	103	4	0
Popcorn, air-popped, 3 cups	67	0	0
Radishes, 1 cup	14	<1	16

Chewy Snacks

	Calories	Fat (g)	Sodium (mg)
Dried apple slices, 4 pieces	60	<1	21
Fruit roll-up, 1/2 ounce roll	50	<1	5
Dried apricots, 7 pieces	60	<1	3

	Calories	Fat (g)	Sodium (mg)
Bagel, 2 halves toasted	150	1	320
English muffin, 2 halves toasted	140	2	180
Cheese veggie pizza, 1/8th pie	164	5	309
Raisins, 2 tablespoons	60	0	0
Rice cake, 1	35	0	0
Flour tortilla, 1 small broiled with 1/2 teaspoon reduced fat margarine and sprinkled with chili powder	72	3	n/a

Savory or Salty

	Calories	Fat (g)	Sodium (mg)
Bean dip, 1/4 cup with raw veggies	90	6	n/a
Lean roast beef, 1 ounce	40	2	560
Cheese, reduced fat, 1 ounce	50	2	410
Mozzarella cheese, 1 ounce part-skim	80	5	190
Chicken, white meat canned, 1/4 cup	45	1	115
Crab, 3 ounces	60	<1	270
Taco sauce, 1/4 cup, with raw veggies	15	0	440
Ham, 95% lean, 1 ounce	29	1	349
Pretzels, 1 ounce	110	2	470
Tuna, 1/4 cup packed in water	30	<1	155
Turkey, 1 ounce white meat (no skin)	51	2	12

Sweet Snacks

	Calories	Fat (g)	Sodium (mg)
Cinnamon bagel, 2 halves toasted	166	1	320
Banana, 1 9-inch whole	105	<1	0
Blueberries, 3/4 cup fresh	61	<1	69
Angel food cake, 1/12 cake	140	0	130
Chocolate angel food cake, 1/12 cake	140	0	300
Confetti angel food cake, 1/12 cake	140	0	310
Lemon custard angel food cake, 1/12 cake	140	0	210
Strawberry angel food cake, 1/12 cake	140	0	160
Life Savers hard candy, 1 piece	10	0	0
Jellied candy, 1 ounce	100	0	10

	CALORIES	FAT (G)	SODIUM (MG)
Licorice, 1 ounce	100	<1	95
Bran or corn flake cereal, 1 ounce	90	1	150
Bing cherries, 12	60	2	1
Animal crackers, 7	80	2	87
Molasses cookies, 1	65	2	65
Vanilla wafers, 6	110	4	70
Chunky fruit in juice, 1/2 cup	50	0	10
Sugar-free gelatin, 1/2 cup	4	0	35
Grapes, 15	60	0	6
Cone for sherbet, 1	20	0	35
Sherbet, 1/4 cup	55	<1	n/a
Jelly or jam, 2 teaspoons	35	0	0
Kiwi fruit, 1	55	<1	4
Melon, 1 cup chunks or balls	55	<1	53
Nectarine, 1 fresh	67	<1	0
Orange, 1 fresh	65	<1	0
Peach, 1 large fresh	60	<1	0
Pear, 1 fresh	60	<1	1
Pineapple, 1/2 cup canned in juice	60	<1	1
Sugar-free pudding, 1/2 cup	70	0	65
Plums, 2 fresh	60	0	0
Raspberries, 1 cup fresh	60	0	0
Strawberries, 1 1/4 cups fresh	60	0	0

Chocolate Snacks

	CALORIES	FAT (G)	SODIUM (MG)
Cocoa Krispies cereal, 1 ounce dry	110	0	190
Chocolate nonfat milk, 1 cup	140	<1	155
Alba Fit and Frosty, 1 serving	76	<1	206
Chocolate Malt Flavor Carnation Instant Breakfast made with 1 cup skim milk	215	2	285
Chocolate nonfat pudding pop, 1	80	2	80
Frozen or Creamy Snacks			
Fruit and Creme Bar, 1 serving	90	1	20
Sorbet, 1/4 cup	60	1	6

	Calories	Fat (g)	Sodium (mg)
Lemon frozen fruit bar (such as Shamitoffs), 1	50	<1	1
Fruit and juice bar (such as Dole), 1	70	1	6
Popsicle, 1	60	<1	0
Ice milk, 1/2 cup	110	3	n/a
Sherbet, 1/4 cup	60	<1	6
Yogurt, frozen, 1/3 cup	70	<1	34
Applesauce, no sugar added, 1/2 cup	53	0	0
Cottage cheese, 1% fat, 1/4 cup	45	1	185
Fruit yogurt, sugar-free/nonfat, 1 cup	100	<1	120

Thirst Quenching Snacks

	Calories	Fat (g)	Sodium (mg)
Low-calorie cranberry juice, 1/2 cup	24	0	4
Grape juice, 1/3 cup (mix with Diet 7 Up)	60	0	0
Apple cider, 1/2 cup	60	0	0
Light beer, 1 can	96	0	7
Grapefruit juice, 1/2 cup	60	0	2
Sugar-free lemonade, 1 cup	4	0	0
Skim milk, 1 cup	86	<1	126
Orange or pineapple juice, 1/2 cup	60	0	0
Sugar-free soft drinks, 1 can	2-12	0	6-95
V-8 juice, 6 ounces	35	0	345

Warm Snacks

	Calories	Fat (g)	Sodium (mg)
Vegetable bouillon, 1 packet low-sodium	11	<1	10
Oatmeal, 1/2 cup no salt added	69	1	1
Coffee or decaffeinated coffee, 1 cup	5	0	1
Tea or herb tea	2	0	0
Vegetable beef soup, 1 cup	150	2	1140
Chicken noodle soup, 1 cup	120	4	980
Hot tomato juice, 6 ounces	30	0	550

Low-Fat, High-Calcium Foods

A 1994 report from the American Medical Association called attention to the large percentage of Americans that fail to meet currently recommended guidelines for optimal calcium intake. Furthermore, the report identified the preferred source of calcium to be calcium-rich foods such as dairy products. Osteoporosis affects more than 25 million people in the United States and is the major cause of bone fractures in post-menopausal women.

The AMA recommends calcium intake as follows:

Adults 25 to 65 years of age: 1000 milligrams/day

Post-menopausal women not taking estrogen: 1500 milligrams/day

These levels are higher than the 1989 Recommended Daily Allowance.

Use this list to maximize calcium and minimize fat:

	Calories	Fat (g)	Calcium (mg)
Skim milk, 1 cup	85	0	302
1% milk, 1 cup	100	3	300
2% cottage cheese, 1 cup	205	4	285
Nonfat cottage cheese, 1 cup	125	0	46
Nonfat yogurt, 1 cup	125	0	452
2% yogurt, 1 cup	145	4	415
Nonfat ice milk, 1/2 cup	93	3	137

Low-Fat Breakfasts

The trick with any low-fat breakfast is to include some protein so it sticks with you until midday. You won't be thinking about food all morning with these menu ideas.

1/2 cup orange juice

1 toasted blueberry bagel with 2 tablespoons reduced-fat cream cheese

305 calories, 3 gm. fat

Power Shake:
1 cup nonfat vanilla yogurt
1/2 banana
1/2 cup pineapple juice

> 220 calories, 0 gm. fat

2/3 cup reduced-fat granola
1 sliced peach
1 cup skim milk

> 300 calories, 4 gm. fat

1/2 cup tomato juice
1/2 cup fat-free egg substitute with 1 tablespoon Parmesan cheese
1 wheat toast with 1 teaspoon 40% vegetable oil margarine

> 210 calories, 3 gm. fat

1/2 cup cranberry juice
1 reduced-fat raisin bran muffin
1 ounce reduced-fat string cheese

> 260 calories, 7 gm. fat

1 cup nonfat strawberry yogurt
1 toasted English muffin with 1 teaspoon 40% vegetable oil margarine
300 calories, 2 gm. fat
1 toasted waffle topped with 1/2 cup nonfat yogurt and 1 tablespoon raspberry preserves

> 235 calories, 0 gm. fat

Low-Fat Picnics and Camp Food

Use the following ideas as you plan your next picnic or campout menu:

1. Add life to salads by substituting brown rice, cracked wheat, or couscous for white pasta. Toss in chickpeas or other beans for fiber.

2. Use colorful veggies such as cherry tomatoes and yellow peppers for eye appeal in your salads and appetizers.
3. Fold fresh apricot and peach chunks into chicken salad to extend the flavor but not the fat.
4. Use vinegar-based salad dressings instead of the rich creamy ones.
5. Treat the family to a variety of breads for sandwich meals such as mini French loaves, whole grain pita breads or sourdough rolls.
6. Use focaccia (Italian flat bread) for an interesting sandwich base, layering thin strips of low-fat cheese with garden-fresh veggies and fresh basil and oregano.
7. Beat the heat with fruit-based coolers. Use equal parts lemon-flavored mineral water with pineapple juice or lime-flavored mineral water with cranberry juice.
8. Freeze melon chunks, strawberries, bananas, and grapes, and serve them as appetizers for hungry campers.
9. Keep loads of low-sugar, low-caffeine beverages on hand such as ice water, mineral water, fruit juice, and tomato juice.
10. Offer baked chips with salsa. Toss fresh tomatoes, peppers, and onions with commercial salsa to extend the nutrition and dilute the sodium.

Low-Fat Brown Bag Lunches

When school starts, pack a low-fat lunch that wins a gold star.
1. Use the first letter of your child's name and cut sandwiches, low-fat cheese slices and fresh fruits into that shape.
2. Surprise the rascals with a variety of breads such as bagels, pita bread, tortillas, tiny sandwich rolls, or sliced French breads. Bake low-fat banana bread in ice cream cones.
3. Insist on 100 percent fruit juice for those drink boxes.

4. Add a spinach leaf or sliced cucumber to the low-fat lunch meat sandwich.
5. Freeze sandwiches on Sunday night for every day of the next week. You can freeze just about anything you would put on a sandwich except salad veggies, eggs, mayonnaise, and cream cheese.
6. Throw in a low-fat granola bar for dessert.
7. Celebrate Fridays or stressful test days with a snack-size candy bar.
8. Use a thermal container to include refrigerated yogurt or cottage cheese once a week.
9. Use up leftover chicken breast, roast beef, or meat loaf on the kid's lunch sandwiches. Send the leftover pizza along to school.
10. Get out of the carrot and celery rut with sliced jicama, cherry tomatoes, and yellow pepper strips.

Lean Grilling

The outdoor barbecue is the centerpiece of all-American low-fat summer dining. In the last decade, much caution has been urged regarding heavy consumption of charred foods. While there is no evidence that the occasional summer cookout will increase cancer risk, it's a good idea to follow these rules:

1. Before grilling meat, trim every bit of excess fat from the meat and remove skin from the poultry. Use nonfat flavoring in your marinades such as vinegar, fruit or vegetable juice, wine, herbs, and spices. Many marinade recipes call for oil, which is unnecessary.
2. Cook all foods a minimum of six inches above the coals or lava rock.
3. Avoid charring or burning foods. Do not let flames come in contact with food and do not consume the burned part of the food. Mutagens form as the food is charred and they have an ability to cause cell damage. When greasy meats drip onto the coals, a potent carcinogen

known as benzopyrene is formed. It rises in the smokes and is carried back to the food.

4. Add barbecue sauces containing honey, syrup, or sugar during the final minutes of cooking to prevent charring. Baste meats with a low-fat or nonfat broth, lemon juice, or herb-flavored wine instead of butter.

5. Always serve cooked food on a clean platter, not the one that held the raw food.

Low-Fat Office Treats

It's your turn to bring office treats. Watch their mouths water with these low-fat temptations:

1. A fresh fruit platter with nonfat lemon yogurt as a dipper. Fruits easiest to transport without bouncing and browning: bunches of grapes, slices of cantaloupe and honeydew melon, Bing cherries, orange slices, and wedges of kiwi.

2. Mini fat-free chocolate bars with skim milk

3. Low-fat muffins with orange-pineapple juice

4. Low-fat sesame crackers with fat-free string cheese and rolled slices of smoked turkey

5. Chocolate angel food cake with ice milk and fresh raspberries

Menus in a Pinch

If the kitchen is not your favorite place for leisure, here are some quick menus for everyday use that require common ingredients from A Low-Fat Shopping List (see pages 31 to 41). When you get home late and have nothing planned for dinner, turn to this section. You'll feel in control again.

A basic menu can be created around an entree, one accompaniment, and a dessert. Add milk and bread, and it's a banquet. Impulse eating doesn't have to be high fat, as you'll see from the following idea lists.

Entrée Ideas in a Pinch

All measurements are for approximately four servings. All measurements are approximate. Use your own discretion when adding seasonings. Work with your own kitchen inventory to make substitutions for vegetable or meat ingredients in this section.

Using pasta. The beauty of pasta is that you can start it cooking and 8 minutes later, it's just right. Use those 8 minutes to fix the rest of the meal. For perfect pasta, bring 2 quarts of water in a one-gallon pot to a boil. Do not use a small pan because it will boil over and you'll be cleaning up a messy stove. Add 8 ounces of pasta, and boil rapidly (keep the bubbles coming to ensure tender noodles). Boil for 8 to 12 minutes or follow package directions. Set the timer so it doesn't overcook. Drain noodles in a colander and rinse with cold water, tossing as you rinse.

Mozzarella Macaroni
8 ounces dry macaroni, cooked and
  tossed with
8 ounces no-added-salt tomato sauce
2 teaspoons dried basil
8 ounces shredded part-skim
  mozzarella cheese

Calories per 1/4 recipe: 337
Fat: 6 gm. Cholesterol: 15 mg.
Sodium: 163 mg.
For exchange diets, count: 3 starch, 2 vegetable, 1 lean meat

Crab Spaghetti
8 ounces dry spaghetti, cooked and
  tossed with
8 ounces mock crab, flaked

5 ounces (or one-half of a small can)
Campbell's Special Request cream of
mushroom soup
2 teaspoons dried cilantro and/or 1
tablespoon green chilies

Calories per 1/4 recipe: 322
Fat: 4 gm. Cholesterol: 12 mg.
Sodium: 652 mg.
For exchange diets, count: 3 starch,
1 vegetable, 2 lean meat

Asparagus Fettuccini
8 ounces dry fettuccini, cooked and
tossed with
1 pound steamed asparagus cuts
4 ounces Parmesan cheese

Calories per 1/4 recipe: 368
Fat: 8 gm. Cholesterol: 19 mg.
Sodium: 457 mg.
For exchange diets, count: 2 vegetable,
2 lean meat, 2 1/2 starch

Tuna or Chicken Linguini
8 ounces dry linguini, cooked and
tossed with
8 ounces drained water-packed tuna or
chicken
1 cup steamed green peas
5 ounces Campbell's Special Request
cream of mushroom soup

Calories per 1/4 recipe: 356
Fat: 4 gm. Cholesterol: 18 mg.
Sodium: 351 mg.
For exchange diets, count: 3 starch, 1 lean
meat, 2 vegetable

Using flour tortillas. Flour tortillas are made for stuffing. For quickest results, stuff them, roll seam side down, and place in a pan that has been sprayed with cooking spray. Put them in the microwave for 2 1/2 to 4 minutes. Conventional baking at 375°F. for 20 minutes also works, too. Always serve chopped lettuce and/or tomatoes on the side. For a topping, try part-skim ricotta or nonfat cottage cheese that has been pureed in a blender.

Ham and Vegetable Tortilla
Stuff 8 6-inch flour tortillas with a
    mixture of:
8 ounces slivered lean ham
2 ounces shredded part-skim cheese of
    choice
2 cups steamed vegetables of choice

Calories per 1/4 recipe: 323
Fat: 15 gm. Cholesterol: 35 mg.
Sodium: 430 mg.
For exchange diets, count: 2 starch, 1 fat, 2 lean
meat

Chicken and Chili Tortilla
Stuff 8 6-inch flour tortillas with a
    mixture of:
8 ounces cooked chicken pieces
5 ounces Campbell's Special Request
cream of chicken soup
2 tablespoons green chilies

Calories per 1/4 recipe: 257
Fat: 6 gm. Cholesterol: 41 mg.
Sodium: 497 mg.
For exchange diets, count: 2 starch, 2 lean meat

Tortillas with Leftovers
Stuff 8 6-inch flour tortillas with a
mixture of:
8 ounces any leftover meat such as
   sirloin
1/4 cup chopped onion
1/4 cup chopped green pepper
   8 ounces no-added-salt tomato sauce
   2 teaspoons taco seasoning

> Calories per 1/4 recipe: 250
> Fat: 4 gm. Cholesterol: 40 mg.
> Sodium: 356 mg.
> For exchange diets, count: 1 vegetable, 2
> starch, 1 lean meat

Kidney Bean Tortilla
Stuff 8 6-inch flour tortillas with a mixture
of:
   16-ounce can drained kidney beans
   1/2 cup chopped scallions
   2 tablespoons green chilies
   4 ounces shredded part-skim cheese

> Calories per 1/4 recipe: 327
> Fat: 7 gm. Cholesterol: 15 mg.
> Sodium: 866 mg.
> For exchange diets, count: 2 starch, 2 veg-
> etable, 2 lean meat

Using vegetables. It's easy to get the nutritional benefits of vegetables with these entrées.

Chicken-Topped Potatoes
Bake 4 potatoes. Lay the potatoes flat and
slice across them both ways, creating a

middle cavity. Stuff with a mixture of:
8 ounces cooked chicken pieces
5 ounces Campbell's Special Request
cream of celery soup
2 tablespoons green chilies or scallions
Cover and microwave for 3 minutes on high
power.

Calories per 1/4 recipe: 338
Fat: 4 gm. Cholesterol: 44 mg.
Sodium: 234 mg.
For exchange diets, count: 3 starch, 2 lean meat

Snappy Stuffed Peppers
Clean 4 peppers and remove seeds. Mix the
following together and stuff the peppers:
1 cup quick rice
1/2 cup water
8 ounces no-added-salt tomato sauce
8 ounces shredded mozzarella cheese
2 teaspoons basil
Cover stuffed peppers and microwave for
15 minutes on 50 percent power.

Calories per 1/4 recipe: 300
Fat: 10 gm. Cholesterol: 30 mg.
Sodium: 629 mg.
For exchange diets, count: 2 lean meat,
2 starch, 1 vegetable

Leftover Vegetable Stir-Fry
Combine the following in a no-stick skillet:
4 cups leftover steamed vegetables
2 cups drained canned chicken or
salmon
2 teaspoons dill weed
1 tablespoon vegetable oil

Stir-fry until heated through.

Calories per 1/4 recipe: 130
Fat: 5 gm. Cholesterol: 44 mg.
Sodium: 39 mg.
For exchange diets, count: 1 vegetable,
2 lean meat

Broiled Asparagus Main Dish
1 pound asparagus, cleaned, stemmed,
and steamed until tender
Place on broiler-proof pan and top with:
8 ounces shredded part-skim farmer
cheese
1 cup croutons
Broil for 5 minutes or until cheese bubbles.

Calories per 1/4 recipe: 238
Fat: 10 gm. Cholesterol: 30 mg.
Sodium: 417 mg.
For exchange diets, count: 3 vegetable,
2 lean meat, 1 fat

Using Meats. When you have a main meat and need something
quick to dress it up, try the following:

Ham Steak Marinade
Mix 1/4 cup each of Worcestershire sauce,
brown sugar, and lemon juice. Marinate 1
pound lean ham steak for 20 minutes, then
broil.

Calories per 1/4 recipe: 191
Fat: 4 gm. Cholesterol: 74 mg.
Sodium: 1388 mg.
For exchange diets, count: 3 lean meat,
1/2 starch

★ ★ ★

Round Steak in Beer

Mix 1/2 teaspoon garlic powder, 1 teaspoon sugar, and 1 can beer. Marinate 1 pound lean trimmed round steak 20 minutes, then broil.

Calories per 1/4 recipe: 192
Fat: 4 gm. Cholesterol: 72 mg.
Sodium: 56 mg.
For exchange diets, count: 3 lean meat,
1/2 starch

★ ★ ★

Teriyaki White Fish

Marinate 1 pound white fish fillets in 1/2 cup teriyaki sauce for 20 minutes, then broil.

Calories per 1/4 recipe: 119
Fat: 1 gm. Cholesterol: 47 mg.
Sodium: 1446 mg.
For exchange diets, count: 2 lean meat

★ ★ ★

Italian Grilled Chicken

Marinate 1 pound skinless chicken pieces in 1/2 cup reduced-calorie Italian dressing for 20 minutes, then broil.

Calories per 1/4 recipe: 169
Fat: 6 gm. Cholesterol: 69 mg.
Sodium: 297 mg.
For exchange diets, count: 3 lean meat

Italian Steamed Chicken

Place 3 pounds of skinned chicken pieces in microwave casserole dish. Mix 8 ounces no-added-salt tomato sauce with 1/2 teaspoon garlic powder and 1 teaspoon each of oregano, basil, sugar, and lemon juice. Pour sauce over chicken and cover. Microwave at 70 percent power for 15 to 18 minutes.

Calories per 1/4 recipe: 163
Fat: 4 gm. Cholesterol: 67 mg.
Sodium: 73 mg.
For exchange diets, count: 3 lean meat

Chili Meat Loaf

Mix 1 pound lean ground turkey, pork, or beef with 1 tablespoon chili powder. Place in microwave pan and microwave for 8 to 10 minutes on high power. Drain well.

Calories per 1/4 recipe
(using ground turkey): 129
Fat: 2 gm. Cholesterol: 67 mg.
Sodium: 71 mg.
For exchange diets, count: 3 lean meat

Chicken or Fish Fillets

Pat 1 pound of skinless, boneless chicken pieces or fish fillets dry. Roll in skim milk and baking mix such as Bisquick. Place on baking sheet and dot each piece with 1/2 teaspoon margarine. Season with lemon pepper, garlic powder, or paprika. Bake fish for 20 to 25 minutes and chicken for 40 to 45 minutes at 400°F.

Calories per 1/4 recipe: 191
Fat: 5 gm. Cholesterol: 67 mg.
Sodium: 232 mg.
For exchange diets, count: 3 lean meat,
1/2 starch

Accompaniments in a Pinch. These accompaniments quickly complete a main meal. All measurements are for four servings.

Coleslaw in a Jiffy

Mix 2 cups shredded cabbage with 1/2 cup reduced-calorie coleslaw dressing.

Calories per 1/4 recipe: 53
Fat: 2 gm. Cholesterol: 2 mg.
Sodium: 260 mg.
For exchange diets, count: 2 vegetable

Pea Salad

Mix 1 cup each of thawed green peas, tomatoes, and celery with 1/2 cup reduced-calorie Thousand Island dressing.

Calories per 1/4 recipe: 89
Fat: 1 gm. Cholesterol: 2 mg.
Sodium: 322 mg.
For exchange diets, count: 1 starch

Old-Fashioned Cukes

Slice 2 cucumbers and 1 onion into a shallow bowl and cover with 1 teaspoon salt and 1 tray of ice cubes. Allow to sit for 30 minutes. Meanwhile mix 1/4 cup sugar and 1/2 cup vinegar. Drain vegetables and combine in a bowl with dressing. This will keep in the refrigerator for 3 days.

Calories per 1/4 recipe: 72
Fat: 0 Cholesterol: 0
Sodium: 0
For exchange diets, count: 1 fruit, 1 vegetable

★ ★ ★

Tomato Medley

Slice 1 tomato, 1 cucumber, and 1 green
pepper into a salad bowl. Pour 1/2 cup
reduced-calorie creamy Italian dressing
over the top.

Calories per 1/4 recipe: 59
Fat: 3 gm. Cholesterol: 2 mg.
Sodium: 243 mg.
For exchange diets, count: 1 vegetable, 1/2 fat

★ ★ ★

Sugar and Sprouts

Steam 2 cups Brussels sprouts, then dot
with 2 teaspoons lemon juice and 2 tablespoons brown sugar.

Calories per 1/4 recipe: 50
Fat: 0 Cholesterol: 0
Sodium: 0
For exchange diets, count: 2 vegetable

★ ★ ★

Stuffed Squash

Combine 1/2 cup raisins or finely chopped
apples with 2 tablespoons brown sugar.
Stuff into 2 halves of an acorn squash.
Place in a casserole dish, cover, and
microwave for 12 to 15 minutes on high
power.

Calories per 1/4 recipe: 127
Fat: <1 gm. Cholesterol: 0

Sodium: 5 mg.
For exchange diets, count: 2 starch

Low-Fat Stuffing on the Stove
The commercial stuffing mixes are high in
sodium that can't be removed, but you can
control the fat content. Add just 1/4 of the
margarine called for in package directions.
In most cases this will be just 1 tablespoon
instead of 1/4 cup. Substitute chicken broth
for the remaining fat.

Calories per 1/2-cup serving: 117
Fat: 2 gm. Cholesterol: n/a
Sodium: 580 mg.
For exchange diets, count: 1 starch, 1 veg-
etable, 1/2 fat

Desserts in a Pinch. If you're the type that likes a sweet at the
end of the meal, this list will quickly delight you.

Fruits in Syrup
Mix 2 cups fresh, canned, or frozen fruit
with 2 tablespoons lemon juice and 2 tablespoons grenadine.

Calories per 1/4 recipe: 80
Fat: 0 Cholesterol: 0
Sodium: 0
For exchange diets, count: 1 1/2 fruit

Fruits in Wine

Mix 2 cups fresh, canned, or frozen fruit
with 2 tablespoons white wine and 2 tablespoons sugar.

Calories per 1/4 recipe: 80
Fat: 0 Cholesterol: 0
Sodium: 0
For exchange diets, count: 1 1/2 fruit

Iced Coffee

Pour your favorite coffee into a mug and
top with 1/4 cup ice milk.

Calories per serving: 46
Fat: 1 gm. Cholesterol: 4 mg.
Sodium: 26 mg.
For exchange diets, count: 1/2 starch

Fruit and Cream

Heat 1 cup applesauce, pineapple sauce, or
cranberry relish for 3 minutes on high
power in the microwave. Use as a topping
for 2 cups of ice milk or frozen yogurt.

Calories per 1/4 recipe: 140
Fat: 3 gm. Cholesterol: 9 mg.
Sodium: 54 mg.
For exchange diets, count: 2 fruit, 1/2 fat

★ ★ ★

Apples in Maple Syrup
Peel and core 4 apples suited to baking
(Winesaps, Jonathans, or McIntosh vari-
eties are best). Place apples in a baking
dish, then drizzle with 1/2 cup maple syrup.
Cover and microwave for 6 to 9 minutes on
high power.

Calories per 1/4 recipe: 110
Fat: <1 gm. Cholesterol: 0
Sodium: 8 mg.
For exchange diets, count: 2 fruit

If You Have Diabetes
★ ★ ★

If you have diabetes, your dietitian has prescribed a food plan best suited for you to control your blood glucose. The four most widely used food plans to manage diabetes are:

The Exchange Lists for Meal Planning

Carbohydrate Counting

No Concentrated Sweets Diet and

The Food Guide Pyramid with emphasis on avoiding foods with sugar

All four of these food plans are low in total fat and saturated fat, and that is important because diabetes is a risk factor for coronary artery disease. Persons with diabetes are wise to carefully control their blood cholesterol and to maintain a healthy weight.

Using Food Exchanges

The Exchange Lists for Meal Planning is a popular and useful tool to control total carbohydrates and fat. The system was developed by The American Dietetic Association and the American Diabetes Association in 1950 and has been continually updated and improved, with the latest revision coming in 1995. The concept of using food groups to control calories and fat is common for several weight loss programs, including Weight Watchers. While there are some minor differences in various exchange plans, the principle is the same: You control total calories and fat by choosing foods from food groups in specific portion sizes.

Foods are grouped into six lists called exchange lists. Each list is a group of measured foods of approximately the same nutrient value. Therefore, foods on each list can be substituted or "exchanged" with other foods on the same list. All of the recipes in this cookbook have been translated into food exchange values for readers using this system.

The following chart shows the amount of nutrients in one serving from each group:

GROUP	CARBOHYDRATE	PROTEIN (G)	FAT (G)	CALORIES
Carbohydrate Group				
Starch	15	3	<1	80
Fruit	15	0	0	60
Milk				
Skim	12	8	0-3	90
Low-fat	12	8	5	120
Whole	12	8	8	150
Other carbohydrates	15	varies	varies	varies
Vegetables	5	2	0	25
Meat and Meat Substitute Group				
Very lean	0	7	0-1	35
Lean	0	7	3	55
Medium-fat	0	7	5	75
High-fat	0	7	8	100
Fat Group	—	—	5	45

From these lists, a daily food plan is created to meet the individual's need for nutrients.

Basic Daily Food Exchange Allowances to Control Calories and Fat

EXCHANGES	1200	1400	1600	1800	2000
Breakfast					
Starch	2	2	2	2	2
Fruit	1	1	2	2	2
Skim milk	1	1	1	1	1
Fat	1	1	1	1	1
Lunch					

Starch	2	2	2	2	3
EXCHANGES	1200	1400	1600	1800	2000
Fruit	1	1	1	1	1
Skim milk	0	0	0	1/2	1/2
Lean meat	3	3	3	3	3
Vegetable	1	1	1	1	1
Fat	1	1	1	2	2
Dinner					
Starch	1	2	2	3	3
Fruit	1	1	1	1	1
Skim milk	0	0	0	1/2	1/2
Lean meat	2	2	3	3	3
Vegetable	1	2	2	2	2
Fat	0	1	1	1	1
Snack					
Starch	0	0	1	1	1
Fruit	1	1	1	1	2
Skim milk	1	1	1	1	1
Fat	0	0	0	0	1

From these basic daily prescriptions, a dietitian will individualize a menu for you.

All recipes in this book are presented in food exchange form to easily fit into a food exchange system.

If you need a copy of The Exchange Lists for Meal Planning, talk with your dietitian or call the American Dietetic Association at 1-800-366-1655 to order one.

No Concentrated Sweets Diet

The No Concentrated Sweets Diet is a list of foods allowed and food to avoid to control blood glucose. The foods to avoid listing means that when shopping or cooking or dining out, those foods are routinely avoided. Low-sugar, low-fat substitutions are recommended. Most of the recipes in this cookbook are allowed on the No Concentrated Sweets Diet.

Carbohydrate Counting

Carbohydrate counting is based on the idea that carbohydrate intake is the main consideration in determining meal-related insulin requirements for persons with diabetes.

The process of counting grams of carbohydrate is simple. Food counting books provide carbohydrate counts and most food labels state the number of grams of carbohydrate per serving. All of the recipes in this cookbook include the carbohydrate count.

The Food Guide Pyramid

The Food Guide Pyramid is a popular illustration of low-fat foods to eat. The Pyramid promotes the idea of using grains, fruits, and vegetables to form the base of the diet. As the Pyramid ascends to the peak, less emphasis is placed on high-fat, high-sugar foods.

The Food Guide Pyramid may be used successfully by persons with diabetes to promote blood glucose control. Reducing fats, oils, and sweets as well as fat-containing meats, cheeses, and dairy products, while increasing fat-free grains, fruits, and vegetables may be the single most effective dietary prescription for persons with diabetes to embrace. The recipes in this book fit the Pyramid.

If you would like examples of menus and additional recipes to fit with these diabetic food plans, please refer to my book *Diabetic Low-Fat & No-Fat Meals in Minutes* available from Chronimed Publishing at 1-800-848-2793.

★ ★ ★

Spring & Summer

Menus & Recipes

A Month of Low-Fat Dinner Menus for Spring and Summer
★ ★ ★

These dinner menus feature common foods and selected recipes from this book (noted with an asterisk). Use the dinner menus together with breakfast and lunch menus on page 78 to create a 40-gram fat (or 1500-calorie) diet plan.

Week One

1 serving *White Fish Creole
1/2 cup quick rice
1 cup fresh greens with 2 T. no-oil dressing
1 serving *Mile High Peach Pie
1 cup skim milk

1 serving *Layered Summer Salad
2 large breadsticks
1/4 cantaloupe marinated in ginger ale
1 cup skim milk

1 serving *Sirloin Barbecue
1/2 cup steamed carrots
1 serving *Party Potato Salad
15 fresh green grapes
1 cup skim milk

1 serving *Garden Pizza
1 serving *Old-Fashioned Cucumbers
1/2 frozen banana
1 cup skim milk

1 serving *Mediterranean Cod
baked potato with margarine
1 cup fresh greens with 1 serving *Lemon and Basil Dressing
1/2 cup sorbet
1 cup skim milk

1 serving *Baked Burrito
1 serving *Tex-Mex Slaw
1/2 cup fresh pineapple slices
1 cup skim milk

1 serving *Turkey Roll-Ups over tender cooked fettucini

4 cherry tomatoes
1/2 cup frozen yogurt
1 cup skim milk

Week Two

1 serving *Meat Loaves Italiano
1/2 cup steamed potatoes
1 serving *Lemon Zucchini
1 slice angel food cake with 1 cup fresh strawberries
1 cup skim milk

1/3 cup grape juice
1 serving *Easy Seafood Salad
1 serving *Onion Cheese Supper Bread
1/2 cup sugar-free vanilla pudding with raisins
1 cup skim milk

1 serving *Cornflake Chicken
1/2 cup mashed potatoes with 1 tsp. margarine
1 serving *Eggplant and Tomato Parmesan
12 bing cherries
1 cup skim milk

1/2 cup no-added-salt tomato juice
1 serving *Broccoli and Cheese Enchiladas
4 carrot sticks
15 red grapes
1 cup skim milk

1 serving *Pizza Salad
1 kaiser roll with 1/2 tsp. margarine
1 Granny Smith apple
1 cup skim milk

1 serving *Shrimp Casserole
1 serving *Cucumbers with Honey
Dressing
1 slice wheat toast
1/2 cup orange slices marinated in
wine cooler
1 cup skim milk

1 serving *Grilled Pork Kabobs
1 slice French bread
1 serving *Twenty-Calorie Molded
Salad
1 serving *Lemon Poke Cake
1 cup skim milk

Week Three

1 serving *Spring Turkey Salad
1 toasted onion bagel with 1 tsp.
margarine
1 serving *Blueberry and Pineapple
Dessert Cups
1 cup skim milk

1 serving *Bean Casserole Olé
1 serving *Cornbread with Chilies
1 cup tomato slices
1/2 cup cranberry juice
1 cup skim milk

3-ounce lean broiled hamburger on a
wheat bun
1 serving *Carrot Marinade
1 cup sliced watermelon
1 cup skim milk

1 serving *Fifteen Minute Bean
Casserole
1 *Apricot Muffin
1 cup nonfat vanilla yogurt over 1/2
cup blueberries

1 serving *Chicken Divan
1 slice rye bread with margarine
1 serving *Summer Vegetable Mold
1 nectarine
1 cup skim milk

1 serving *Pork and Black Bean
Stir-Fry
4 radishes
1 serving *Honey of a Waldorf Salad
6 vanilla wafers
1 cup skim milk

1 serving *Bayou Fish Stew
1 slice sourdough bread
1 cup fresh veggies with 1 tablespoon reduced-calorie dressing
1/2 cup raspberry sherbet
1 cup skim milk

Week Four

1 serving *Tortilla Cheeseburgers
1 cup fresh greens with 1 serving
*Quick Homemade Italian Dressing
1/2 cup sliced oranges
1 cup skim milk

1 serving *Mediterranean Supper
1 slice white bread from frozen
dough with 1 tsp. margarine
1/2 cup applesauce over 1/2 cup ice
milk
1 cup skim milk

1 serving *Seafood and Summer
Vegetables
1 slice broiled garlic toast
1 serving *Creamy Strawberry
Squares
1 cup skim milk

1 serving *Mexican Turkey Salad
1 broiled flour tortilla with 1 tsp.
margarine
1 serving *Honeydew Whip
1 cup skim milk

3-ounce sautéed chicken breast
1 baked potato
1 serving *Escalloped Cabbage
1 fresh pear
1 cup skim milk

1 serving *Hot Crab with Vegetables
1 wheat roll with 1 tsp. margarine
1/2 cup fresh pineapple over 1/2 cup
lime sherbet
1 cup skim milk

1 serving *Zucchini Lasagna
1 cup fresh greens with 1 tablespoon
reduced-calorie Italian dressing
1 serving *Fat-Free Frozen Fruit
Cups
1 cup skim milk

A Week of Breakfast and Lunch Menus for Spring and Summer
★ ★ ★

Use these breakfast and lunch menus together with the dinner menu suggestions on page 76 to create a 40-gm. fat (or 1500 calorie) diet plan.

Breakfast	Lunch	Snack
	Monday	
1/2 c. oatmeal with 2 Tbsp. raisins 1 slice wheat toast & 1 tsp. margarine 1/2 c. skim milk	1 oz. farmer cheese & 1 oz. lean turkey on 2 slices rye bread with 1 tsp. margarine and mustard 1/2 c. tomato juice 1 large apple 1/2 c. skim milk	1 oz. pretzels 1 orange
	Tuesday	
1 whole bagel toasted with 2 tsp. peanut butter 1/2 c. grapefruit juice 1/2 c. skim milk	1 large baked potato topped with 1/2 c. browned ground beef and 1/4 c. tomato sauce 1/4 cantaloupe 1/2 c. vanilla yogurt on top	4 squares graham crackers 1/2 c. apple juice
	Wednesday	
3/4 c. flaked cereal with 1/2 banana 1 slice French bread toasted with 1 tsp. margarine 1/2 c. skim milk	1/2 c. tuna with 1 c. fresh chopped vegetables and 1 Tbsp. no-oil dressing 8 wheat crackers 1 Granny Smith apple 1/2 c. skim milk	5 melba rounds 1/2 c. pineapple juice

Breakfast	Lunch	Snack

Thursday

1 English muffin toasted with 2 tsp. margarine 1/2 c. orange juice 1/2 c. skim milk	2 small soft shell tacos with 2 oz. seasoned ground turkey 1 c. chopped lettuce & tomato 1 fresh pear 1/2 c. skim milk	3 cups air popcorn 1 apple

Friday

1/2 c. bran cereal 1 slice raisin toast with 1 tsp. margarine 1/2 c. pineapple chunks 1/2 c. skim milk	2 oz. grilled breast of chicken on a bun with mustard 1 c. steamed green beans with 1 tsp. margarine 12 grapes 1/2 c. skim milk	7 animal crackers 2 plums

Saturday

1/2 c. Maltomeal 1 bran muffin 1/2 c. pineapple juice 1/2 c. skim milk	1 c. tomato soup 4 wheat crackers 1/2 c. low-fat cottage cheese 1/2 c. mixed fruit 1/2 c. skim milk	1/4 c. sherbet with 1 kiwi fruit

Sunday

2 small pancakes with 1/2 c. applesauce and cinnamon on top 1/2 c. skim milk	2 oz. lean ham 2 large breadsticks radishes, carrots & celery 1 c. watermelon chunks 1/2 c. skim milk	1/2 c. blueberries 1 molasses cookie

Special Occasion Menus for Spring and Summer
★ ★ ★

Confirmation or First Communion Dinner
*Hawaiian Pork
Baked potatoes
Fresh vegetables with
*Creamy Cucumber Dressing
Wheat dinner rolls with margarine
*Strawberry Alaska

Easter Sunday
*Gourmet Chicken with Cheese
Steamed broccoli
*Glazed Lemon Muffins
*Easter Salad
*Spring Parfait

Memorial Day
*Grilled Pork à l'Orange
*Green Bean and Dilly Stir-Fry
*Wild Rice Salad
*Rhubarb Crunch

Ladies' Luncheon
*Fresh Mushroom Soup with Ry-Krisp Crackers
*Chicken Chestnut Salad
*Fancy Marinated Tomatoes
*Tortoni Cafetta

*Recipe included. Check index for page number.

Special Occasion Menus for Spring and Summer
★ ★ ★

Graduation Buffet
*Blue Cheese Dip for Veggies
*Cocktail Crab Dip with wheat crackers
*Love My Cheddar Cheese Ball with breadsticks
*Curried Chicken Salad
*Lasagna Salad
*Wild Rice and Vegetable Salad
*Pineapple in Poppyseed Dressing
*Cheesecake with Rhubarb Sauce

Golf Outing
*Crab and Artichoke Dip
*Lemon Chicken for Company
*Antipasto Salad
*Summer Vegetable Medley
*Stand Up for Strawberry Pie

Fourth of July
*Western Broil
*Fabulous French Bread
*Party Potato Salad
*Lean Bean Salad
*Oatbran Crunchies

Family Reunion
*Roast Pork Loin with Cumberland Sauce
*Italian Potato Salad
*Summer Baked Beans
*Lemon Strawberry Supreme

*Recipe included. Check index for page number.

Special Occasion Menus for Spring and Summer
★ ★ ★

Summer Brunch
Cran-Raspberry Cocktail with Ginger Ale
*Eggs for a Bunch
*Asparagus Chef Salad
Assorted Fresh Fruits with *Lemon Fluff
*Summer Herb Buttermilk Bread
*Oatbran Blueberry Muffins
*Coffee Lovers' Cheesecake

Kid's Birthday Party
*Party Popcorn
*Deep Dish Pizza
*Want More Salad
*Zucchini Brownies
*Moonbeam Punch

Labor Day Cookout
*Cajun Fish on the Grill
*Sinless Scalloped Corn
*Cucumbers with Honey Dressing
*Fabulous French Bread
*Brownie Banana Split Dessert

For Casual Summer Evening Entertaining
*My Favorite Gazpacho
*Barbecued Shrimp
*Stuffed Tomato Salad
*Marinated Mushrooms
*Strawberries 'n Creme

*Recipe included. Check index for page number.

Blue Cheese Dip for Veggies

Preparation time: 10 minutes
Yield: 1/2 cup or 4 2-tablespoon servings

★ ★ ★

1/3 cup low-fat cottage cheese
1 ounce blue cheese
2 tablespoons nonfat yogurt
1 1/2 teaspoons minced scallion

Place all ingredients in a blender; blend until smooth. Chill and serve with raw vegetable dippers such as carrots, celery, broccoli, radishes, cauliflower, asparagus, and cherry tomatoes.

Calories per 2-tablespoon serving: 44
Fat: 2 g.
Cholesterol: 6 mg.
Sodium: 188 mg.

For exchange diets, count: 1 fat

Cocktail Crab Dip

Preparation time: 30 minutes
Yield: 1 1/2 cups or 6 1/4-cup servings

★ ★ ★

1/4 cup toasted almonds
4 ounces light cream cheese (look for 50%
    fat reduced)
2 tablespoons minced onion
1 teaspoon horseradish
1 teaspoon lemon juice
Dash of Worcestershire sauce
1/8 teaspoon salt
1/8 teaspoon pepper
1/4 cup skim milk
4 ounces shredded crab or mock crab

Preheat oven to 375°F. Spread almonds in a flat pan and place in oven for 10 minutes. Remove when browned. Combine all other ingredients and place in a casserole dish. Place almonds on top. Bake for 20 minutes or until bubbly. Serve with low-fat wheat crackers.

Calories per 1/4-cup serving: 115
Fat: 7 g.
Cholesterol: 13 mg.
Sodium: 150 mg.

For exchange diets, count: 1 fat, 1 lean meat

Crab and Artichoke Dip

Preparation time: 20 minutes
Yield: 16 1/4-cup servings + 4 bread dippers

1 round loaf white bread
Dip:
8 ounces nonfat cream cheese, softened
1/2 cup light mayonnaise
2 tablespoons Dijon mustard
1/2 teaspoon cayenne pepper
1/2 teaspoon garlic powder
8-ounce can artichoke hearts, drained and
    chopped
8 ounces cooked crabmeat, fresh or frozen
1/4 cup nonfat cheddar cheese, shredded

Slice the top off the loaf of bread. Hollow out the loaf, and cut the
bread into 1-inch cubes. Set aside. Mix cream cheese, mayonnaise, mustard, cayenne pepper, and garlic powder until smooth.
Fold in artichoke hearts and crab. Gently warm crab mixture in
the microwave on 70 percent power for 5 minutes, then transfer
to the hollowed out loaf of bread. Sprinkle with shredded cheese
and serve warm or cold with bread cube dippers.

Calories per 1/4 cup dip + 4 bread cube serving: 121
Fat: 2 g.
Cholesterol: 19 mg.
Sodium: 190 mg.

For exchange diets, count: 1 starch, 1 lean meat

Fresh Mushroom Soup
Preparation time: 25 minutes
Yield: 4 1 1/2-cup servings

1 1/2 pounds fresh mushrooms
8 scallions
1/2 cup red wine
1/2 teaspoon thyme
1/4 teaspoon black pepper
1 tablespoon Dijon mustard
1 quart fat-free no-added-salt chicken
   broth
1 cup plain nonfat yogurt

Chop mushrooms and scallions into bite-sized pieces. Place in nonstick Dutch oven and cook with red wine until tender. Add thyme, pepper, mustard, and chicken broth. Bring to a boil and simmer for 15 minutes. Add yogurt, stirring just to blend, and serve.

Calories per 1 1/2-cup serving: 105
Fat: 0
Cholesterol: 0
Sodium: 145 mg.

For exchange diets, count: 1 starch, 1 vegetable

Homemade Low-Fat Granola
Preparation time: 10 minutes
Baking time: 40 minutes
Cooling time: 2 hours
Yield: 16 1/2-cup servings

---

5 cups rolled oats
1/2 cup raw wheat germ
1/2 cup honey
1/4 cup reduced-fat margarine
1 teaspoon cinnamon
1 teaspoon vanilla
1/2 cup cold water
1 cup golden raisins
1 cup banana chips

Preheat oven to 300°F. In a large mixing bowl, combine rolled oats, and wheat germ. Combine honey, margarine, and cinnamon, and add to dry ingredients stirring until well mixed. Mix the vanilla and water, and add to the oat mixture slowly, mixing until crumbly. Pour mixture into a 15 by 8-inch baking sheet. Bake for 40 minutes, stirring every 10 minutes. Turn oven off, leave the oven door ajar, and allow the granola to cool in the oven. When it is room temperature, transfer it to a covered container and stir in the raisins and banana chips.

Calories per 1/2-cup serving: 162
Fat: 4 g.
Cholesterol: 0
Sodium: 4 mg.

For exchange diets, count: 1 starch, 1 fruit,
1/2 fat

Lemon Fluff for Fresh Fruits

Preparation time: 5 minutes
Yield: 6 1/4-cup servings

1/2 cup marshmallow cream
1 cup (8-ounce carton) nonfat, sugar-free
lemon-flavored yogurt

Place marshmallow cream in a mixing bowl. Microwave on high power for 45 seconds to soften. Blend yogurt into the cream with a wire whisk until smooth. Refrigerate and serve with assorted fresh fruit dippers.

Calories per 1/4-cup serving: 35
Fat: 0
Cholesterol: 0
Sodium: 36 mg.

For exchange diets, count: 1/2 fruit

Appetizers and Beverages

Love My Cheddar Cheese Ball

Preparation time: 50 minutes
Yield: 2 cups or 8 1/4-cup servings

★ ★ ★

1 cup nonfat cottage cheese
4 ounces light cheddar cheese (label says
  part-skim)
1 tablespoon chopped pimiento
1 1/2 teaspoons minced onion
1/2 teaspoon Worcestershire sauce
1/8 teaspoon cayenne
2 tablespoons chopped fresh parsley

Place cottage cheese in a blender. Blend until smooth. Grate cheddar cheese. Combine all ingredients except parsley in a medium-size bowl. Chill in the freezer for 30 minutes and then form mixture into a ball. Roll in parsley and serve on a plate with low-fat wheat crackers.

Calories per 1/4-cup serving: 55
Fat: 2 g.
Cholesterol: 9 mg.
Sodium: 244 mg. (To reduce sodium, use low-
sodium cheese.)

For exchange diets, count: 1/2 fat, 1/2 skim milk

My Favorite Gazpacho
Preparation time: 50 minutes
Yield: 8 3/4-cup servings

4 large ripe tomatoes, peeled, seeded, and
  chopped
1 cup no-added-salt tomato juice
1 cup chopped and peeled cucumber
1 avocado, peeled and chopped
1 red bell pepper, chopped
2 teaspoons chopped jalapeño pepper
1/4 cup chopped scallions
2 tablespoons lemon juice
1/2 teaspoon garlic powder
1/4 teaspoon salt (optional)
1 teaspoon sugar or substitute

Combine all ingredients and marinate in the refrigerator for at
least 30 minutes. Serve as a salad or use as a dip with tortillas.
Gazpacho keeps well for 3 days in the refrigerator.

Calories per 3/4 cup-serving: 75
Fat: 4 g.
Cholesterol: 0
Sodium: 80 mg. with salt; 19 mg. without salt

For exchange diets, count: 2 vegetable, 1 fat

Note: To make a crunchy low-fat tortilla, spray flour tortillas
with cooking spray, sprinkle with chili powder, and bake at
200°F. for 15 minutes. Cool before serving.

Party Popcorn

Preparation time: 1 hour, 15 minutes
Yield: 2 quarts or 4 2-cup servings

★ ★ ★

8 cups popped corn
1 tablespoon dill weed
2 teaspoons finely grated lemon rind
1/4 teaspoon garlic powder
1/2 teaspoon pepper
2 tablespoons margarine, melted

Place popped corn in a 3-quart baking pan. Mix seasonings with melted margarine. Pour over popped corn and stir. Bake at 200°F. for 1 hour, stirring every 15 minutes. Cool to room temperature and transfer to an air-tight container. To use after several days, simply rewarm in the oven at 200°F. for 10 minutes.

Calories per 2-cup serving: 96
Fat: 6 g.
Cholesterol: 0
Sodium: 66 mg.

For exchange diets, count: 1/2 starch, 1 fat

Summer's Here Fruit Punch

Preparation time: 10 minutes
Yield: 12 1-cup servings

1 quart pineapple juice
1 quart sugar-free lemonade
1 quart iced tea

Mix liquids together in a 3-quart pitcher. Serve over ice cubes and garnish with a pineapple spear.

Calories per 1-cup serving: 46
Fat: 0
Cholesterol: 0
Sodium: 2 mg.

For exchange diets, count: 1 fruit

Vitality Punch for Brunch

Preparation time: 15 minutes
Yield: 12 1-cup servings

---

4 bananas, peeled and sliced into chunks
1/4 cup lemon juice
12-ounce can frozen pineapple-orange
   juice concentrate
32 ounces (3 cans) water
2 tablespoons grenadine
1 teaspoon almond extract
1 quart crushed ice

Combine bananas and lemon juice in a blender or food processor and purée smooth. Transfer mixture to a 3-quart pitcher and add remaining ingredients. Pour into tall tumblers and garnish with an orange slice.

Calories per 1-cup serving: 104
Fat: 0
Cholesterol: 0
Sodium: 8 mg.

For exchange diets, count: 1 1/2 fruit

Apricot Muffins

Preparation time: 45 minutes
Yield: 24 muffins

★ ★ ★

---

2 cups flour
1/4 cup white sugar
1/2 cup brown sugar
1 tablespoon baking powder
3/4 teaspoon salt
2 teaspoons pumpkin pie spice
1/2 cup oatmeal
1 cup chopped dried apricots
1/2 cup chopped walnuts
1 egg or 1/4 cup liquid egg substitute
1 1/2 cups skim milk
1/3 cup vegetable oil

Preheat oven to 350°F. Combine flour, brown sugar, baking powder, salt, pumpkin pie spice, and oatmeal in a large bowl. Stir in apricots and walnuts. Use an egg beater to combine eggs, milk, and oil in a small bowl. Pour liquid into dry ingredients, stirring just to moisten. Spoon batter into greased or lined muffin cups, filling two-thirds full. Bake for 25 to 30 minutes or until muffins are brown.

Calories per muffin: 119
Fat: 5 g.
Cholesterol: 14 mg. with egg; 0 mg. with substitute
Sodium: 120 mg.

For exchange diets, count: 1 starch, 1 fat

Note: If you do not have pumpkin pie spice on hand, substitute: 1 teaspoon cinnamon, 1/2 teaspoon ginger, 1/4 teaspoon nutmeg, and 1/8 teaspoon ground cloves.

Blueberry Lemon Loaf

Preparation time: 15 min.; Baking time: 1 hour, 15 min.
Yield: 1 loaf or 16 1-slice servings

★ ★ ★

Nonstick cooking spray
1 1/2 cups flour
1 teaspoon baking powder
1/4 teaspoon salt
1/4 cup reduced-fat margarine
1/4 cup nonfat sour cream
1 cup sugar
2 eggs or 1/2 cup liquid egg substitute
2 teaspoons finely grated lemon rind
1/2 cup skim milk
1 1/2 cups fresh blueberries, washed and
  stemmed
Glaze:
1/3 cup sugar
3 tablespoons lemon juice

Preheat oven to 325°F. In a large mixing bowl, mix flour, baking powder, and salt together. In a medium-size bowl, cream margarine, sour cream, and sugar together until light and fluffy. Beat in eggs or liquid egg substitute. Add flour mixture and lemon rind alternately with milk. Gently fold in berries and pour into a 5 by 9-inch loaf pan that has been sprayed with cooking spray. Bake for 1 hour and 15 minutes or until bread tests done. Combine 1/3 cup sugar and lemon juice in a glass measure. Microwave on high power for 3 minutes. Pierce holes in top of bread with a wooden pick. Pour glaze over the bread. Cool in the pan for 30 minutes, then remove and cool on a wire rack.

Calories per slice: 141; Fat: 4 g.
Cholesterol: 39 mg. with egg;
1 mg. with substitute; Sodium: 103 mg.

For exchange diets, count: 1 1/2 starch, 1/2 fat

Cornbread with Chilies

Preparation time: 45 minutes
Yield: 8-inch square pan or 12 squares

★ ★ ★

Nonstick cooking spray
1 cup flour
1 cup cornmeal
2 tablespoons sugar
4 teaspoons baking powder
1/4 teaspoon salt
1 egg or 1/4 cup liquid egg substitute
1 cup skim milk
2 tablespoons vegetable oil
2 tablespoons diced green chilies (may use
    canned or fresh)

Preheat oven to 375°F. Combine flour, cornmeal, sugar, baking powder, and salt in a large bowl. Using an egg beater, combine egg, skim milk, and oil. Pour liquid into the dry ingredients. Add chilies. Stir just until blended. Batter will be lumpy. Pour into an 8-inch square pan that has been sprayed with cooking spray. Bake for 25 minutes or until an inserted toothpick returns clean.

Calories per square: 119
Fat: 3 g.
Cholesterol: 21 mg. with egg;
1 mg. with substitute
Sodium: 166 mg.

For exchange diets, count: 1 starch, 1 fat

Fabulous French Bread

Preparation time: 90 minutes
Yield: 2 loaves or 40 slices

Cornmeal to dust pans
2 packages dry yeast
1/2 cup water
1/2 teaspoon sugar
2 tablespoons sugar
2 tablespoons margarine
2 teaspoons salt
2 cups boiling water
7 1/2 cups flour

Dust 2 French bread loaf pans with cornmeal. Dissolve yeast in 1/2 cup water and stir in 1/2 teaspoon sugar. Combine 2 tablespoons sugar, margarine, salt, and boiling water in a large mixing bowl. Cool to lukewarm and stir in yeast mixture. Slowly add flour, processing with food processor or electric mixer or by hand until dough is smooth and elastic. Cover and allow to rise until double in bulk. Form into 2 loaves. Preheat oven to 400°F. Place a pan of boiling water in the bottom of the oven. Bake for 20 minutes. Cool for 10 minutes, then remove loaves from pan and cool on a rack.

Calories per slice: 96
Fat: 1 g.
Cholesterol: 0
Sodium: 107 mg.

For exchange diets, count: 1 starch

Speed Alert: This recipe takes 90 minutes when bread is allowed to rise in warm place.

Glazed Lemon Muffins
Preparation time: 40 minutes
Yield: 18 muffins

2/3 cup sugar
1/3 cup vegetable oil
1 egg or 1/4 cup liquid egg substitute
1 cup low-fat lemon yogurt
1 tablespoon grated fresh lemon peel
1 teaspoon soda
2 cups flour
Glaze:
1/4 cup lemon juice
2 tablespoons sugar

Preheat oven to 375°F. In a mixing bowl, cream sugar and oil. Beat in egg, yogurt, and lemon peel. Combine soda and flour, then stir into batter just until all is moistened. Spoon batter into greased or lined muffin tins. Bake for 20 minutes. To glaze: Use a toothpick to poke 5 holes in each muffin. Combine lemon juice and sugar in a glass measuring cup and microwave for 25 seconds to dissolve sugar. Stir. Pour a small amount of glaze over each muffin.

Calories per muffin: 125
Fat: 4 g.
Cholesterol: 15 mg. with egg;
1 mg. with substitute
Sodium: 45 mg.

For exchange diets, count: 1 starch, 1 fat

Oat Bran Muffins
with Blueberries or Raspberries
Preparation time: 40 minutes
Yield: 12 muffins

1/4 cup whole wheat flour
3/4 cup white flour
1/2 cup brown sugar
1 cup oat bran cereal
4 teaspoons baking powder
1/4 teaspoon salt
1 cup skim milk
1 teaspoon vanilla
1 egg or 1/4 cup liquid egg substitute
1/3 cup liquid vegetable oil
1 cup drained berries

Preheat oven to 400°F. Combine dry ingredients in a mixing bowl. Stir well. Using an egg beater, combine milk, vanilla, egg, and oil. Pour into dry ingredients and add drained blueberries or raspberries. Stir just until moistened. Spoon batter into greased or lined muffin cups and bake for 20 minutes.

Calories per muffin: 112
Fat: 6 g.
Cholesterol: 21 mg. with egg;
1 mg. with substitute
Sodium: 83 mg.

For exchange diets, count: 1 starch, 1 fat

Onion Cheese Supper Bread

Preparation time: 35 minutes
Yield: 8 slices

Nonstick cooking spray
1 egg, beaten
1/2 cup skim milk
1/2 cup onion, chopped
1 1/2 cups biscuit mix
2 tablespoons parsley, chopped
1 cup part-skim American cheese,
 shredded, divided

Preheat oven to 400°F. In a small mixing bowl, combine egg and milk using an egg beater. In a large mixing bowl, combine onion, biscuit mix, parsley, and 1/2 of the shredded cheese. Pour liquid into the large bowl and stir just until moist. Spread dough into an 8-inch round pan that has been sprayed with cooking spray. Spread remaining cheese over the top. Bake for 20 minutes.

Calories per slice: 135
Fat: 6 g.
Cholesterol: 42 mg. with egg;
20 mg. with substitute
Sodium: 222 mg.

For exchange diets, count: 1 starch, 1 fat

Strawberry-Rhubarb Muffins

Preparation time: 40 minutes
Yield: 12 large muffins

1 3/4 cups flour
3/4 cup sugar
2 1/2 teaspoons baking powder
3/4 teaspoon salt
1 egg or 1/4 cup liquid egg substitute
1/2 cup skim milk
1/2 cup nonfat sour cream
3 tablespoons vegetable oil
3/4 cup minced fresh rhubarb
3/4 cup sliced strawberries
Topping:
1/4 cup sugar

Preheat oven to 400°F. Prepare muffin tins with paper liners or cooking spray. Combine flour, sugar, baking powder, and salt in a large bowl. Beat together egg or liquid egg substitute, milk, sour cream, and oil in a small bowl, then stir into the flour mixture with a fork just until moist. Gently fold in rhubarb and strawberries. Fill prepared muffin tins, then sprinkle each muffin with 1 teaspoon of sugar. Bake for 20 to 25 minutes.

Calories per muffin: 183
Fat: 4 g.
Cholesterol: 17 mg. with egg;
2 mg. with substitute
Sodium: 228 mg.

For exchange diets, count: 1 1/2 starch, 1 fat

Summer Herb Buttermilk Bread

Preparation time: 55 minutes
Yield: 1 loaf or 18 slices

Nonstick cooking spray
2 cups whole wheat flour
2 cups white flour
1 teaspoon salt
2 teaspoons sugar
1 teaspoon baking soda
1 teaspoon baking powder
3 tablespoons margarine
1 teaspoon oil
1 teaspoon each dried basil, sage,
    tarragon, and chives or 2 tablespoons
    each fresh herbs (may substitute other
    favorite herbs)
2 cups buttermilk

Preheat oven to 375°F. In a large bowl, combine first six dry ingredients. Add margarine and work into mixture until crumbly. Put oil in small glass dish, and microwave 15 seconds. Stir in herbs. This helps to bring out the flavor. Add herbs and buttermilk to crumbly mixture and mix until well blended. Spread dough into a loaf pan that has been sprayed with cooking spray. Bake for 35 to 45 minutes, or until the middle of the loaf is firm to the touch. Cool on a rack.

Calories per slice: 122
Fat: 3 g.
Cholesterol: 2 mg.
Sodium: 234 mg.

For exchange diets, count: 1 starch, 1 fat

Antipasto Salad

Preparation time: 15 minutes
Yield: 4 1-cup servings

---

1 small head Boston lettuce
16-ounce can artichoke hearts in water
2 stalks celery, sliced thin
1/2 cup sliced radishes
1 tablespoon chopped red onion
1/4 cup reduced-calorie Italian dressing

Wash and drain lettuce, then tear into bite-sized pieces. Drain artichokes and combine with celery, radishes, onion, and dressing in a mixing bowl. Divide lettuce onto 4 serving plates and spoon vegetables and dressing over the top. Serve.

Calories per 1-cup serving: 68
Fat: 3 g.
Cholesterol: 1 mg.
Sodium: 191 mg.

For exchange diets, count: 3 vegetable

Asparagus Vinaigrette

Preparation time: 40 minutes
Yield: 4 1-cup servings

2 pounds fresh asparagus
1 tablespoon water
1 onion, chopped fine
1/4 teaspoon garlic powder
1/2 teaspoon salt, optional
1 1/2 teaspoons Dijon mustard
2 tablespoons lemon juice
1 tablespoon vegetable oil
1 teaspoon red wine
1/2 teaspoon vinegar
1/4 cup chopped fresh parsley

Trim and wash asparagus, then steam in microwave with water
in a covered microwave dish on high power for 5 minutes. Place
spears in a flat shallow serving dish and sprinkle with onion.
Combine all other ingredients except parsley in a blender container. Blend, then pour over the asparagus. Chill in refrigerator for 20 minutes, garnish with parsley, and serve.

Calories per 1-cup serving: 95
Fat: 4 g.
Cholesterol: 0
Sodium: 179 mg. with salt; 57 mg. without salt

For exchange diets, count: 2 vegetables, 1 fat

Carrot Marinade

Preparation time: 20 minutes
Yield: 8 3/4-cup servings

★ ★ ★

---

1 1/2 pounds carrots, cut into coins
1 tablespoon water
1/2 green pepper, chopped fine
1 scallion, sliced fine
8-ounces no-added-salt tomato sauce
1/4 cup vinegar
2 tablespoons brown sugar
1 teaspoon prepared mustard
1 tablespoon Worcestershire sauce
1/2 teaspoon celery seed

Place carrots and water in microwave-safe 2-quart dish. Cover with plastic wrap and microwave on high for 3 minutes. Drain well. Transfer carrots to a 2-quart salad bowl. Add green pepper and scallion. Combine tomato sauce, vinegar, brown sugar, mustard, Worcestershire sauce, and celery seed in a shaker container and pour over vegetables, tossing to coat. This salad keeps well in the refrigerator for 4 days.

Calories per 3/4-cup serving: 77
Fat: <1 g.
Cholesterol: 0
Sodium: 71 mg.

For exchange diets, count: 1 starch

Creamy Cucumber Salad Dressing

Preparation time: 15 minutes
Yield: 8 2-tablespoon servings

1/2 cup cucumber, coarsely chopped
1 tablespoon minced fresh dill
1/2 teaspoon white pepper
1/2 teaspoon garlic powder
1 tablespoon lemon juice
3/4 cup nonfat yogurt
1 tablespoon vegetable oil
1/4 teaspoon salt
1 teaspoon sugar

Combine cucumber, dill, pepper, and garlic powder in a blender. Blend until creamy. Transfer to a mixing bowl and whisk in remaining ingredients; refrigerate until ready to serve. This dressing keeps well in the refrigerator for 4 days.

Calories per 2-tablespoon serving: 31
Fat: 2 g.
Cholesterol: <1 mg.
Sodium: 83 mg.

For exchange diets, count: 1 vegetable

Cucumbers with Honey Dressing

Preparation time: 15 minutes
Yield: 8 3/4-cup servings

3 large cucumbers, peeled and sliced thin
1/2 red onion, sliced finely
1 small can mandarin oranges, drained
   well
Dressing:
3 tablespoons orange juice
1 tablespoon lemon juice
1 tablespoon honey
2 teaspoons Dijon mustard
2 teaspoons grated orange rind
1/4 teaspoon salt (optional)
1 tablespoon vegetable oil

Combine cucumbers, onion, and oranges in a 3-quart salad bowl.
Mix ingredients for dressing in a shaker container and pour over
salad ingredients just before serving, tossing to coat.

Calories per 3/4-cup serving: 51
Fat: 2 g.
Cholesterol: 0
Sodium: 79 mg. with salt; 18 mg. without salt

For exchange diets, count: 1 vegetable, 1/2 fat

Easter Salad

Preparation time: 20 minutes
Yield: 8 2-cup servings

4 cups torn lettuce
4 cups torn spinach
1/4 cup sliced mushrooms
1/4 cup sliced red onion
2 cups sliced oranges
2 slices bacon, broiled and crumbled
Dressing:
1/3 cup vinegar
1 tablespoon oil
1/2 teaspoon sugar
1/4 teaspoon salt, optional
1/8 teaspoon dry mustard

In a large salad bowl, combine lettuce, spinach, mushrooms, onion, oranges, and bacon. In a shaker container, combine ingredients for dressing. Pour over salad ingredients, mixing well and serve.

Calories per 2-cup serving: 111
Fat: 4 g.
Cholesterol: 2 mg.
Sodium: 125 mg. with salt; 64 mg. without salt

For exchange diets, count: 1/2 fruit, 1 vegetable,
1 fat

Easy Fat-Free Coleslaw

Preparation time: 20 minutes
Chilling time: 1 hour
Yield: 8 3/4-cup servings

4 cups shredded cabbage
1 large carrot, peeled and shredded
1 large green pepper, seeded and diced
   fine
2 green onions, diced fine
1 stalk celery, diced fine

Dressing:
1/2 cup fat-free mayonnaise
2 tablespoons vinegar
1 tablespoon sugar or equivalent sugar
   substitute
1/2 teaspoon salt (optional)
1/2 teaspoon black pepper
1/2 teaspoon celery seed

In a large salad bowl, combine cabbage and vegetables. In a small bowl, use a whisk to mix ingredients for dressing. Pour dressing over salad ingredients, mixing well. Refrigerate at least 1 hour before serving.

Calories per 3/4-cup serving: 33
Fat: 0
Cholesterol: 0
Sodium: 326 mg. with salt; 193 mg. without salt

For exchange diets, count: 1 vegetable

Fancy Marinated Tomatoes

Preparation time: 60 minutes
Yield: 4 1-tomato servings

4 firm, ripe tomatoes
1/4 cup snipped parsley
1/2 teaspoon garlic powder
1/4 teaspoon salt
1 teaspoon sugar
1/4 teaspoon pepper
1 tablespoon vegetable oil
1 tablespoon wine vinegar
1 teaspoon Dijon mustard

Remove stems from the tomatoes and turn tomatoes upside down. Cut partially through each tomato vertically in 3/4-inch slices. For each tomato, spoon 1 teaspoon of parsley between the slices and place stem-side down in a shallow serving dish. Combine remaining ingredients and pour over tomatoes. Cover and chill at least 30 minutes. Allow to stand at room temperature for 15 minutes before serving.

Calories per 1-tomato serving: 59
Fat: 3 g.
Cholesterol: 0
Sodium: 160 mg.

For exchange diets, count: 1 vegetable, 1 fat

Honey of a Waldorf Salad

Preparation time: 15 minutes
Yield: 8 1/2-cup servings

2 cups chopped apples
1 tablespoon lemon juice
1/2 cup celery, finely diced
1/3 cup chopped walnuts
1/2 cup sliced green grapes
1/4 cup light mayonnaise
2 tablespoons honey

Place chopped apples in a salad bowl. To retard browning, sprinkle the lemon juice over the apples, and stir. Add all remaining ingredients, and stir to mix.

Calories per 1/2-cup serving: 120
Fat: 7 g.
Cholesterol: 2 mg.
Sodium: 25 mg.

For exchange diets, count: 1 fruit, 1 1/2 fat

Jelled Rhubarb Salad

Preparation time: 15 minutes
Chilling time: 4 hours
Yield: 12 1/2-cup servings

2 cups finely chopped rhubarb
2 cups apple juice, divided
2 3-ounce packages sugar-free raspberry
   gelatin
2 bananas, finely chopped
1/2 cup crushed pineapple
Topping:
1/2 cup fat-free sour cream
1 tablespoon sugar or equivalent sugar
   substitute
1/2 teaspoon vanilla
2 tablespoons chopped pecans

Combine rhubarb and 1 cup of apple juice in a saucepan. Bring the mixture to a boil, then simmer for 10 minutes. Remove mixture from the heat and stir in gelatin until completely dissolved. Then stir in remaining 1 cup of chilled apple juice. Cool mixture in the refrigerator until partially set, about 1 hour. Stir in banana and pineapple, and transfer to an 8-inch square dish. Refrigerate 3 hours. In a small bowl, combine ingredients for the topping. Spread over salad before serving. Cut salad into 12 squares.

Calories per 1/2-cup serving: 64
Fat: 1 g.
Cholesterol: 0
Sodium: 16 mg.

For exchange diets, count: 1 fruit

Lean Bean Salad

Preparation time: 15 minutes
Yield: 8 1/2-cup servings

16-ounce can garbanzo beans
15-ounce can French-style green beans (no
    salt added)
1 small red onion, chopped
1 tablespoon fresh or dried parsley
1 tablespoon vegetable oil
1/4 cup vinegar
2 tablespoons sugar
1 teaspoon garlic powder
1/2 teaspoon black pepper
1/4 cup Parmesan cheese

Drain beans well. Combine all other ingredients in a 2-quart
salad bowl. Add beans. May be chilled or served immediately.
This keeps well for 5 days.

Calories per 1/2-cup serving: 118
Fat: 3 g.
Cholesterol: 2 mg.
Sodium: 58 mg.

For exchange diets, count: 1 lean meat,
1 vegetable

Lemon and Basil Salad Dressing

Preparation time: 10 minutes
Yield: 1 cup or 16 1-tablespoon servings

1/3 cup lemon juice
1/2 teaspoon basil
1 1/2 teaspoons dry mustard
1 teaspoon sugar
1/4 teaspoon salt
1/4 teaspoon garlic powder
1/4 teaspoon pepper
1/2 cup vegetable oil

Combine all ingredients except oil in a blender or shaker container. Add oil. Store in a covered container for up to 3 weeks in the refrigerator. Use over fresh greens or raw vegetables.

Calories per 1-tablespoon serving: 34
Fat: 4 g.
Cholesterol: 0
Sodium: 31 mg.

For exchange diets, count: 1 fat

Marinated Mushroom Salad

Preparation time: 50 minutes
Yield: 4 1/2-cup servings

1/2 cup red wine vinegar
1/3 cup water
2 teaspoons vegetable oil
1/2 teaspoon garlic powder
1/2 teaspoon basil
1/4 teaspoon thyme
Dash cayenne pepper
12 ounces fresh mushrooms, cleaned and
    sliced thin

Combine everything except mushrooms in a saucepan. Bring to a boil, then simmer for 5 minutes. Add mushrooms. Remove from heat and cover for 5 minutes. Transfer to a salad bowl. Cover. Chill for at least 30 minutes. Serve with slotted spoon. Can be made a day ahead; keeps for 3 days.

Calories per 1/2-cup serving: 49
Fat: 3 g.
Cholesterol: 0
Sodium: 15 mg.

For exchange diets, count: 1 vegetable, 1/2 fat

Old-Fashioned Cucumbers
Preparation time: 55 minutes
Yield: 4 1-cup servings

1 quart fresh cucumbers, peeled and
  sliced thin
1 medium onion, cut into slices
1 teaspoon salt
Ice cubes
1/4 cup vinegar
1/4 cup sugar
1/2 teaspoon celery seed

Wash and prepare cucumbers and onion, and layer in a shallow bowl. Sprinkle with salt, and cover with a tray of ice cubes. Allow to marinate for at least 30 minutes. Drain well, squeezing liquid from cucumbers. Combine vinegar, sugar, and celery seed in a shaker container. Pour over vegetables, and chill at least 15 minutes. This keeps 3 days.

Calories per 1-cup serving: 73
Fat: 0
Cholesterol: 0
Sodium: 61 mg.

For exchange diets, count: 1 vegetable, 1/2 fruit

Overnight Layered Spinach Salad

Preparation time: 15 minutes
Chilling time: 8 to 24 hours
Yield: 4 2-cup servings

1/2 pound fresh spinach, washed, drained
   dry and torn into bite-sized pieces
1 red pepper, finely chopped
2 green onions, finely chopped
8-ounce can mandarin oranges, drained
4 strips bacon, broiled until crisp, then
   diced
1/2 cup fat-free Caesar salad dressing
   (such as Hidden Valley)

Layer ingredients in a 7 by 11-inch glass dish. Cover and refrigerate overnight.

Calories per 2-cup serving: 114
Fat: 3 g.
Cholesterol: 5 mg
Sodium: 132 mg.

For exchange diets, count: 3 vegetable, 1 fat

Speed Alert: This recipe requires overnight chilling.

Quick Homemade Italian Dressing
Preparation time: 5 minutes
Yield: 8 1-tablespoon servings

1/4 cup red wine vinegar
1/4 cup no-added-salt vegetable broth
1 tablespoon olive oil
1 tablespoon Italian seasoning blend
1 teaspoon sugar
1/4 teaspoon salt
1/8 teaspoon ground black pepper

Combine all ingredients in a shaker container, and chill. This salad dressing keeps for up to 6 weeks in the refrigerator.

Calories per 1-tablespoon serving: 14
Fat: 1 g.
Cholesterol: 0
Sodium: 66 mg.

For exchange diets, count: as a free food

Red, White, and Blue Salad
Preparation time: 10 minutes
Yield: 8 2/3-cup servings

1 cup sliced strawberries
1 cup blueberries
1 large banana, sliced
1 cup white miniature marshmallows
1 cup sugar-free nonfat vanilla yogurt
Garnish:
2 tablespoons coconut

Combine first five ingredients in a clear glass salad bowl, using a spatula to gently mix. Garnish the top with coconut and chill or serve immediately.

Calories per 2/3-cup serving: 73
Fat: 1 g.
Cholesterol: 0
Sodium: 26 mg.

For exchange diets, count: 1 fruit

Salads

Summer Vegetable Mold

Preparation time: 2 hours
Yield: 8 3/4-cup servings

6 cherry tomatoes
2 packages sugar-free lemon gelatin
2 cups boiling water
1 cup cold water
3 tablespoons vinegar
1/2 cup diced and seeded cucumber
1/4 cup green pepper, chopped fine
1 scallion, chopped fine

Cut cherry tomatoes in half and set them aside. Pour gelatin into a small mixing bowl. Add the boiling water and stir to dissolve the gelatin. Add cold water and vinegar. Pour 1 cup of the gelatin mixture into a 2-quart mold. Chill for 30 minutes. Add remaining vegetables to gelatin left in the bowl and chill for 1 hour. When first layer of gelatin in mold has set for 30 minutes, press 12 cherry tomato halves into the mold. Allow to set 30 minutes more. Then spoon remaining gelatin and vegetables over the tomatoes and chill for 1 more hour. Unmold by placing the mold in hot water for 30 to 45 seconds; cut into 8 slices.

Calories per 3/4-cup serving: 27
Fat: 0
Cholesterol: 0
Sodium: 8 mg.

For exchange diets, count: 1 vegetable

Speed Alert: This recipe requires 2 hours for gelatin to set.

Sweet and Sour Tomatoes

Preparation time: 15 minutes
Chilling time: 2 hours
Yield: 8 1-cup servings

6 large home-grown tomatoes, peeled and
   chopped, and juice discarded
2 green onions, chopped
2 stalks celery, diced
1 yellow or green pepper, seeded and diced
1/4 cup sugar or equivalent sugar
   substitute
1/4 cup cider vinegar
1/4 teaspoon pepper

Combine all ingredients in a large salad bowl. Cover and refrigerate at least 2 hours before serving.

Calories per 1-cup serving: 48
Fat: 0
Cholesterol: 0
Sodium: 17 mg.

For exchange diets, count: 2 vegetable

Speed Alert: This recipe requires 2 hours for flavors to blend.

Twenty Calorie Molded Salad

Preparation time: 2 hours
Yield: 4 1-cup servings

---

1 cup boiling water
2 3-ounce packages sugar-free or regular
  lemon gelatin
1 tablespoon lemon juice
6 large ice cubes
1 cup chopped celery
1 cup shredded cabbage and carrots

Pour boiling water over gelatin in a bowl, stirring until gelatin is dissolved. Stir in lemon juice and ice cubes, and chill for 1 hour or until mixture is thick. Stir in vegetables, and transfer to an 8-inch square pan or 1-quart salad bowl. Chill for 1 hour more, and cut into 4 servings.

Calories per 1-cup serving: 22 (using sugar-free
gelatin)
Fat: 0
Cholesterol: 0
Sodium: 41 mg.

For exchange diets, count: 1 vegetable

Speed Alert: This recipe requires 2 hours for gelatin to set.

Tex-Mex Slaw

Preparation time: 20 minutes
Yield: 8 1-cup servings

1/2 head green cabbage
1 red onion
12 ounces frozen whole kernel corn
1 cup taco sauce
1/3 cup light mayonnaise
16-ounce can black beans, drained

Shred cabbage to desired texture. Transfer to a salad bowl.
Shred onion and add to cabbage. Steam frozen corn for 3 minutes, then drain. Combine taco sauce and mayonnaise. Toss cabbage, drained beans, and corn with taco sauce dressing just
before serving.

Calories per 1-cup serving: 120
Fat: 3 g.
Cholesterol: 3 mg.
Sodium: 69 mg.

For exchange diets, count: 1 vegetable, 1 fat,
1/2 starch

Want More Salad
Kids love it!
Preparation time: 20 minutes
Yield: 4 3/4-cup servings

---

2 Granny Smith apples, cut fine
3 stalks celery, chopped fine
1/4 cup raisins
2 tablespoons sunflower seeds
7 ounces pineapple chunks in juice,
 drained well

Dressing:
1/4 cup light mayonnaise
1/4 cup plain nonfat yogurt
2 tablespoons orange juice
2 packages Equal sugar substitute or
 2 teaspoons sugar

Combine first five ingredients in a salad bowl. Combine dressing ingredients, and pour over salad. Toss, and refrigerate or serve. This keeps well for 2 days.

Calories per 3/4-cup serving: 155
Fat: 6 g.
Cholesterol: 11 mg.
Sodium: 155 mg.

For exchange diets, count: 1 fat, 1 1/2 fruit

Asparagus Chef Salad

Preparation time: 35 minutes
Yield: 4 1-cup servings

---

2 1/2 pounds asparagus, trimmed
2 tablespoons water
8 ounces mushrooms, sliced
2 ounces part-skim Swiss cheese, cut into
   julienne strips
2 ounces lean ham, cut into julienne strips
1 tablespoon finely chopped onion
1 orange, peeled and cubed
Dressing:
1 package lemon and herb salad dressing
   mix
2 tablespoons water
1/4 cup vinegar
1/4 cup vegetable oil

Chop asparagus into bite-sized pieces and place in a microwave-proof casserole dish. Add water, cover, and microwave for 2 minutes. Drain. Measure remaining ingredients into a salad bowl. Add asparagus when completely cool. Combine dressing ingredients in a shaker container. Add approximately 1/3 of the dressing to the salad. Save remaining dressing for greens and fresh vegetables.

Calories per 1-cup serving: 151
Fat: 5 g.
Cholesterol: 25 mg.
Sodium: 347 mg.

For exchange diets, count: 2 vegetable,
1 lean meat, 1 fat

Baked Burrito

Preparation time: 35 minutes
Yield: 8 8-ounce servings

---

1 pound lean ground beef
4 ounces part-skim American cheese
1/4 cup chopped scallions
8 10-inch flour tortillas
Mexican Sauce:
8 ounces no-added-salt tomato sauce
1/4 teaspoon garlic powder
1/2 teaspoon cumin
1/8 teaspoon cayenne powder (optional)
1/2 teaspoon dried jalapeño peppers
    (optional)
1 tablespoon lemon juice
1 tablespoon sugar

Preheat oven to 350°F. Brown and drain the ground beef. Meanwhile, shred the cheese and chop the scallions. Mix the sauce ingredients together and pour over drained beef, stirring to mix. Place 1/2 cup beef mixture in each tortilla; fold and place seam side down on a baking sheet. Top with cheese and scallions. Bake 15 minutes. Serve with lettuce and tomatoes. These burritos freeze well on baking sheets or in baking dishes.

Calories per 1-burrito serving: 212
Fat: 6 g.
Cholesterol: 57 mg.
Sodium: 180 mg.

For exchange diets, count: 2 lean meat,
1 starch, 1 vegetable

Bayou Fish Stew

If you've never tried fish stew, you're in for a special discovery!
Preparation time: 45 minutes
Yield: 4 1 1/2-cup servings

Nonstick cooking spray
1 pound white fish, thawed (haddock, cod,
  or trout are great)
1 tablespoon water
2 scallions, chopped
4 ounces fresh mushrooms, sliced
1 small zucchini, sliced
1 green pepper, chopped
12 ounces chunky tomatoes
1 cup quick rice
1/2 teaspoon garlic powder
1/2 teaspoon cumin
Cayenne to taste
8 ounces no-added-salt tomato sauce
1 teaspoon basil
1 teaspoon Worcestershire sauce

Steam fish with water in the microwave for 3 minutes. Cool and cut into small cubes. Sauté scallions, mushrooms, zucchini, and pepper in a Dutch oven that has been sprayed with cooking spray. Add fish and all remaining ingredients to vegetables, and simmer for 30 minutes. Or microwave uncovered in a 3-quart casserole dish for 15 minutes.

Calories per 1 1/2-cup serving: 320
Fat: 8 g.
Cholesterol: 62 mg.
Sodium: 40 mg.

For exchange diets, count: 3 lean meat, 2 vegetable, 1 starch

Bean Casserole Olé

Preparation time: 55 minutes
Yield: 8 1 1/2-cup servings

---

1 cup chopped onion
1 green pepper, diced
2 tablespoons margarine
2 15-ounce cans pinto or kidney beans
4 teaspoons chili powder
1 teaspoon garlic powder
1 teaspoon dried jalapeño pepper
  (optional)
14-ounce can chopped tomatoes or 2 cups
  fresh tomatoes
4 strips bacon
1/2 cup shredded part-skim American
  cheese
1/2 cup shredded part-skim Monterey jack
  cheese

Preheat oven to 350°F. Sauté onion and pepper in the margarine in a skillet. Combine the sautéed vegetables, beans, seasonings, and tomatoes in a 3-quart baking dish. Stir well. Bake for 35 minutes. Broil bacon until crisp, and crumble. Sprinkle the casserole with cheese and bacon, and bake for 5 more minutes. Serve. Leftovers freeze well.

Calories per 1 1/2-cup serving: 349
Fat: 11 g.
Cholesterol: 28 mg.
Sodium: 392 mg.

For exchange diets, count: 2 meat, 2 starch,
1 fat, 1 vegetable

Bowtie Pasta Salad with Asparagus, Peaches, and Chicken

This combination sounds wild, but it tastes wonderful!
Preparation time: 20 minutes
Chilling time: 1 hour
Yield: 8 1 1/2-cup servings

★ ★ ★

---

1 pound asparagus, chopped
1 tablespoon water
8 ounces bowtie pasta, cooked and drained
1 green onion
16-ounce can diced peaches, drained
8 ounces cooked white meat chicken, cut
    into chunks
1/2 cup your favorite fat-free salad
    dressing

Place asparagus in a glass bowl. Sprinkle with water. Cover and microwave on high power for 4 minutes. Remove cover from bowl. Meanwhile, cook pasta according to package directions, taking care not to overcook. Rinse and drain pasta. In a large salad bowl, combine steamed asparagus, cooked pasta, and all remaining ingredients. Cover and chill at least 1 hour before serving.

Recipe tested with Quick Homemade
Italian Dressing, page 118.
Calories per 1 1/2-cup serving: 171
Fat: 1 g.
Cholesterol: 18 mg.
Sodium: 184 mg.

For exchange diets, count: 1 very lean meat,
1 starch, 2 vegetable

Broccoli and Cheese Enchiladas

Preparation time: 40 minutes
Yield: 8 servings

★ ★ ★

Nonstick cooking spray
1 medium onion, chopped
1 tablespoon margarine
10-ounce package frozen spinach
2 cups frozen broccoli
4 ounces shredded part-skim mozzarella
  cheese, divided
1 cup part-skim ricotta cheese
1/2 cup picante sauce
1 teaspoon cumin
1/4 teaspoon garlic powder
8 flour tortillas

Preheat oven to 350°F. Sauté onion in margarine until tender. Meanwhile, microwave spinach and broccoli 3 minutes on high power to thaw. Drain well. In a mixing bowl, combine onion, vegetables, 1/2 cup of mozzarella cheese, ricotta cheese, picante sauce, cumin, and garlic powder. Spoon 1/2 cup filling onto each tortilla and roll up. Place seam side down in a baking dish that has been sprayed with cooking spray. Top with remaining mozzarella cheese. Bake for 20 minutes. Serve with shredded lettuce and tomatoes.

Calories per 1-enchilada serving: 212
Fat: 8 g.
Cholesterol: 17 mg.
Sodium: 348 mg. (To reduce sodium, use no-added-
salt tomato sauce instead of picante sauce.)

For exchange diets, count: 2 meat, 1 vegetable, 1 starch

Chicken Chestnut Salad

Preparation time: 15 minutes
Yield: 4 1-cup servings

2 cups chunked white meat of chicken (or
    turkey)
1/2 cup peeled and chopped cucumber
1/2 cup diced celery
1/2 cup water chestnuts, drained and
    sliced
1/4 cup diced green pepper
1/4 cup diced scallions
1/4 cup diced pimiento
1/4 cup light mayonnaise
Salad greens of choice
Paprika for garnish

Toss first seven ingredients with mayonnaise. Serve on fresh
greens and garnish with paprika.

Calories per 1-cup serving: 146
Fat: 9 g.
Cholesterol: 36 mg.
Sodium: 153 mg.

For exchange diets, count: 2 lean meat,
2 vegetable

Curried Chicken Salad

Preparation time: 20 minutes
Yield: 4 2-cup servings

1/2 cup plain nonfat yogurt
1 tablespoon peanut butter
1 tablespoon sugar
2 tablespoons skim milk
2 teaspoons curry powder
6 cups torn mixed greens
2 cups diced cooked chicken
1 cup shredded green cabbage
1 cup shredded red cabbage
11 ounces mandarin oranges, drained well
1 ounce peanuts, chopped
1 tablespoon chopped scallions

Combine yogurt, peanut butter, sugar, milk, and curry in a shaker container. In a salad bowl, arrange greens, chicken, cabbage, oranges, peanuts, and scallions. Toss salad with dressing, and serve.

Calories per 2-cup serving: 282
Fat: 12 g.
Cholesterol: 52 mg.
Sodium: 85 mg.

For exchange diets, count: 3 lean meat, 1 fat,
1 starch

Deep Dish Pizza

Preparation time: 60 minutes
Yield: 12 slices

1-pound loaf frozen white or wheat bread
   dough
1 tablespoon vegetable oil
8 ounces part-skim mozzarella cheese,
   shredded
8 ounces lean ground pork, browned
1/2 cup chopped onion
1/2 cup chopped green pepper
8 ounces no-added-salt tomato sauce
1/2 teaspoon garlic powder
1/2 teaspoon fennel
1/4 teaspoon pepper
1 teaspoon basil
1 teaspoon oregano
1/2 teaspoon sugar

Thaw frozen dough the day before in the refrigerator or thaw in the oven. (To thaw in the oven, preheat the oven to 200°F. Turn off oven. Place oiled bread dough in oiled 15 by 8-inch or 12-inch round pan. Cover with a towel and leave for 45 minutes in the oven.) Preheat oven to 450°F. Work thawed dough to the edges and part way up the sides of the pan. Sprinkle first with cheese, then pork, onions, and pepper. Combine tomato sauce with seasonings, and pour over all. Bake for 40 minutes or until edges are browned and the middle has risen. Remove from oven and allow to stand for 10 minutes. Cut and serve. Freeze or refrigerate leftovers.

Calories per slice: 229; Fat: 10 g.
Cholesterol: 22 mg. Sodium: 293 mg.

For exchange diets, count: 2 lean meat, 1 1/2 starch, 1 fat

Easy Seafood Salad

Preparation time: 15 minutes
Yield: 4 1-cup servings

1 cup salad shrimp, cooked
1 cup crab or flaked mock crab
1/2 cup chopped celery
1/4 cup chopped pimiento
2 tablespoons minced onion
1 cup green peas, thawed
1/2 cup reduced-calorie Thousand Island
  dressing
1 teaspoon lemon juice
1/4 teaspoon pepper
1/4 teaspoon marjoram
1/4 cup plain nonfat yogurt

Combine shrimp, crab, celery, pimiento, onion, and peas in a serving bowl. In shaker container, mix salad dressing, lemon juice, pepper, marjoram, and yogurt. Pour dressing over salad, toss, and serve.

Calories per 1-cup serving: 154
Fat: 4 g.
Cholesterol: 63 mg.
Sodium: 388 mg.

For exchange diets, count: 1 starch,
1 1/2 lean meat

Eggs for a Bunch

Preparation time: 60 minutes
Yield: 8 3-inch squares

Nonstick cooking spray
12 slices white or French bread, crusts
    removed
4 ounces lean ham, cubed
2 cups skim milk
8 eggs or 2 cups liquid egg substitute
1/4 cup minced onion
1/2 teaspoon dry mustard
1/4 teaspoon paprika
1/4 teaspoon salt
1 tablespoon dried parsley

Preheat oven to 400°F. Cut bread into cubes and spread over the bottom of a 7 by 11-inch or 9 by 12-inch pan that has been sprayed with cooking spray. Sprinkle ham on top of bread. Using a mixer or blender, combine milk, eggs, onion, mustard, paprika, and salt. Pour over ham. Sprinkle with parsley. Bake for 35 to 40 minutes, or refrigerate overnight and bake in the morning. Perfect for brunch.

Calories per 3-inch square: 245
Fat: 7 g.
Cholesterol: 266 mg. with eggs; 15 mg. with
substitute
Sodium: 377 mg.

For exchange diets, count: 2 lean meat,
1 1/2 starch

Fifteen Minute Bean Casserole for Potluck

Preparation time: 15 minutes
Yield: 8 3/4-cup servings

16-ounce can pork and beans
16-ounce can black beans
16-ounce can pinto or kidney beans,
    drained
1/2 cup diced lean ham, smoked turkey, or
    Canadian bacon
2 tablespoons dried onion
1/2 cup chunky no-added-salt salsa

Combine ingredients in a casserole dish and stir to blend. Cover and microwave on 70 percent power for 7 minutes, stopping to stir once. Remove from microwave and broil under low flame for 5 minutes to brown the top of the casserole.

Calories per 3/4-cup serving: 183
Fat: 1 g.
Cholesterol: 3 mg.
Sodium: 358 mg.

For exchange diets, count: 1 very lean meat,
2 starch

Nutrition Alert: This recipe is high in sodium. It is intended for occasional use only. Substitute roast turkey for ham to reduce the sodium.

Garden Pizza

Preparation time: 40 minutes
Yield: 8 slices

Nonstick cooking spray
1 Robin Hood pizza crust mix, prepared
   according to package directions
2 cups sliced mushrooms
1 1/2 cups shredded carrots
1 cup finely sliced zucchini
1/2 cup chopped onions
1 tablespoon vegetable oil
8 ounces no-added-salt tomato sauce
1/4 teaspoon garlic
1/4 teaspoon fennel
1 teaspoon basil
1 teaspoon oregano
1 teaspoon brown sugar
1 cup part-skim mozzarella cheese
1/2 cup Parmesan cheese

Preheat oven to 425°F. Spray a 14-inch round pizza crisper pan with cooking spray. Press prepared crust onto pan. Bake for 14 to 16 minutes. Meanwhile, sauté mushrooms, carrots, zucchini, and onion in oil over medium heat for 3 minutes. When crust is prebaked, sprinkle with vegetables, sauce, seasonings, and both kinds of cheese. Bake for 15 more minutes. Remove from oven; cool for 3 minutes before slicing.

Calories per slice: 190
Fat: 7 g.
Cholesterol: 12 mg.
Sodium: 245 mg.

Continued on next page

Main-Dish Salads and Casseroles

Garden Pizza
(continued)

For exchange diets, count: 1 starch, 1 1/2 lean
meat, 1 vegetable

This recipe may be easily frozen after fully prepared. To use later, thaw at room temperature, place on a pizza crisper pan, and heat at 300°F. for 15 minutes.

Hot Crab with Vegetables
Preparation time: 25 minutes
Yield: 8 1 1/2-cup servings

6 medium tomatoes
1 cup evaporated skim milk
2 tablespoons margarine
2 tablespoons lemon juice
1/8 teaspoon nutmeg
1/4 teaspoon salt
1/2 teaspoon pepper
2 cups or 16 ounces imitation crab
1/4 pound mushrooms
1/2 cup frozen peas
1/2 cup vegetable spiral pasta
1/4 cup Parmesan cheese

Skin and chop tomatoes. Cook tomatoes for 5 minutes. Add milk and margarine, and cook for 10 minutes. Add lemon juice, nutmeg, salt, and pepper. Stir in crab, and remove from heat. Meanwhile, steam mushrooms and peas. Cook spiral pasta for 8 minutes in boiling water. Drain the pasta. Mix crab into the sauce; then combine with pasta and vegetables in a large serving bowl. Sprinkle with cheese, and serve.

Calories per 1 1/2-cup serving: 382
Fat: 11 g.
Cholesterol: 65 mg.
Sodium: 336 mg. with salt; 214 mg. without salt

For exchange diets, count: 4 lean meat, 2 starch

Cindy's Lasagna Salad

Preparation time: 25 minutes
Yield: 4 8-ounce servings

8 lasagna noodles, cooked and drained
1 tablespoon vegetable oil
1 cup low-fat cottage cheese
2 ounces shredded mozzarella cheese
16 fresh spinach leaves, chopped
1/2 teaspoon garlic powder
1 teaspoon basil
1/4 teaspoon black pepper
1 cup chopped tomatoes
1/2 cup low-calorie Italian dressing

Brush cooked noodles with oil. Combine cheeses, spinach, and garlic powder. Spread cheese mixture over noodles. Season with basil and pepper. Roll up noodles. Place on serving platter. Sprinkle with chopped tomatoes and your choice of low-calorie Italian dressing.

Calories per 2-noodle serving: 325
Fat: 10 g.
Cholesterol: 17 mg.
Sodium: 291 mg.

For exchange diets, count: 3 lean meat, 2 starch

Main-Dish Salads and Casseroles

Layered Summer Salad
Preparation time: 25 minutes
Yield: 4 1 1/2-cup servings

---

3 cups shredded lettuce or fresh greens of
   choice
1/2 cup low-calorie buttermilk dressing,
   divided
2 strips bacon, broiled and crumbled
2 cups cherry tomatoes, halved
2 ounces part-skim mozzarella cheese,
   cubed
8 ounces turkey or chicken, cooked and
   cubed

In a 3-quart salad bowl, layer the ingredients as follows: lettuce,
1/4 cup dressing, bacon, tomatoes, cheese, turkey or chicken, and
remaining 1/4 cup of dressing. Serve immediately or refrigerate
overnight.

Calories per 1 1/2-cup serving: 208
Fat: 8 g.
Cholesterol: 57 mg.
Sodium: 637

For exchange diets, count: 3 lean meat,
1 vegetable

Nutrition Alert: This recipe is high in sodium. Reduce the sodium
by omitting bacon and by using low-sodium cheese.

Make Ahead Cheesy Chicken Casserole

Preparation time: 10 minutes
Baking time: 1 hour, 15 minutes
Yield: 8 1 1/4-cup servings

10-ounce can white meat chicken,
    undrained
2 10-ounce cans reduced fat cream of
    chicken soup
1 cup skim milk
2 cups macaroni, uncooked
4 ounces fat-free cheddar cheese,
    shredded

Mix all ingredients together and spread into an 11 by 7-inch
casserole dish. Cover dish and refrigerate overnight. Bake at
350°F. for 1 hour and 15 minutes. Remove cover during the last
15 minutes of cooking.

Calories per 1 1/4-cup serving: 186
Fat: 4 g.
Cholesterol: 4 mg.
Sodium: 522 mg. (*To reduce sodium, substitute
reduced-sodium chicken and reduced-sodium
cream of chicken soup.)

For exchange diets, count: 2 very lean meat,
1 1/2 starch

Mexican Turkey Salad

Preparation time: 20 minutes
Yield: 4 1 1/2-cup servings

1 cup quick rice
1 cup water
1 ripe tomato, diced
1 green pepper, chopped
2 tablespoons green chilies
2 cups cooked turkey
Dressing:
1/2 cup nonfat yogurt
1 tablespoon vegetable oil
1 1/2 teaspoons chili powder
1/2 teaspoon cumin
1/2 teaspoon sugar
1/4 teaspoon garlic powder
1/4 teaspoon salt (optional)

Combine rice and water in a 1-quart microwave dish, cover tightly, and microwave on high for 3 minutes. Meanwhile, prepare vegetables. When rice is cooked, rinse quickly with cold water and transfer to colander to drain. In a salad bowl, combine vegetables, turkey, and rice. In shaker container, blend ingredients for dressing, and pour over salad just before serving.

Calories per 1 1/2-cup serving: 248
Fat: 5 g.
Cholesterol: 35 mg.
Sodium: 130 mg. with salt; 58 mg. without salt

For exchange diets, count: 1 1/2 starch,
2 lean meat, 1 vegetable

Continued on next page

Main-Dish Salads and Casseroles

Mexican Turkey Salad
(continued)

This recipe may be easily doubled. If using for a meal several days later, simply combine the turkey, rice, and vegetables in a covered plastic container and mix with dressing just before serving.

Main-Dish Salads and Casseroles

Pizza Salad
Preparation time: 20 minutes
Yield: 4 1 1/2-cup servings

---

4 cups chopped fresh lettuce or greens
2 large tomatoes, cut into wedges
8 large mushrooms, sliced
4 ounces part-skim mozzarella cheese,
  shredded
1/2 cup diced lean ham
1 tablespoon vegetable oil
1/4 cup red wine vinegar
1/4 teaspoon sugar
1 tablespoon Italian spice blend

Layer lettuce, tomato, mushrooms, cheese, and ham on salad plates. Combine oil, vinegar, sugar, and spices in a shaker container. Shake dressing over salad and serve.

Calories per 1 1/2-cup serving: 161
Fat: 11 g.
Cholesterol: 22 mg.
Sodium: 349 mg.

For exchange diets, count: 2 lean meat,
1 vegetable, 1 fat

Pork and Black Bean Stir-Fry

Preparation time: 20 minutes
Yield: 8 1 1/2-cup servings

1 teaspoon vegetable oil
1 pound lean pork (such as loin), cut into
  strips
2 tablespoons chili powder
1 small onion
1/4 teaspoon garlic powder
16-ounce can black beans, drained
1 pint cherry tomatoes, cut in half
1 cup frozen corn, thawed
1 tablespoon lemon juice
1/4 teaspoon salt, optional

Heat oil in a large skillet over medium heat. Stir-fry pork with
chili powder until pork is browned and cooked through, about 3
minutes. Set pork aside. Add onion and garlic powder to the pan
and stir-fry for 1 minute. Add remaining ingredients and stir-fry
for 3 more minutes. Stir in pork, heat through, and serve. Leftovers may be frozen for a later meal. Reheat in the microwave.

Calories per 1 1/2-cup serving: 270
Fat: 8 g.
Cholesterol: 59 mg.
Sodium: 45 mg. without salt; 112 mg. with salt

For exchange diets, count: 1 vegetable,
1 starch, 3 lean meat

Quiche Lorraine in a Fat-Free Crust

Preparation time: 15 minutes
Baking time: 55 minutes
Yield: 8 servings

Crust:
1 1/2 cups cooked brown rice
1 beaten egg or 1/4 cup liquid egg
    substitute
1 teaspoon caraway seed

Filling:
1 large yellow onion, peeled and chopped
4 ounces fat-free Swiss cheese, shredded
8 slices bacon, cooked crisp and diced fine
1 tablespoon flour
3 large beaten eggs or 3/4 cup liquid egg
    substitute
1 cup skim milk
1/2 teaspoon white pepper

Preheat oven to 400°F. Mix cooked brown rice, egg, and caraway seed together. Press into a 9-inch nonstick pie pan, and bake for 15 minutes. Remove from oven and spread onion, cheese, and bacon on crust. In a small mixing bowl, beat flour, eggs, milk, and pepper together until well mixed. Bake in preheated 425°F. oven for 10 minutes, then reduce heat to 350°F. and bake 30 minutes longer.

Calories per slice: 155
Fat: 6 g.
Cholesterol: 115 mg. with egg;
50 mg. with substitute
Sodium: 161 mg.

For exchange diets, count: 1 lean meat,
1 starch, 1 vegetable

Salmon Pasta Salad

Preparation time: 15 minutes
Yield: 8 1 1/4-cup servings

---

1 pound canned salmon, drained and
   flaked
8 ounces shell macaroni, cooked according
   to package directions and drained
1 rib celery, finely chopped
Dressing:
1/4 cup lemon juice
1 tablespoon olive oil
1/4 cup fresh basil leaves
1/2 teaspoon minced garlic
1/4 teaspoon pepper
1/4 cup Parmesan cheese

Combine salmon, macaroni, and celery in a salad bowl. In a food
processor or blender, process ingredients for the dressing until
basil leaves are chopped fine and the mixture is well blended.
Pour dressing over the salad ingredients, and toss to coat. Serve
on a bed of dark greens, and garnish with fresh lemon.

Calories per 1 1/4-cup serving: 195
Fat: 6 g.
Cholesterol: 20 mg.
Sodium: 261

For exchange diets, count: 1 starch, 2 lean meat

Main-Dish Salads and Casseroles

Seafood and Summer Vegetables

Preparation time: 45 minutes
Yield: 4 2-cup servings

★ ★ ★

1 tablespoon vegetable oil
4 small red-skinned potatoes, sliced
1/2 red onion, sliced
1/4 teaspoon garlic powder
1/2 teaspoon thyme
1/4 teaspoon salt (optional)
1/2 teaspoon white pepper
4 lemon slices
1 pound perch or haddock, thawed
1 zucchini, sliced thin
1 green pepper, chopped
1 tomato, chopped
1/4 cup white wine

Preheat oven to 375°F. Heat oil in a skillet; add potatoes, onion, garlic, thyme, salt, and pepper. Cover, and cook 15 minutes, stirring occasionally. Meanwhile, place lemon slices in a 9 by 9-inch baking dish. Place fish over lemon, and top with sliced zucchini, green pepper, and tomato. Pour on wine. Spoon potato mixture with liquid over tomatoes. Cover and bake for 25 minutes or microwave the covered dish at 70 percent power for 11 to 12 minutes until vegetables are tender.

Calories per 3-ounce fish and 1 cup vegetable
serving: 272
Fat: 8 g.
Cholesterol: 68 mg.
Sodium: 226 mg. with salt; 104 mg. without salt.

For exchange diets, count: 1 starch,
3 lean meat, 1 vegetable

Shoe Peg Tuna Salad

Preparation time: 15 minutes
Yield: 4 1-cup servings

2 7-ounce cans water packed tuna,
    drained
12-ounce can Shoe Peg corn, drained
1/4 cup sweet pickle relish
1 teaspoon dried onion
1/2 cup fat-free mayonnaise

Combine all ingredients in a mixing bowl. Chill until serving
time.

Calories per 1-cup serving: 198
Fat: 2 g.
Cholesterol: 35 mg.
Sodium: 773 mg. (To reduce sodium, use low-
sodium tuna, and substitute fresh cucumber for
the relish.)

For exchange diets, count: 3 very lean meat,
1 starch, 1 vegetable

Shrimp Casserole

Preparation time: 45 minutes
Yield: 4 1 1/2-cup servings

★ ★ ★

Nonstick cooking spray
1/2 cup celery, chopped
1 cup onions, chopped
2 tablespoons margarine
1/4 teaspoon celery seed
16-ounce can chopped tomatoes
1/4 cup ketchup
2 teaspoons horseradish
2 teaspoons Worcestershire sauce
Red pepper sauce as desired
1/2 cup soda cracker crumbs, crushed
1 beaten egg or 1/4 cup liquid egg
    substitute
1 pound shrimp, thawed
1 teaspoon dried parsley

Preheat oven to 375°F. Sauté celery and onion in margarine in a 2-quart Dutch oven. Stir in all remaining ingredients, and transfer to a shallow 2-quart casserole dish sprayed with cooking spray. Bake for 25 minutes or microwave 12 to 15 minutes until mixture is evenly browned and thickened.

Calories per 1 1/2-cup serving: 255
Fat: 9 g.
Cholesterol: 214 mg. with egg; 150 mg. with
substitute
Sodium: 436 mg.

For exchange diets, count: 3 lean meat,
1 1/2 starch

Main-Dish Salads and Casseroles

Spring Turkey Salad

Preparation time: 20 minutes
Yield: 4 1 1/2-cup servings

1/4 cup light mayonnaise
2 tablespoons honey
1/4 teaspoon ginger
1/2 cup diced celery
2 cups chopped turkey
11-ounce can mandarin oranges, drained
1 cup chopped apple
1 cup grape halves
8 ounces pineapple chunks, drained

In a serving bowl, combine mayonnaise, honey, and ginger, mixing well. Add remaining ingredients and mix lightly. Chill or serve.

Calories per 1 1/2-cup serving: 243
Fat: 6 g.
Cholesterol: 47 mg.
Sodium: 70 mg.

For exchange diets, count: 2 fruit, 2 lean meat

Turkey Roll-Ups

This cold entree is perfect for summer evenings.
Preparation time: 45 minutes
Yield: 4 8-ounce servings

★ ★ ★

12 broccoli spears
24 carrot sticks
1 tablespoon water
12 slices turkey breast (approximately 1
 pound)
1 tablespoon vegetable oil
2 tablespoons white wine vinegar
2 tablespoons sesame seeds
1/4 teaspoon salt (optional)
1 teaspoon sugar
1/4 teaspoon pepper

Wash and prepare broccoli and carrots for steaming. Steam with
1 tablespoon water in covered dish in the microwave for 4 minutes. Drain. Chill. Wrap 1 slice of turkey around a bundle of 2
carrot sticks and 1 spear of broccoli, and place seam side down
in a serving dish. Chill for at least 15 minutes. Combine oil, vinegar, sesame seeds, salt, sugar, and pepper in shaker container.
Pour over turkey roll-ups just before serving.

Calories per 3 roll-up serving: 305
Fat: 6 g.
Cholesterol: 73 mg.
Sodium: 280 mg. with salt; 158 mg. without salt

For exchange diets, count: 1 starch,
3 lean meat, 2 vegetable

Veggie Baked Omelet for Brunch

Preparation time: 15 minutes
Baking time: 35 to 40 minutes
Yield: 8 servings

Nonstick cooking spray
2 cups stir-fry or San Francisco-blend
    frozen veggies
1/2 pound reduced-fat pork sausage,
    cooked and drained well
4-ounce can chopped green chilies,
    drained
6 eggs or 1 1/2 cups liquid egg substitute
2 cups nonfat cottage cheese
4 ounces nonfat cheddar cheese, shredded
1/4 cup flour
1 teaspoon baking powder
1/4 teaspoon salt
1/2 teaspoon pepper

Preheat oven to 350°F. Spray a 9 by 13-inch baking pan with
cooking spray. Spread frozen veggies over the bottom of the pan.
Sprinkle sausage and chilies over the veggies. In a large mixing
bowl or food processor, blend all remaining ingredients until
smooth. Pour over the sausage and veggies, and bake uncovered
for 35 to 40 minutes. Rest at room temperature for 5 minutes,
then cut into 8 squares. Remove servings with a spatula and
serve veggie side up. Garnish with a red apple ring or slice.

Calories per serving: 208
Fat: 10 g. with egg, 5 g. with egg substitute
Cholesterol: 190 mg. with egg, 30 mg. with egg substitute
Sodium: 545 mg. (*To reduce sodium, omit salt and
substitute diced cooked pork for the sausage.)

For exchange diets, count: 1/2 skim milk, 1 vegetable, 2 lean meat, 1 fat

Zucchini Lasagna Casserole
Preparation time: 55 minutes using microwave method
Yield: 4 1 1/2-cup servings

Nonstick cooking spray
1 pound lean ground beef, browned and
    drained
1 onion, chopped
1 green pepper, chopped
4 ounces mushrooms, sliced
1/2 teaspoon vegetable oil
4 small zucchini, peeled and sliced thin
    lengthwise
8 ounces no-added-salt tomato sauce
1/4 teaspoon garlic powder
1/4 teaspoon fennel
1/4 teaspoon pepper
1 teaspoon basil
1 teaspoon oregano
2/3 cup low-fat cottage cheese
2 ounces mozzarella cheese, shredded
1/3 cup Parmesan cheese

Preheat oven to 375°F. (Recipe can be microwaved if you prefer.)
Sauté onion, pepper, and mushrooms in oil in a Dutch oven or
microwave 4 minutes in a 2-quart casserole dish. Meanwhile,
steam sliced zucchini 6 minutes on stovetop or microwave with
1 tablespoon water for 3 minutes in covered container. Stir meat,
tomato sauce, and seasonings into sautéed vegetables. Combine
cottage cheese and mozzarella cheese in a separate bowl. Spray
an 8-inch square baking dish with cooking spray. Layer zucchini,
cheese mixture, and meat sauce twice. Sprinkle Parmesan
cheese over last meat layer. Bake for 45 minutes or microwave
20 minutes. This can be assembled and frozen for later use.

Continued on next page

Main-Dish Salads and Casseroles

Zucchini Lasagna Casserole
(continued)

Calories per 1 1/2-cup serving: 298
Fat: 9 g.
Cholesterol: 77 mg.
Sodium: 421 mg.

For exchange diets, count: 3 lean meat,
1 skim milk, 2 vegetable

Barbecued Shrimp

Preparation time: 15 minutes
Yield: 4 4-ounce servings

---

1 pound fresh shrimp, peeled and
    deveined (or 1 pound frozen shrimp,
    thawed)
1/4 cup barbecue sauce
2 tablespoons chunky salsa

Place shrimp on a flat baking sheet. Place 3 inches under broiler
or above hot coals. Cook for 4 minutes, then turn over. Combine
barbecue sauce and salsa in a small bowl, then spread over
shrimp. Cook for 2 to 4 more minutes or until shrimp are opaque
and curled up. Do not overcook, or the shrimp will be tough.
Serve with rice.

Calories per 4-ounce serving: 145
Fat: 2 g.
Cholesterol: 172 mg.
Sodium: 400 mg. (*To reduce sodium, use low-
sodium barbecue sauce.)

For exchange diets, count: 4 very lean meat

Broiled Salmon Steaks

Preparation time: 25 minutes
Yield: 4 4-ounce servings

Nonstick cooking spray
1 pound salmon steaks, thawed (may
  substitute halibut or cod)
1 tablespoon fresh chives, chopped
1/4 teaspoon pepper
1 tablespoon lemon juice
1/4 teaspoon marjoram

Place salmon steak on baking sheet which has been sprayed
with cooking spray. Sprinkle remaining ingredients over fish.
Broil over medium flame for 20 minutes or until salmon flakes
with a fork. For microwave, cook uncovered for 6 minutes.

Calories per 4-ounce serving: 220
Fat: 7 g.
Cholesterol: 35 mg.
Sodium: 45 mg.

For exchange diets, count: 4 lean meat

Broiled Tuna Basted with Pineapple Sauce

Preparation time: 15 minutes
Yield: 4 4-ounce servings

1 pound fresh tuna steaks (or 1 pound
  frozen tuna fillets, thawed)
Sauce:
1/2 cup crushed pineapple in juice
1 tablespoon brown sugar
1 green onion, cut into chunks
2 tablespoons reduced-sodium soy sauce

Place tuna fillets on a flat baking sheet. Combine pineapple, brown sugar, onion, and soy sauce in a blender, and process until smooth. Place tuna fillets 3 inches under broiler or above hot coals. Cook for 6 minutes, then turn over. Spread pineapple sauce over the tuna fillets. Cook for 2 to 4 more minutes or until tuna steaks are flaky when pierced with a fork.

Calories per 4-ounce serving: 135
Fat: 1 g.
Cholesterol: 49 mg.
Sodium: 297 mg.

For exchange diets, count: 4 very lean meat

Cajun Fish on the Grill

Preparation time: 15 minutes
Yield: 4 4-ounce servings

Nonstick cooking spray
1 pound firm white fish of choice
1 teaspoon Cajun or Creole seasoning,
    divided (use a commercial seasoning
    blend or see recipe on page 173)
2 tablespoons lemon juice
1 tablespoon fresh minced basil
    or 1 teaspoon dried basil

Thaw fillets. Cover grate of grill with aluminum foil. Spray foil with cooking spray. Sprinkle 1/2 teaspoon Cajun seasoning over foil. Place fillets over seasoning. Grill for 5 minutes. Sprinkle tops of fish with remaining Cajun seasoning. Turn fillets. Grill for 5 to 10 more minutes, depending on thickness of fillets. Dot with lemon juice, and sprinkle with basil just before serving.

Calories per 4-ounce serving: 220
Fat: 4 g.
Cholesterol: 72 mg.
Sodium: 71 mg. with sodium-free Cajun
seasoning, (Check sodium content of
seasoning. This will vary.)

For exchange diets, count: 4 lean meat

Chicken Divan

Preparation time: 35 minutes
Yield: 4 1-cup servings

★ ★ ★

1 large bunch broccoli
1 tablespoon water
1 pound skinned chicken pieces or 4
    skinned breasts
1 cup quick rice
1 cup no-added-salt chicken broth
1 cup nonfat plain yogurt
2 tablespoons reduced-calorie mayonnaise
1 tablespoon flour
1 tablespoon lemon juice
1 teaspoon curry powder
Fresh parsley for garnish

Preheat oven to 375°F. (Recipe can be microwaved if you prefer.) Wash broccoli and cut off the full spears. Microwave spears in 1 tablespoon water in covered microwave dish until color changes (about 3 minutes). Drain in a colander. Combine chicken, rice, and broth. Microwave covered for 8 minutes. In the meantime, combine yogurt, mayonnaise, flour, lemon juice, and curry powder in a small bowl. When chicken and rice are done, place broccoli spears on top. Pour curry dressing over broccoli. Cover. Bake for 15 minutes or microwave for 8 minutes. Serve.

Calories per 1-cup serving: 358; Fat: 8 g.
Cholesterol: 89 mg. Sodium: 277 mg.

For exchange diets, count: 1 starch, 3 lean
meat, 2 vegetable, 1/2 skim milk

Cornflake Chicken or Fish

Preparation time: 35 minutes for fish; 55 minutes for chicken
Yield: 4 3-ounce servings

2 egg whites, whipped
1 1/2 cups evaporated skim milk
1 teaspoon poultry seasoning
3 cups crushed cornflakes
1 pound chicken pieces, skinned, or 1
    pound frozen fish fillets

Preheat oven to 400°F. Combine egg whites, milk, and seasoning in a mixing bowl. Whip for 2 minutes. Meanwhile, crush cornflakes in a plastic bag. Dip chicken or fish in milk, then shake in cornflakes and place on a baking sheet. For chicken, bake for 35 to 45 minutes. For fish, reduce time to 15 to 20 minutes.

Calories per 3-ounce serving: 160 (fish); 215 (chicken)
Fat: 3g. (fish); 9 g. (chicken)
Cholesterol: 51 mg. (fish); 66 mg. (chicken)
Sodium: 230 mg.

For exchange diets, count: 3 lean meat, 1/2 starch

Gourmet Chicken with Cheese

Preparation time: 50 minutes
Yield: 4 4-ounce servings

1/2 cup part-skim ricotta cheese
1/4 cup shredded part-skim mozzarella
   cheese
4 tablespoons Parmesan cheese, divided
1 tablespoon bread crumbs
1/2 teaspoon basil
2 chicken breasts, split and boned

Preheat oven to 350°F. Combine ricotta, mozzarella, 2 table-spoons Parmesan, bread crumbs, and basil in a small bowl. Carefully separate skin from flesh of each chicken breast, leaving one side of skin attached. Spoon half of cheese mixture between skin and flesh of each breast half. Pull skin edges under breast, and secure with wooden toothpicks. Place chicken, skin side up, in a shallow baking pan. Bake uncovered until chicken is cooked through and golden brown, about 35 minutes. Sprinkle with remaining Parmesan cheese. Serve.

Calories per 4-ounce serving: 275
Fat: 10 g.
Cholesterol: 95 mg.
Sodium: 306 mg.

For exchange diets, count: 1 skim milk,
4 lean meat

To save calories, cholesterol, and fat, do not eat the skin. The chicken can be prepared, stuffed, and frozen.

Honey Lime Salmon Fillets

Preparation time: 5 minutes
Marinating time: 30 minutes to 24 hours
Cooking time: 10 minutes
Yield: 4 4-ounce servings

1 pound fresh salmon steaks (or 1 pound
  frozen salmon steaks, thawed)
Marinade:
1/4 cup lime juice
1 tablespoon olive oil
1 tablespoon honey
1 teaspoon ground ginger
1/4 teaspoon black pepper

Combine ingredients for the marinade in a shallow pan. Place
salmon steaks in the marinade and spoon marinade over the
steaks, coating well. Cover and refrigerate at least 30 minutes or
up to 24 hours. Place salmon steaks 3 inches under broiler or
above hot coals. Cook for 6 minutes, then turn over. Cook for 2
to 4 more minutes or until salmon steaks are flaky when pierced
with a fork.

Calories per 4-ounce serving: 163
Fat: 7 g.
Cholesterol: 47 mg.
Sodium: 49 mg.

For exchange diets, count: 3 lean meat

Kiwi Orange Snapper

Preparation time: 20 minutes
Yield: 4 4-ounce servings

---

1 pound red snapper fillets
Sauce:
1 tablespoon olive oil
1 tablespoon frozen orange juice
    concentrate
1 fresh kiwifruit, peeled and cut into
    chunks
1 teaspoon ground ginger
1/2 teaspoon minced garlic
1/2 teaspoon white pepper

Place red snapper fillets on a baking sheet. In a blender or food processor, combine the ingredients for the sauce, and process until smooth. Cook the snapper fillets 3 inches below the broiler or above hot coals for 6 minutes. Turn over and baste with the sauce. Continue cooking for 4 to 6 more minutes until the fillets appear flaky when pierced with a fork.

Calories per 4-ounce serving: 142
Fat: 4 g.
Cholesterol: 31 mg.
Sodium: 55 mg.

For exchange diets, count: 4 very lean meat

Lemon Chicken for Company

Preparation time: 60 minutes
Yield: 4 4-ounce servings

4 boned and skinned chicken breasts
Juice of 1 lemon
1 tablespoon vegetable oil
1/2 cup flour
1/4 teaspoon salt
1/2 teaspoon paprika
1/4 teaspoon pepper
1 tablespoon grated lemon peel
2 tablespoons brown sugar
1 tablespoon water
1 lemon, sliced thin

Place chicken breasts in a flat pan, and cover with fresh lemon juice, reserving 1 tablespoon for later use. Cover and marinate in the refrigerator for at least 20 minutes. Preheat oven to 425°F. Pour oil in a shallow baking pan and place in the oven until it heats up. Meanwhile, combine flour, salt, paprika, and pepper in a plastic bag. Remove chicken from marinade and place it in the plastic bag, shaking to coat. Reduce oven temperature to 350°F., and place chicken on baking pan with heated oil. Mix grated lemon peel with brown sugar, and sprinkle over chicken. Combine water and 1 tablespoon reserved lemon juice, and sprinkle over chicken. Place one lemon slice on each breast. Bake uncovered for 35 to 40 minutes.

Calories per 4-ounce serving: 236 ; Fat: 6 g.
Cholesterol: 65 mg. Sodium: 344 mg. with salt;
222 mg. without salt

For exchange diets, count: 3 lean meat, 1 starch

Mediterranean Cod

Preparation time: 15 minutes
Yield: 4 4-ounce servings

---

1 medium onion, sliced
1 tablespoon vegetable oil
1/4 teaspoon garlic powder
15-ounce can Italian-style stewed
  tomatoes
1/4 cup salsa
1/4 teaspoon cinnamon
1 pound cod, cut into 4 portions

In a 1 1/2-quart microwave dish, microwave onion, oil, and garlic for 3 minutes. Drain, and stir in tomatoes, salsa, and cinnamon. Place cod fillets in tomato mixture. Cover and microwave on high power for 4 to 6 minutes or until fish is flaky.

Calories per 4-ounce serving: 167
Fat: 5 g.
Cholesterol: 47 mg.
Sodium: 310 mg.

For exchange diets, count: 3 lean meat

No-Salt Seasoning Blends for Poultry or Fish

Review the four different blends and choose the one that includes your favorite spices.

Everything But the Kitchen Sink Blend

Yield: about 1 cup

1/4 cup dried parsley
1/4 cup marjoram
2 1/2 tablespoons dried basil
1 1/2 tablespoons sesame seeds
1 1/2 tablespoons chile pepper flakes
1 1/2 tablespoons celery seed
2 1/2 teaspoons dried savory
2 1/2 teaspoons powdered sage
2 1/4 teaspoons dried thyme
2 teaspoons dried onion
2 teaspoons dill weed
1 1/4 teaspoons black pepper
3/4 teaspoon dried minced garlic

Lemon Herb Blend

Yield: about 3/4 cup

4 1/2 tablespoons dried basil
3 3/4 tablespoons dried oregano
1 1/2 tablespoons black pepper
1 1/2 tablespoons granulated onion
1 1/2 tablespoons whole celery seed
1/2 teaspoon dried minced garlic
1 tablespoon lemon rind, finely grated

Italian Blend

Yield: about 1/2 cup

2 tablespoons dried basil
2 tablespoons dried oregano
2 teaspoons fennel
1 tablespoon dried parsley
1 teaspoon powdered marjoram
1 teaspoon minced dried garlic

Onion-Paprika Blend

Yield: about 1/3 cup

5 teaspoons onion powder
1 tablespoon paprika
1 tablespoon garlic powder
1 tablespoon dry mustard
1 tablespoon thyme
1/2 teaspoon white pepper
1/2 teaspoon celery seed

Orange Teriyaki Marinade for Chicken

Preparation time: 10 minutes
Marinating time: at least 30 minutes up to 24 hours
Grilling time: 10 minutes
Yield: 4 4-ounce servings

1 pound chicken breast fillets, skinned
   and boned
Marinade:
1 green onion, finely chopped
1/2 teaspoon minced dried garlic
2 tablespoons reduced-sodium teriyaki
   sauce
1/4 cup all-fruit orange marmalade
1 tablespoon water

Combine ingredients for marinade in a shallow pan, stirring to blend. Add chicken breasts, and spoon marinade over the chicken. Marinate at least 30 minutes or up to 24 hours. Grill chicken breasts 3 inches over hot coals, about 5 minutes on each side.

Calories per 4-ounce serving: 170
Fat: 3 g.
Cholesterol: 73 mg.
Sodium: 241 mg.

For exchange diets, count: 3 lean meat

Pecan Crusted Chicken

Preparation time: 10 minutes
Baking time: 25 minutes
Yield: 4 4-ounce servings

Nonstick cooking spray
1 pound chicken breast fillets, skinned
and boned
Crust:
1 whole egg or 1/4 cup liquid egg
substitute
2 tablespoons honey mustard
2 tablespoons finely chopped pecans
1/4 teaspoon cayenne pepper

Preheat oven to 375°F. Combine ingredients for crust in a shallow bowl. Dip chicken breasts into the mixture, then arrange on a baking sheet that has been sprayed with cooking spray. Bake for 20 to 25 minutes or until chicken is tender when pierced with a fork.

Calories per 4-ounce serving: 192
Fat: 5 g.
Cholesterol: 116 mg. with egg;
73 mg. with substitute
Sodium: 160 mg.

For exchange diets, count: 4 lean meat

Smoked Turkey on the Grill

Preparation time: 10 minutes
Marinating time: at least 30 minutes up to 24 hours
Grilling time: 10 minutes
Yield: 4 4-ounce servings

1 pound smoked turkey breast fillets
Marinade:
2 tablespoons teriyaki sauce
1/4 cup apple juice
Sauce:
1/4 cup barbecue sauce
1 tablespoon chunky salsa

Combine ingredients for marinade in a shallow pan, stirring to blend. Add turkey breasts, and spoon marinade over the top. Marinate at least 30 minutes or up to 24 hours. Grill turkey breasts 3 inches over hot coals, about 4 minutes on each side. Stir sauce ingredients together. Baste fillets with sauce during last minute of grilling. Smoked turkey is fully cooked as purchased, so the grilling process is just to heat the meat through.

Calories per 4-ounce serving: 163
Fat: 3 g.
Cholesterol: 67 mg.
Sodium: 654 mg.

For exchange diets, count: 4 very lean meat,
1/2 fruit

White Fish Creole

Preparation time: 30 minutes
Yield: 4 4-ounce servings

---

1 pound Blue Hake Loins or other white
    fish fillet, thawed or frozen
2 teaspoons margarine
1 cup chopped fresh tomatoes
Creole Seasoning (Yield = 1/3 cup):
2 tablespoons paprika
1 1/2 teaspoons salt (optional)
2 teaspoons black pepper
2 teaspoons red pepper
2 teaspoons white pepper
1 teaspoon thyme

Preheat oven to 400°F. Place 4 frozen fish fillets on a baking sheet, and top each with 1/2 teaspoon margarine. Combine ingredients for seasoning in a shaker container. Sprinkle over fish (about 1/2 teaspoon per fillet). Label remaining seasoning, and save for later use on vegetables, corn on the cob, or meats. Bake fillets for 20 minutes. (If fillets are thawed, reduce baking time to 15 minutes.) Sprinkle chopped tomatoes over fillets, and bake 5 more minutes.

Calories per 4-ounce serving: 220
Fat: 8 g.
Cholesterol: 80 mg.
Sodium: 350 mg. (To reduce sodium, omit salt.)

For exchange diets, count: 4 lean meat

Grilled Pork à l'Orange

Preparation time: 30 minutes
Yield: 4 3-ounce servings

1 pound lean pork chops, scored in a criss-
  cross pattern
1/4 cup frozen orange juice concentrate
1 tablespoon brown sugar
1/4 teaspoon ground cloves
1 tablespoon Dijon mustard

Trim pork well. Broil or grill until nearly done (7 to 10 minutes on each side). Combine other ingredients and pour 1/2 of the mixture over chops. Broil or grill 2 more minutes. Turn and pour remaining sauce on other side. Broil or grill 2 more minutes. Serve. Garnish with an orange slice.

Calories per 3-ounce serving: 241
Fat: 9 g. Cholesterol: 83 mg.
Sodium: 115 mg.

For exchange diets, count: 1 starch, 3 lean meat

Marinated Pork Kabobs

Preparation time: 50 minutes
Yield: 4 4-ounce servings

---

1 pound boneless lean pork shoulder, well
    trimmed and cubed
1/2 cup ketchup
2 tablespoons lemon juice
2 tablespoons brown sugar
1 teaspoon reduced-sodium soy sauce
1 teaspoon minced onion
4 small onions, halved
1 green pepper, cut into wedges
1 tomato cut into wedges or 8 cherry
    tomatoes
15-ounce can whole potatoes

To prepare marinade, combine ketchup, lemon juice, brown
sugar, soy sauce, and minced onion in a bowl. Add pork cubes,
and marinate for at least 30 minutes. Remove meat from bowl.
Thread pork cubes, onion, pepper, tomato, and potatoes onto 4
skewers. Broil or grill for 5 to 7 minutes on each side. While
kabobs are grilling, transfer leftover marinade to saucepan and
bring to a boil. Reduce heat to simmer. Pour marinade over
kabobs just before serving.

Calories per 4-ounce serving: 260
Fat: 12 g. Cholesterol: 82 mg.
Sodium: 242 mg.

For exchange diets, count: 3 lean meat,
1 vegetable, 1 starch

Hawaiian Pork

Preparation time: 10 minutes
Marinating time: 30 minutes to 24 hours
Cooking time: 50 minutes
Yield: 8 4-ounce servings

2 pounds lean pork loin, well trimmed
1/3 cup lemon juice
2 tablespoons vegetable oil
2 tablespoons shredded onion
1/4 teaspoon garlic powder
1/4 teaspoon salt
1 teaspoon ginger
1 1/2 teaspoons curry powder
1/2 cup pineapple juice

Place pork loin in a shallow pan. Combine remaining ingredients, and pour over loin. Cover and marinate in the refrigerator for at least 30 minutes or up to 24 hours. Broil or grill the loin for 15 to 25 minutes on each side, placing meat 4 to 6 inches from heat element. Pork is done when an internal temperature of 170°F. is reached. Baste with marinade twice during grilling. This meat is tasty as a leftover.

Calories per 4-ounce serving: 249
Fat: 15 g. Cholesterol: 83 mg.
Sodium: 118 mg.

For exchange diets, count: 4 lean meat, 1 fat

Speed Alert: Depending on thickness of pork loin, this recipe may take up to 90 minutes.

Meat Loaves Italiano

Preparation time: 20 minutes
Yield: 4 4-ounce servings

1 pound lean ground beef
1 teaspoon basil
1/4 teaspoon garlic powder
1/4 teaspoon fennel
1/2 teaspoon oregano
1/4 teaspoon brown sugar
8 ounces no-added-salt tomato sauce
2 ounces mozzarella cheese, grated

Combine meat with basil, garlic powder, fennel, oregano, and brown sugar in a bowl. Mix well, then shape into 4 loaves. Put on microwave meat tray, and microwave for 4 minutes on high or broil in oven or on grill for 20 to 25 minutes. Drain well, then transfer to oven-safe meat platter. Pour tomato sauce over loaves, top with cheese, and broil for 4 to 6 minutes. Garnish with fresh parsley before serving. Recipe can be doubled, cooked, and frozen.

Calories per 4-ounce serving: 203
Fat: 6 g. Cholesterol: 76 mg.
Sodium: 121 mg.

For exchange diets, count: 3 lean meat

Roast Pork Loin with Cumberland Sauce

Preparation time: 50 minutes
Yield: 8 4-ounce servings

---

2 pounds pork loin, well trimmed
2 tablespoons lemon juice
2 tablespoons cornstarch
1 small can fruit cocktail in juice
1/4 cup frozen orange juice concentrate
1/4 cup currant jelly
2 tablespoons sherry
1/2 teaspoon ginger

Grill loin 4 to 6 inches from flame on grill or broiler. Cook for 15 to 25 minutes on each side. Meanwhile, in a small saucepan, combine lemon juice and cornstarch. Drain juice from fruit cocktail and reserve juice. Add orange juice concentrate, jelly, sherry, ginger, and reserved juice to the saucepan. Heat the mixture, stirring constantly until it thickens. Pour in fruit. Serve hot with grilled meat.

Calories per 4-ounce serving: 290
Fat: 12 g. Cholesterol: 80 mg.
Sodium: 60 mg.

For exchange diets, count: 4 lean meat, 1 fruit

Salt-Free Homemade Mustard

Commercial mustards have 150 mg. sodium per tablespoon.
This delicious mustard saves sodium and cents!
Preparation time: 40 minutes
Yield: 1 cup or 16 1-tablespoon servings

1/4 cup dry mustard
1/4 cup white wine vinegar
1/3 cup white wine
1 tablespoon sugar
3 egg yolks or 3/4 cup liquid egg
    substitute

Blend together all ingredients except egg yolks. Let this mixture marinate for 30 minutes. Beat egg yolks into the mixture with an egg beater. Transfer to a double boiler or a saucepan with a heavy bottom. Cook over medium heat, stirring constantly until slightly thickened, about 5 minutes. Remove from heat. Cool and store in a covered container for up to 1 month. Use with grilled red meats or cold sandwiches.

Calories per 1-tablespoon serving: 18
Fat: <1 g. Cholesterol: 32 mg. with eggs, 0 with
liquid egg substitute
Sodium: 21 mg.

For exchange diets, count: as a free food

Sirloin Barbecue
Preparation time: 10 minutes
Marinating time: 30 minutes to 24 hours
Cooking time: 25 minutes
Yield: 8 4-ounce servings

2 pounds sirloin, well trimmed
1/2 teaspoon salt
1/4 teaspoon pepper
1 tablespoon vegetable oil
1/3 cup water
8-ounce can tomato sauce
1/2 cup chopped onion
1/2 teaspoon garlic powder
2 tablespoons lemon juice
2 tablespoons vinegar
2 tablespoons brown sugar
1 teaspoon dry mustard

Place sirloin in a shallow pan. Combine remaining ingredients, and pour over meat. Cover and marinate for at least 30 minutes (or up to 24 hours) in the refrigerator. Broil or grill sirloin for 12 minutes on each side, placing meat 4 inches from heat. Brush with marinade during last 5 minutes of cooking. This meat is tasty as a leftover.

Calories per 4-ounce serving: 229
Fat: 9 g. Cholesterol: 72 mg.
Sodium: 374 mg. (*To reduce sodium, use no-added-salt tomato sauce.)

For exchange diets, count: 4 lean meat

Three Pepper Beef Kabobs

*Nancy Degner, chief recipe designer with the Iowa
Cattleman's Association, recommends beef sirloin
or tip steak cubes or strips for this favorite.*
Preparation time: 30 minutes
Yield: 4 4-ounce beef + 3/4-cup vegetable servings

---

1 tablespoon lemon juice
1 tablespoon water
2 teaspoons Dijon mustard
1 teaspoon honey
1/2 teaspoon dried oregano
1/4 teaspoon pepper
1 pound boneless beef sirloin steak, cut
    into 1-inch cubes
1 large green bell pepper, cut into 1-inch
    pieces
1 large red bell pepper, cut into 1-inch
    pieces
1 large yellow bell pepper, cut into 1-inch
    pieces
8 large mushrooms

In a shallow bowl, whisk together lemon juice, water, mustard,
honey, oregano, and pepper. Add beef, peppers, and mushrooms,
stirring to coat. Alternately thread pieces of beef, bell pepper,
and mushrooms on each of 4 12-inch skewers. Place kabobs on
rack in broiler pan so surface of meat is 3 to 4 inches from heat.
Broil 9 to 12 minutes for medium rare, turning occasionally.
Serve with steamed rice or a baked potato.

Calories per serving: 194
Fat: 7 g. Cholesterol: 76 mg. Sodium: 133 mg.

For exchange diets, count: 4 very lean meat, 2 vegetables

Tortilla Cheeseburgers
Preparation time: 30 minutes
Yield: 4 4-ounce servings

1 pound lean ground beef
1/2 teaspoon cumin
1/8 teaspoon pepper
4 flour tortillas, warmed
1/2 cup chopped tomato
1/2 cup chopped lettuce
1/2 cup part-skim cheddar cheese,
    shredded

Combine ground beef, cumin, and pepper, mixing lightly. Form into 4 patties. Place on a broiler pan or on the grill about 3 to 4 inches from the heat. Broil to desired doneness, turning once. Top half of each tortilla with equal portions of tomato, lettuce, and cheese. Place burger on top and fold tortilla.

Calories per filled tortilla: 299
Fat: 9 g. Cholesterol: 66 mg.
Sodium: 337 mg.

For exchange diets, count: 4 lean meat, 1 starch

Western Broil

Preparation time: 10 minutes
Marinating time: 30 minutes to 24 hours
Cooking time: 20 minutes
Yield: 4 8-ounce servings

1 pound round steak, cut 1-inch thick
1/2 cup light soy sauce
2 tablespoons honey
1 tablespoon lemon juice
2 scallions, finely chopped
1/4 teaspoon garlic powder
3/4 cup sliced carrots, steamed
1 1/2 cups pea pods, steamed

Combine soy sauce, honey, lemon juice, scallions, and garlic powder in a small bowl. Place steak in a pie pan and pour marinade over the steak, turning to coat. Marinate in the refrigerator for at least 30 minutes or up to 24 hours. Discard the marinade. Place steak on a broiler rack, so surface of meat is 3 inches from the heat. Broil for 20 minutes, turning once. Meanwhile, arrange carrots and peas around outside edges of a serving platter. Carve beef into 4 servings and place in the middle of platter.

Calories per 8-ounce serving: 240
Fat: 6 g. Cholesterol: 72 mg.
Sodium: 692 mg. (*To reduce sodium, use
1/4 cup light soy sauce.)

For exchange diets, count: 4 lean meat,
1 vegetable

Eggplant and Tomato Parmesan
Preparation time: 50 minutes
Yield: 4 1-cup servings

Nonstick cooking spray
1 medium eggplant (or zucchini), peeled
2 medium tomatoes, chopped
6 ounces no-added-salt V-8 juice
1/2 cup oatmeal or bread crumbs
1 teaspoon basil
1/4 teaspoon oregano
1/2 teaspoon garlic powder
1/2 cup or 2 ounces shredded part-skim
  mozzarella cheese
2 tablespoons Parmesan cheese

Preheat oven to 350°F. (Recipe can be microwaved if you prefer.)
Spray an 8-inch square baking dish with cooking spray. Cut eggplant lengthwise into 1/2-inch slices. Place slices in the baking
dish; top with tomatoes. In a small bowl, combine all other ingredients except cheeses. Spread oatmeal mixture over vegetables,
and cover evenly with cheeses. Bake for 35 minutes until golden
brown or microwave on high power for 15 minutes.

Calories per 1-cup serving: 144
Fat: 4 g. Cholesterol: 10 mg.
Sodium: 118 mg.

For exchange diets, count: 2 vegetable, 1/2
starch, 1 lean meat

Escalloped Cabbage

Preparation time: 55 minutes
Yield: 8 1-cup servings

3 quarts water
1 small head cabbage
2 tablespoons margarine
1/4 cup flour
1 cup skim milk
1 teaspoon salt-free seasoning for
   vegetables, such as Lawry's or
   Parsley Patch
1/2 teaspoon caraway seed
1 ounce mozzarella cheese
1/2 teaspoon salt (optional)
1/2 cup salad croutons

Preheat oven to 350°F. Bring water to a boil in a 4-quart pan. Wash cabbage and slice into bite-sized chunks. Place cabbage in boiling water, and cook for 15 minutes. Drain. Meanwhile, melt margarine in a small skillet or saucepan, and stir in flour. Gradually add milk, and cook over medium heat until thickened. Stir in seasoning, caraway seed, cheese, and optional salt. Spoon cabbage into a 3-quart baking dish. Fold in sauce, and top with croutons. Bake for 20 minutes. This may be prepared and frozen for later use.

Calories per 1-cup serving: 113
Fat: 3 g. Cholesterol: 9 mg.
Sodium: 169 mg. with salt, 107 mg. without salt

For exchange diets, count: 1 starch, 1 fat

Fresh Spinach with Lemon and Garlic

This elegant vegetable recipe was discovered in St. Louis.
Preparation time: 10 minutes
Yield: 4 1-cup servings

1 pound fresh spinach, washed and
   drained
1/2 teaspoon minced garlic
1 whole fresh lemon, quartered

Place fresh spinach leaves in a microwave-safe casserole dish.
Sprinkle with minced garlic. Cover and microwave on high
power for 6 minutes. Remove cover, squeeze fresh lemon juice
over the spinach, and serve piping hot.

Calories per 1-cup serving: 54
Fat: 0 Cholesterol: 0
Sodium: 36 mg.

For exchange diets, count: 2 vegetable

Green Bean and Dilly Stir-Fry

Preparation time: 20 minutes
Yield: 4 1-cup servings

1 1/2 pounds green beans, washed and
   trimmed
2 tablespoons water
4 teaspoons vegetable oil
6 scallions, sliced
1/4 cup chopped fresh dill
3 tablespoons red wine vinegar
1/2 teaspoon salt (optional)

Place beans in a microwave dish with 2 tablespoons water. Cover
and microwave on high power for 5 minutes. Drain. Heat oil in
a large skillet over high heat. Add beans and stir-fry for 4 minutes, until brown specks appear on beans. Add scallions, dill,
vinegar, and salt. Cook for 8 more minutes over medium heat.
Serve hot.

Calories per 1-cup serving: 108
Fat: 5 g. Cholesterol: 0
Sodium: 285 mg. with salt; 41 mg. without salt

For exchange diets, count: 2 vegetable, 1 fat

Grilled Vegetable Kabobs

Preparation time: 20 minutes
Yield: 4 1-cup servings

---

1 medium zucchini, cut diagonally into
   1/2-inch thick slices
1 medium yellow squash, cut diagonally
   into 1/2-inch thick slices
1 red onion, cut into quarters
8 cherry tomatoes
1 tablespoon Dijon mustard
1 tablespoon apple juice

Alternately thread vegetables onto four 12-inch skewers. Combine mustard and apple juice in a small dish. Grill vegetables for 4 to 5 minutes four inches from medium coals or broiler flame. Brush with mustard and apple juice; turn and grill the other side. Brush with remaining mustard and apple juice, and serve with red meats, poultry, or fish.

Calories per 1-cup serving: 50
Fat: 1 g. Cholesterol: 0
Sodium: 58 mg.

For exchange diets, count: 2 vegetables

Italian Potato Salad

Preparation time: 45 minutes
Yield: 4 1-cup servings

2 cups cooked potato chunks
2 tablespoons water
1 cup steamed pea pods
1/2 cup sliced radishes
2 tablespoons chopped scallions or chives
1/2 cup reduced-calorie Italian dressing

Wash potatoes; slice potatoes into a microwave dish. Add 2 tablespoons water, then steam until tender (about 10 minutes on high power). Steam pea pods in same fashion in covered microwave dish for 3 minutes. Drain potatoes and pea pods, and rinse with cold water. Transfer to a serving bowl. Combine with radishes and scallions or chives. Chill 15 minutes. Toss with dressing just before serving.

Calories per 1-cup serving: 108
Fat: 3 g. Cholesterol: 0
Sodium: 236 mg.

For exchange diets, count: 1 starch, 1 vegetable, 1/2 fat

Lemon Zucchini

Preparation time: 15 minutes
Yield: 4 1-cup servings

---

4 small zucchini, peeled and sliced thin
2 tablespoons water
2 tablespoons chopped onion
1/3 cup chopped parsley
1 tablespoon margarine
1/2 teaspoon grated lemon peel
2 tablespoons lemon juice

In a covered dish, combine zucchini with water. Cover and microwave on high power for 5 minutes. Drain. Meanwhile, sauté onion and parsley in margarine in a skillet. Stir in lemon peel and juice. Add steamed zucchini to the pan, and toss. Serve hot.

Calories per 1-cup serving: 36
Fat: 3 g. Cholesterol: 0
Sodium: 1 mg.

For exchange diets, count: 1 vegetable, 1/2 fat

Party Potato Salad

Preparation time: 30 minutes
Yield: 8 1/2-cup servings

3 cups peeled and diced potatoes (about 5
   potatoes)
1/2 cup frozen peas, thawed
1/4 cup diced red pepper
1 tablespoon onion, chopped
1 hard-cooked egg, diced
Dressing:
1/2 cup nonfat yogurt
1/2 cup light or reduced-calorie
   mayonnaise
1 teaspoon sugar
1 tablespoon Dijon or regular prepared
   mustard
1/4 teaspoon salt
1/2 teaspoon pepper

Steam potatoes until tender. This requires about 25 minutes on
the stovetop or about 10 minutes in the microwave (with 2 tablespoons water in a covered dish). Combine potatoes with remaining salad ingredients in a 2-quart salad bowl. Combine dressing
ingredients, and pour over vegetables. Toss until well blended.
Serve immediately or chill for 24 hours.

Calories per 1/2-cup serving: 132
Fat: 6 g. Cholesterol: 42 mg.
Sodium: 193 mg.

For exchange diets, count: 1 starch, 1 fat

Sinless Scalloped Corn
Preparation time: 30 minutes
Yield: 4 3/4-cup servings

★ ★ ★

Nonstick cooking spray
2 cups whole kernel corn (or 16-ounce
    package frozen corn)
1/8 cup chopped onion
1/4 cup skim milk
1 egg or 1/4 cup liquid egg substitute
1/4 teaspoon pepper
4 wheat crackers with unsalted tops,
    crushed

Preheat oven to 350°F. (Recipe can be microwaved if you prefer.)
If corn is frozen, defrost until the kernels are loose. Put corn into
a 1-quart casserole dish sprayed with cooking spray. Add
remaining ingredients. Stir well. Microwave on high power for
20 minutes until mixture is thick, or bake for 45 minutes. This
freezes well.

Calories per 3/4-cup serving: 113
Fat: 3 g. Cholesterol: 63 mg. with egg; 0 with
substitute
Sodium: 39 mg.

For exchange diets, count: 1 1/2 starch

Vegetables and Starches

Stuffed Tomatoes

Preparation time: 15 minutes
Yield: 4 whole tomato servings

1/2 cup orzo (rice-shaped pasta)
1/2 cup shredded farmer cheese
1/4 cup diced celery
1 teaspoon dill weed
1 tablespoon vegetable oil
1 teaspoon lemon juice
1/2 teaspoon salt (optional)
1/4 teaspoon pepper
4 large tomatoes

Cook orzo according to package directions, taking care not to overcook. Drain and rinse under cold water. In a medium mixing bowl, combine orzo with all remaining ingredients except tomatoes. Cut tops off tomatoes and scoop out the pulp and seeds. Stuff each tomato with 1/4 of the orzo mixture.

Calories per 1-tomato serving: 144
Fat: 7 g. Cholesterol: 10 mg.
Sodium: 409 mg. with salt; 165 mg. without salt

For exchange diets, count: 1 starch, 1 vegetable,
1 fat

Summer Baked Beans

Preparation time: Start day before; 3 hours day of serving.
Yield: 16 1/2-cup servings

12 ounces dried navy or black beans
1 quart water
1/2 cup chopped onion
1 green pepper, diced
1/2 cup diced celery
12 ounces beer
4 cups water
Sauce:
16 ounces no-added-salt tomato sauce
1/2 teaspoon garlic powder
1/2 teaspoon basil
2 teaspoons Worcestershire sauce
2 teaspoons lemon juice
3 tablespoons brown sugar
1 tablespoon prepared mustard
1/8 teaspoon cayenne pepper (optional)

Soak beans 12 hours or overnight in a 3-quart saucepan with 1 quart water. Drain. Combine beans, vegetables, beer, and 4 cups water in the same saucepan, and simmer for 2 1/2 hours. Preheat oven to 350°F. Drain beans well, and transfer to a 1 1/2-quart baking dish. Combine ingredients for sauce, and stir into beans and vegetables. Bake for 15 to 20 minutes uncovered, or microwave in covered dish for 8 to 10 minutes until heated through. These beans may be fully prepared and frozen.

Calories per 1/2-cup serving: 108
Fat: 1 g. Cholesterol: 0
Sodium: 24 mg.

Vegetables and Starches

For exchange diets, count: 1 starch,
1/2 lean meat

Speed Alert: This recipe must be started the day before, and then requires 3 hours to prepare the day of serving. To save time, purchase cooked beans or use fast-soak method. This calls for covering beans with water, bringing to a boil for 15 minutes, removing from heat, and covering for 45 to 60 minutes. The fast-soak method replaces overnight soaking.

Southern Vegetable Medley

Preparation time: 25 minutes
Yield: 4 1-cup servings

---

1 cup no-added-salt tomato juice
1 1/2 cups whole kernel corn
1 cup sliced, peeled zucchini
2 tablespoons brown sugar

Combine all ingredients, and simmer uncovered on medium heat for 45 minutes or microwave on high power in a deep covered 2-quart casserole dish for 18 minutes. Mixture will thicken.

Calories per 1-cup serving: 109
Fat: 1 g. Cholesterol: 0
Sodium: 16 mg.

For exchange diets, count: 1 starch, 1 vegetable

Wild Rice and Vegetable Salad

Preparation time: 40 minutes
Yield: 4 3/4-cup servings

1/2 cup long grain wild rice
1 cup water
Dash salt
2 tablespoons fresh dill or 1/2 teaspoon
    dill weed
2 tablespoons lemon juice
1 tablespoon vegetable oil
1/2 teaspoon grated lemon peel
1/2 teaspoon Dijon mustard
1/4 teaspoon pepper
1/2 cup fresh carrot slices
1/2 cup chopped fresh broccoli
1/4 cup chopped onion
1/2 cup fresh cauliflower, in small pieces

Cook rice in water with salt until tender—about 20 minutes.
Rinse with cold water and drain well. Combine the next 6 ingredients for dressing in a salad bowl, using a whisk. Add vegetables and rice; toss and serve. This keeps well for several days in
the refrigerator.

Calories per 3/4-cup serving: 130
Fat: 4 g. Cholesterol: 0
Sodium: 43 mg.

For exchange diets, count: 1 starch,
1 vegetable, 1 fat

Wild Rice for Picnics

Preparation time: 35 minutes
Yield: 4 1-cup servings

★ ★ ★

2 cups water
1/2 cup wild rice
8 ounces fresh mushrooms, sliced
1/2 cup scallions, diced
1/2 pound asparagus, chopped
3 medium carrots, sliced thin
1 teaspoon vegetable oil
2 tablespoons oil
1/4 cup vinegar
2 teaspoons sugar
1 1/2 teaspoons dry Good Seasons lemon
   and herb dressing mix

Heat water to boiling and add wild rice. Cook for 25 minutes, then rinse with cold water and drain well. Meanwhile, prepare mushrooms, scallions, asparagus, and carrots. Place 1 teaspoon oil in a 2-quart microwave-safe baking dish. Put sliced vegetables in oil, and cover. Microwave on high power for 6 minutes. Uncover and stir to cool. Combine 2 tablespoons oil, vinegar, sugar, and dressing mix in shaker container. Place drained rice and cooled vegetables in a 2-quart salad bowl and chill. Just before serving, pour dressing on salad, and toss.

Calories per 1-cup serving: 208
Fat: 8 g. Cholesterol: 0
Sodium: 217 mg.

For exchange diets, count: 1 starch,
2 vegetable, 1 fat

Blueberry and Pineapple Dessert Cups
Preparation time: 2 hours
Yield: 4 1-cup servings

---

1 cup pineapple juice
3-ounce package sugar-free lemon gelatin
1 1/2 cups nonfat yogurt
2 cups fresh blueberries

Bring pineapple juice to a boil. Pour over gelatin in a 2-quart bowl, and stir until dissolved. Chill until slightly thickened (about 1 hour). Blend in yogurt and blueberries. Pour into 4 dessert cups, and chill until firm. Garnish with pineapple chunks on a skewer.

Calories per 1-cup serving: 119
Fat: 0 Cholesterol: 0
Sodium: 60 mg.

For exchange diets, count: 1 fruit, 1/2 skim milk

Speed Alert: This recipe requires 2 hours for dessert cups to chill.

Desserts

Bridge Club Dieter's Treat

A recipe made famous by my mother-in-law, Isabelle Smith,
together with Charlotte, Francis, and Lois, packs
160 milligrams of calcium per slice!
Preparation time: 15 minutes
Freezing time: 3 hours
Yield: 6 slices

★ ★ ★

2 8-ounce cartons strawberry-flavored fat-
  free, sugar-free refrigerated yogurt
  (may use raspberry)
3-ounce package sugar-free gelatin (may
  use raspberry)
1 cup reduced-fat whipped topping
1 reduced-fat prepared graham cracker
  crust

In a medium mixing bowl, gently combine yogurt, gelatin powder, and whipped topping. Transfer into prepared crust. Freeze
for 3 hours, then slice and serve. Garnish the plate with a chocolate mint.

Calories per slice: 198
Fat: 5 g. Cholesterol: 2 mg.
Sodium: 285 mg.

For exchange diets, count: 1/2 fruit, 1 starch,
1 fat, 1/2 skim milk

Brownie Banana Split

An all-American birthday treat for party-goers of all ages!
Preparation time: 15 minutes
Baking time and cooling time: 1 hour
Yield: 12 servings—1 banana split each

Brownies:
5-ounce envelope brownie mix (for 9-inch
   square pan)
2 tablespoons vegetable oil
4 tablespoons skim milk or yogurt
Nonstick cooking spray

4 bananas
1 cup strawberry all-fruit spread
4 cups fat-free vanilla frozen yogurt

Preheat oven to 350°F. In a small mixing bowl, combine brownie
mix, oil, and milk. Stir by hand for 50 strokes. Transfer batter
into a 9-inch square pan with has been sprayed with cooking
spray. Bake brownies for 28 to 30 minutes. Brownies will begin
to pull away from the pan when they are done, but may appear
soft in the center. Cool brownies for 30 minutes, then cut into 12
squares. Meanwhile, peel and slice bananas. Microwave fruit
spread in a glass measuring cup on high power for 60 seconds.
Assemble dessert in individual bowls by layering: 1 brownie
square, 1/3 cup frozen yogurt, 1/3 cup fresh banana slices, with
1 1/2 tablespoons warm fruit spread drizzled over the top. Put a
candle in the birthday person's dessert!

Calories per serving: 312; Fat: 4 g.
Cholesterol: 0; Sodium: 50 mg.

For exchange diets, count: 1 1/2 fruit, 1/2 skim milk,
2 starch, 1/2 fat

Coffee Lovers' Cheesecake

Preparation time: 15 minutes
Baking time and cooling time: 3 1/2 hours
Yield: 10 slices

---

1 reduced-fat prepared graham cracker
    crust

Filling:

2 tablespoons instant espresso coffee
    powder or instant coffee
2 tablespoons strong coffee or coffee
    liqueur
1 cup nonfat ricotta cheese
3/4 cup reduced-fat sour cream
8 ounces reduced-fat cream cheese,
    softened
2/3 cup sugar
2 eggs or 1/2 cup egg substitute
2 tablespoons unsweetened cocoa powder

Garnish:

Cinnamon

Preheat oven to 300°F. In a food processor or blender, add ingredients for cheesecake filling one at a time, blending after each addition until smooth. Pour filling into prepared crust, sprinkle with cinnamon, and bake for 1 hour. Turn off the oven, and leave the cheesecake inside with the door closed for 30 minutes longer. Remove the cheesecake from the oven and refrigerate 2 hours. Slice into 10 wedges, dipping a sharp knife in hot water and wiping dry before cutting each slice.

Calories per slice: 236
Fat: 7 g. Cholesterol: 53 mg. with eggs, 0 with substitute
Sodium: 321 mg.

For exchange diets, count: 1 skim milk, 1 starch, 1 fat, 1/2 fruit

Cheesecake with Fruit Sauce

Preparation time: 60 minutes
Yield: 8 slices

★ ★ ★

1 Royal lite cheesecake mix
1/4 cup water
2 cups chopped rhubarb, strawberries,
  cherries, or peaches, or mixture of your
  favorite fruit
1 package sugar-free raspberry gelatin

Prepare cheesecake according to package directions, and refrigerate. Bring water to a boil in a medium saucepan. Add fruit. Cover and simmer for 15 minutes. Stir in gelatin. Chill and serve as a sauce for the cheesecake.

Calories per 1/8 cheesecake
and 1/4 cup sauce: 140
Fat: 4 g. Cholesterol: 0
Sodium: 260 mg.

For exchange diets, count: 1 1/2 starch, 1 fat

Creamy Strawberry Squares

Preparation time: 15 minutes
Chilling time: 3 hours
Yield: 8 slices

★ ★ ★

3-ounce package sugar-free strawberry
   gelatin
1 cup hot water
4 ounces nonfat cream cheese, softened to
   room temperature
1 cup reduced-fat whipped topping
9-ounce can crushed pineapple
1 cup sliced fresh strawberries
Garnish:
8 whole strawberries

In a small mixing bowl, mix gelatin powder with hot water until
gelatin is fully dissolved. Place cream cheese in a blender or food
processor. Slowly pour gelatin mixture into the cream cheese,
processing continuously on low until mixture is completely
creamy and smooth. Gently fold in remaining ingredients, and
transfer to a loaf pan. Chill for 3 hours. Slice and serve squares
with a fresh berry garnish.

Calories per slice: 56
Fat: 1 g. Cholesterol: 0
Sodium: 2 mg.

For exchange diets, count: 1 fruit

Fat-Free Frozen Fruit Cups

These frozen treats satisfy an 8 p.m. sweet tooth.
Preparation time: 10 minutes
Freezing time: 3 hours
Yield: 8 1-cup servings

16-ounce bag frozen whole strawberries
2 large bananas, peeled and sliced
9-ounce can crushed pineapple and juice
12-ounce can sugar-free lemon lime soft
  drink

Combine all ingredients in a large mixing bowl. Ladle 1 cup of fruit and juice into 8 12-ounce disposable plastic cups. Freeze for 3 hours. Microwave on high power for 55 seconds to soften to perfect slushiness.

Calories per 1-cup serving: 67
Fat: 0 Cholesterol: 0
Sodium: 2 mg.

For exchange diets, count: 1 fruit

Speed Alert: This recipe requires 3 hours for freezing.

Lemon Cheesecake
with Fresh Raspberry Topping

Preparation time: 15 minutes
Baking time and cooling time: 3 1/2 hours
Yield: 10 slices

1 reduced-fat prepared graham cracker
  crust
Filling:
1/4 cup frozen lemonade concentrate
1 tablespoon finely grated fresh lemon
  rind
1 cup nonfat ricotta cheese
2 tablespoons cornstarch
3/4 cup reduced-fat sour cream
8 ounces reduced-fat cream cheese,
  softened
2/3 cup sugar
2 eggs or 1/2 cup liquid egg substitute
Garnish:
1 cup fresh raspberries

Preheat oven to 300°F. In a food processor or blender, add ingredients for cheesecake filling one at a time, blending after each addition until smooth. Pour filling into prepared crust, and bake for 1 hour. Turn off the oven and leave the cheesecake inside with the door closed for 30 minutes longer, then remove it from the oven and cool. Refrigerate at least 2 hours. Slice into 10 wedges, dipping a sharp knife in hot water and wiping dry before cutting each slice. Garnish with fresh raspberries.

Desserts

Calories per slice: 236
Fat: 7 g. Cholesterol: 53 mg. with egg;
0 with substitute
Sodium: 321 mg.

For exchange diets, count: 1 skim milk, 1 starch,
1 fat, 1/2 fruit

Honeydew Whip

Preparation time: 15 minutes
Refrigeration time: 4 hours, 30 minutes
Yield: 8 servings

---

1 large honeydew melon
1/4 cup lemon juice
1/4 cup lime juice
1 cup water
2/3 cup sugar
5 envelopes unflavored gelatin
2 tablespoons orange or peach liqueur
1 cup fat-free Cool Whip

In blender, purée small amounts of melon, lemon juice, and lime juice, and pour into a large bowl. Repeat until the whole melon is used. Combine water, 2/3 cup sugar, and gelatin in a small mixing bowl, and let stand for 4 minutes. Microwave this gelatin mixture at full power uncovered for 3 minutes or just to boiling; stir to dissolve the sugar and gelatin. Add to melon, then briskly stir in liqueur. Chill for 30 minutes. Mixture should mound when spooned. Fold Cool Whip into chilled melon mixture, and transfer to a soufflé dish. Refrigerate for 4 hours or place in freezer for 1 1/2 hours and then transfer to refrigerator for 30 minutes. Slice and serve.

Calories per 1/8 of recipe: 156
Fat: 0 Cholesterol: 0
Sodium: 13 mg.

For exchange diets, count: 1 starch, 1 fruit

Speed Alert: This recipe requires a minimum of 2 1/2 hours preparation time.

Lemon Poke Cake

Preparation time: 10 minutes
Baking time: 35 minutes
Chilling time: 3 hours
Yield: 24 squares

1 reduced-fat white cake mix
2 cups boiling pineapple juice
2 3-ounce packages sugar-free lemon
    gelatin
Garnish:
Fresh fruit topping

Prepare cake mix according to package directions using liquid egg substitute in a 9 by 13-inch cake pan. While cake is baking, combine pineapple juice with gelatin powder in a small mixing bowl, stirring until the gelatin is completely dissolved. When cake is done, remove from the oven, and use a fork to pierce the cake at 1/2-inch intervals. Carefully and slowly pour gelatin over the cake. Refrigerate at least 3 hours so gelatin is firm. Slice cake and serve with fresh fruit topping.

Calories per square: 96
Fat: 1 g. Cholesterol: 0
Sodium: 155 mg.

For exchange diets, count: 1 1/2 fruit

Speed Alert: This recipe requires 3 3/4 hours.

Lemon Strawberry Supreme
Preparation time: 15 minutes
Refrigeration time: 2 hours
Yield: 8 slices

Nonstick cooking spray
2 pints strawberries
1/2 cup skim milk
1 envelope unflavored gelatin
1/2 cup sugar
2 tablespoons grated fresh lemon peel
1/4 cup lemon juice
1 1/2 cups nonfat yogurt

Clean strawberries and chill. In a 1-quart saucepan, combine milk and gelatin. Set aside for 5 minutes, then stir in sugar. Stir over low heat until gelatin and sugar are dissolved. Stir in lemon peel and lemon juice. Cool to room temperature, then chill until syrupy, about 15 minutes. Meanwhile, spray a quiche or vegetable dish (with 2-inch deep sides) with cooking spray. Fold yogurt into gelatin mixture and spoon into quiche dish. Cut the strawberries in half and place on top of lemon mixture. Chill at least 1 1/2 hours, then slice and serve.

Calories per slice: 101
Fat: 1 g. Cholesterol: 2 mg.
Sodium: 84 mg.

For exchange diets, count: 2 fruit

Speed Alert: This recipe requires 2 hours.

Desserts

Low-Fat Pie Crust

Use this with your favorite fruit filling.
Preparation time: 15 minutes
Chilling time: 1 hour
Yield: 1 whole pie crust, or 8 slices

★ ★ ★

1/2 cup all-purpose flour
1/4 teaspoon salt
1/4 teaspoon baking powder
1/4 cup soft margarine at room
    temperature

Sift flour, salt, and baking powder together in a deep bowl. Add margarine all at once, and work into the flour mixture with a pastry blender until no flour sticks to the side of the bowl. Shape into a ball, and wrap in wax paper. Refrigerate for 1 hour until thoroughly chilled. Roll out and place in pie pan. Fill and bake as pie recipes direct.

Calories per slice (1/8 pie): 75
Fat: 5 g. Cholesterol: 0
Sodium: 116 mg.

For exchange diets, count: 1 fat, 1/2 starch

Mile High Peach Pie

Preparation time: 30 minutes
Refrigeration time: 1 1/2 hours
Yield: 8 slices

16 2 x 2-inch graham crackers
2 tablespoons margarine
4 fresh peaches
1 cup sugar
2 egg whites
1 teaspoon vanilla
1 teaspoon lemon juice
1 cup whipped topping

Crush crackers in a blender or with a rolling pin, and transfer to a pie pan. Melt margarine, and stir into cracker crumbs, pressing mixture evenly over bottom and up sides of the pan. Peel the peaches, chop fine, and set aside. In a medium mixing bowl, combine sugar, egg whites, vanilla, and lemon juice; beat at medium speed for 15 minutes or until mixture is stiff. Fold in whipped topping and peaches. Pile lightly into prepared crumb shell. Chill for 1 1/2 hours and serve.

Calories per slice: 210
Fat: 5 g. Cholesterol: 0
Sodium: 113 mg.

For exchange diets, count: 1 starch, 1 fat,
1 1/2 fruit

Speed Alert: This recipe requires 2 hours.

This recipe contains uncooked egg white. I thought about taking the recipe out of this second edition because of recent safety concerns regarding consumption of raw egg. Be sure your eggs have been properly handled and refrigerated to reduce risk of contamination.

Oat Bran Crunchies

Preparation time: 30 minutes
Yield: 30 cookies

1/2 cup margarine
1/2 cup brown sugar
1 tablespoon water
1 teaspoon vanilla
1 egg or 1/4 cup liquid egg substitute
1/2 cup flour
1/4 cup whole wheat flour
1/2 teaspoon baking soda
1/4 teaspoon salt
3/4 cup oatmeal
3/4 cup oat flake cereal, lightly crushed
  (such as Honey Bunches of Oats or
  Clusters)
1/4 cup oat bran
2 tablespoons sugar
1 teaspoon cinnamon

Preheat oven to 350°F. Cream margarine and sugar with electric mixer until well blended. Add water, vanilla, and egg, beating well. Combine flours, soda, and salt, and add to creamed mixture. Add oatmeal, oat flake cereal, and oat bran. Drop dough by spoonfuls onto a no-stick baking sheet. Combine 2 tablespoons sugar and 1 teaspoon cinnamon in a small bowl. Dip flat bottom of a glass into the sugar and cinnamon mixture, and use to press dough flat. Bake for 7 minutes until browned. Cool on a wire rack. Store in covered container.

Calories per cookie: 80
Fat: 4 g. Cholesterol: 9 mg. with egg;
0 with substitute
Sodium: 70 mg.

For exchange diets, count: 1/2 starch, 1 fat

Desserts

Pineapple in Poppy Seed Dressing
Preparation time: 15 minutes
Yield: 4 1-cup servings

★ ★ ★

1 fresh pineapple
1/2 cup pineapple juice
1 tablespoon lime juice
2 tablespoons honey
1 tablespoon poppy seed
1 teaspoon grated lime peel

Cut pineapple in half lengthwise through crown. Remove fruit with a curved knife, leaving shells intact. Cut pineapple into chunks. Combine remaining ingredients in a shaker container. Spoon dressing over fruit, and mix. Transfer to pineapple shell, and serve.

Calories per 1-cup serving: 117
Fat: 1 g. Cholesterol: 0
Sodium: 2 mg.

For exchange diets, count: 2 fruit

Rhubarb Crunch

Preparation time: 60 minutes
Yield: 8 1-cup servings

6 cups chopped rhubarb
1 package sugar-free raspberry gelatin
2 teaspoons vanilla
1/2 cup orange juice
2/3 cup flour
1/3 cup oatmeal
1/2 cup brown sugar
1 teaspoon cinnamon
1/4 cup margarine

Preheat oven to 350°F. Combine rhubarb, gelatin, vanilla, and orange juice in a 9-inch square baking dish. Use a pastry blender to combine all remaining ingredients in a small mixing bowl until the mixture is crumbly. Sprinkle crumbs over the rhubarb. Bake for 45 minutes uncovered, just until bubbly. Cool and serve. Use vanilla nonfat yogurt, vanilla ice milk, or vanilla frozen yogurt as a topping.

Calories per 1-cup serving: 178
Fat: 7 g. Cholesterol: 0
Sodium: 117 mg.

For exchange diets, count: 1 starch, 1 fruit, 1 fat

Desserts

Rhubarb Strawberry Crisp

Preparation time: 30 minutes if microwaved,
55 minutes if baked
Yield: 8 1/2-cup servings

★ ★ ★

Nonstick cooking spray
2 1/2 cups strawberries, thinly sliced
1 1/2 cups chopped rhubarb
1 tablespoon cornstarch
1/4 cup sugar
Topping:
1/2 cup oatmeal
1/2 cup flour
1/3 cup brown sugar
1/4 cup margarine
1/2 teaspoon cinnamon

Preheat oven to 350°F. (Recipe can be microwaved if you prefer.)
Spray a 2-quart baking dish with cooking spray. Combine fruits
with cornstarch and sugar in the baking dish. Use a pastry
blender to mix the topping ingredients until crumbly. Sprinkle
topping over fruit. Microwave for 15 minutes on high power or
bake for 40 minutes.

Calories per 1/2-cup serving: 155
Fat: 7 g. Cholesterol: 0
Sodium: 73 mg.

For exchange diets, count: 1 fruit, 1 fat,
1/2 starch

Spring Parfait

Preparation time: 50 minutes
Yield: 4 1-cup servings

10-ounce package frozen raspberries,
 thawed
2 tablespoons lemon juice
1 cup fat-free Cool Whip
1 cup nonfat plain yogurt

Purée berries and lemon juice in blender until smooth. Strain out seeds and set in freezer. Fold Cool Whip into yogurt. Spoon yogurt mixture into 4 dessert glasses or dishes. Spoon chilled berries on top. Freeze at least 30 minutes. Remove from freezer 5 minutes before serving.

Calories per 1-cup serving: 140
Fat: 0 Cholesterol: 0
Sodium: 40 mg.

For exchange diets, count: 1 starch, 1 fruit

Stand Up for Strawberry Pie

Preparation time: 30 minutes
Chilling time: 1 1/2 hours
Yield: 8 slices

Crust:
1 1/2 cups crushed cornflakes
2 tablespoons margarine, melted
1 tablespoon sugar
Filling:
4 cups sliced strawberries
2/3 cup sugar
1 cup water
3 tablespoons cornstarch
3 tablespoons corn syrup
3 tablespoons strawberry gelatin (may use
    sugar-free)
Topping:
8 ounces low-fat vanilla yogurt

Preheat oven to 375°F. Combine ingredients for crust in a 9-inch pie plate. Press into pan, and bake for 10 minutes until browned. Cool. Put sliced berries into the crust. Combine sugar, water, cornstarch, and corn syrup in a saucepan, and boil for 2 minutes, stirring constantly. Remove from heat and stir in gelatin. Pour over berries. Chill for 1 1/2 hours. Top with yogurt before serving.

Calories per serving: 194; Fat: 4 g.
Cholesterol: 2 mg. Sodium: 94 mg.

For exchange diets, count: 2 fruit, 1/2 starch, 1 fat

Speed Alert: This recipe requires 2 hours.

Strawberry Alaska

Preparation time: 2 hours
Yield: 12 servings

1 angel food cake mix
4 cups low-fat frozen strawberry yogurt
3 egg whites
Pinch cream of tartar
Pinch salt
1/3 cup sugar

Prepare and bake cake according to package directions. Cool completely. Let yogurt soften slightly. Frost cake with yogurt. Cover with plastic wrap, and freeze immediately for 20 minutes. In a mixing bowl, beat egg whites until foamy. Add cream of tartar and salt. Gradually add sugar, beating constantly, until stiff. Preheat broiler. Frost cake with meringue. Place cake 3 inches from heat source, and broil for 1 to 2 minutes, until browned. Serve immediately. Leftover dessert may be frozen for use later.

Calories per serving: 221
Fat: 2 g. Cholesterol: 6 mg.
Sodium: 204 mg.

For exchange diets, count: 2 starch, 1 fruit

Speed Alert: This recipe requires 2 hours.

This recipe contains uncooked egg white. I thought about taking the recipe out of this second edition because of recent safety concerns regarding consumption of raw egg. Be sure your eggs have been properly handled and refrigerated to reduce risk of contamination.

Strawberries 'n Creme

Preparation time: 25 minutes
Yield: 4 3/4-cup servings

---

3 cups strawberries, halved
2 tablespoons grenadine
2 teaspoons rum extract
1/4 cup light sour cream
1 cup nonfat vanilla yogurt
1/4 cup sugar
1/4 teaspoon ground nutmeg

Toss strawberries with grenadine and rum extract. Chill for 15 minutes. Before serving, combine sour cream, yogurt, and sugar in a bowl. Spoon berries into individual dessert glasses, top with yogurt mixture, and sprinkle with nutmeg.

Calories per 3/4-cup serving: 169
Fat: 1 g. Cholesterol: 2 mg.
Sodium: 47 mg.

For exchange diets, count: 2 fruit, 1/2 skim milk

Desserts

Tortoni Cafetta

Preparation time: 60 minutes
Yield: 8 1/2-cup servings

6 tablespoons sugar
1 1/2 cups low-fat ricotta cheese
2 teaspoons vanilla
1/2 teaspoon almond extract
1/4 cup cocoa
1 tablespoon instant coffee powder
2 cups fat-free Cool Whip
Almonds for garnish

Blend first six ingredients together in a blender until very smooth. Fold Cool Whip into blended ricotta cheese mixture. Spoon mixture into 8 individual dessert dishes. Freeze for 45 minutes. Remove from freezer 10 minutes before serving. Garnish with almonds.

Calories per 1/2-cup serving: 59
Fat: 1 g. Cholesterol: 1 mg.
Sodium: 150 mg.

For exchange diets, count: 1 starch

Zucchini Brownies
Preparation time: 40 minutes
Yield: 30 2-inch square brownies

Nonstick cooking spray
3 cups peeled and grated zucchini
1 1/2 cups sugar
2/3 cup oil
3 cups flour
1/2 teaspoon salt
2 teaspoons soda
1/3 cup cocoa
3 teaspoons vanilla
1/3 cup coconut
1/2 cup chopped almonds

Preheat oven to 350°F. Mix all ingredients together in a 2-quart mixing bowl. Spray an 8 x 15-inch pan with cooking spray. Spread batter in pan. Bake for 25 minutes or until toothpick inserted in center comes out clean. Dust with powdered sugar when cooled.

Calories per brownie: 137
Fat: 6 g. Cholesterol: 0
Sodium: 92 mg.

For exchange diets, count: 1 starch, 1 fat

Nutrition Alert: This recipe contains a significant amount of sugar, and may not be a good choice for insulin-dependent diabetics. Check with your dietitian if you have questions.

★ ★ ★

Fall & Winter

Menus & Recipes

A Month of Low-Fat Dinner Menus for Fall and Winter

★ ★ ★

The following dinner menus feature common foods and selected recipes from this book (noted with an asterisk). Use the dinner menus together with breakfast and lunch menus on page 228 to create a 40-gram fat (or 1500-calorie) diet plan.

Week One

1 serving *Pizza Rounds
1 c. fresh greens with
2 tablespoons no-oil dressing
1/2 c. frozen peaches
1 c. skim milk

1 serving *California Blend
   Cream Soup
2 large breadsticks
2 oz. part-skim cheese
1 kiwifruit marinated in ginger ale
1 c. skim milk

1 serving *Almond Chicken with
   Vegetables
1/2 cup fresh carrot sticks
15 fresh green grapes
1 c. skim milk

1 serving *Harvest Casserole
1 slice wheat toast
1 c. fresh cucumber slices
1/2 frozen banana
1 c. skim milk

1 serving *Pumpkin Soup
1 toasted bagel with
2 oz. lean ham
1 c. fresh greens with 1 Tbsp. no-oil
   dressing
1/2 c. sorbet
1 c. skim milk

1 serving *Chicken Stroganoff
1 whole wheat roll with 1 tsp. margarine
1 c. shredded cabbage with 1 Tbsp.
   reduced-calorie dressing

1/2 c. pineapple slices
1 c. skim milk

1 serving *Vegetable Enchiladas
1 c. chopped lettuce
4 cherry tomatoes
1/2 c. frozen yogurt
1 c. skim milk

Week Two

1 serving *Turkey Kabobs
1 dinner roll with 1 tsp. margarine
1 slice angel food cake with 1 c.
   strawberries
1 c. skim milk

1 serving *Taco Casserole
1 c. chopped lettuce & tomatoes
1/2 c. sugar-free vanilla pudding
   with raisins
1 c. skim milk

1 serving *Kiwi Orange Snapper
1 baked potato with 1 tsp. margarine
1/2 c. steamed broccoli
1/2 c. cherries
1 c. skim milk
1/2 c. no-added-salt tomato juice

1 serving *Pineapple Chicken
1/2 c. quick rice
4 carrot sticks
15 red grapes
1 c. skim milk

1 serving *Tex-Mex Pork Loaf
1/2 c. squash
1 kaiser roll with 1/2 tsp. margarine
1 Granny Smith apple
1 c. skim milk

1 serving *Chestnut Chicken and Rice
1 cup radishes and cherry tomatoes
1 slice wheat toast
1/2 c. orange slices marinated in
  wine cooler
1 c. skim milk

1 serving *London Broil
1 serving *Baked Potato Chips
1 slice French bread and 1 tsp. margarine
1/2 c. peach and banana slices
1 c. skim milk

Week Three

1 serving *Chicken Cacciatore
1 toasted onion bagel with 1 tsp.
  margarine
1/2 c. blueberries
1 c. skim milk

1 serving *Turkey Salad à l'Orange
4 wheat crackers
1/2 c. cranberry juice
1 c. skim milk

1 serving *Michigan Bean Soup
1 slice wheat toast and 1 tsp. margarine
1 c. melon balls with
1/2 c. lime sherbet on top
1 c. skim milk

1 serving *Fish & Potato Bake
1/2 c. stewed tomatoes
1/2 c. mixed fruit with
1 c. nonfat vanilla yogurt on top
3 oz. grilled chicken breast

1 serving *Rice Creole
1 slice French bread with 1 tsp.
  margarine
1 nectarine
1 c. skim milk

1 serving *Shopper's Chili
6 soda crackers
4 radishes
1/2 c. apple and pineapple chunks
1 c. skim milk

3 oz. grilled halibut steak
1 baked potato with 1 tsp. margarine
1 c. fresh veggies and 1 Tbsp.

reduced-calorie dressing
1 serving *Anita's Pretty Fruit C.s
1 c. skim milk

Week Four

3 oz. broiled hamburger on a wheat
  bun with
lettuce, onion, and tomato
1/2 c. whole kernel corn
1 serving *Perfect Raspberry Chiffon
1 c. skim milk

1 serving *Traditional Pot Roast
1 slice white bread from frozen
  dough with 1 tsp. margarine
1/2 c. applesauce over
1/2 c. ice milk
1 c. skim milk

1 serving *Turkey & Mushroom
  Tetrazzini
1 slice broiled garlic toast
1 fresh orange
1 c. skim milk

1 serving *Baked Potato Burrito
1 c. chopped lettuce and tomato
1/2 c. fruit cocktail with sliced
  bananas
1 c. skim milk

1 serving *Old Fashioned Swiss
  Steak
1/2 c. *Carolyn's Veggie Pilaf
1 fresh pear
1 c. skim milk

1 serving *Chicken Breast Midwest
1 wheat roll with 1 tsp. margarine
1/2 c. fresh pineapple over 1/2 c. lime
  sherbet
1 c. skim milk

1 serving *Fettuccini Low-Fat
  Alfredo
1 c. fresh greens with
1 Tbsp. reduced-calorie Italian
  dressing
1/2 c. frozen yogurt
1 c. skim milk

A Week of Breakfast and Lunch Menus for Fall and Winter

★ ★ ★

Use these breakfast and lunch menus together with the dinner menu suggestions on page 226 to create a 40-gm. fat (or 1500 calorie) diet plan.

Breakfast	Lunch	Snack
	Monday	
3/4 c. Cream of Wheat with 1/2 banana 1 slice French bread toasted with 1 tsp. margarine 1/2 c. skim milk	1/2 c. tuna with 1 tsp. mayo on a warm bun 1 c. steamed California blend veggies 1 Granny Smith apple 1/2 c. skim milk	5 melba rounds 1/2 c. pineapple juice
	Tuesday	
1 English muffin toasted with 2 teaspoons margarine 1/2 c. orange juice 1/2 c. skim milk	2 small soft-shell tacos with 2 oz. seasoned ground turkey 1 c. chopped lettuce and tomato 1 fresh pear 1/2 c. skim milk	3 cups air popcorn 1 apple
	Wednesday	
1/2 c. oatmeal with 2 Tbsp. raisins 1 slice wheat toast with 1 tsp. margarine 1/2 c. skim milk	1 c. chicken noodle soup 2 oz. farmer cheese 1 slice wheat toast 1 large apple 1/2 c. skim milk	1 oz. pretzels 1 orange

Thursday

1 whole bagel toasted with 2 tsp. peanut butter 1/2 c. grapefruit juice 1/2 c. skim milk	1 large baked potato topped with 1/2 c. browned ground beef and 1/4 c. tomato sauce 1/2 c. strawberries with 1/2 c. vanilla yogurt on top	4 squares graham crackers 1/2 c. apple juice

Friday

2 small pancakes with 1/2 c. applesauce and cinnamon on top 1/2 c. skim milk	2 oz. lean ham with 1 c. fresh veggies stuffed into 1 large pita bread 1 c. vegetable soup 1/2 grapefruit 1/2 c. skim milk	1/2 c. blueberries 1 molasses cookie

Saturday

1/2 c. Maltomeal 1 bran muffin 1/2 c. pineapple juice 1/2 c. skim milk	1 c. tomato soup 4 wheat crackers 1/2 c. low-fat cottage cheese 1/2 c. mixed fruit 1/2 c. skim milk	1/4 c. sherbet with 1 kiwi fruit

Sunday

1/2 c. bran cereal 1 slice raisin toast with 1 tsp. margarine 1/2 c. pineapple chunks 1/2 c. skim milk	2 oz. grilled breast of chicken on a bun with mustard 1 c. steamed green beans with 1 tsp. margarine 12 grapes 1/2 c. skim milk	7 animal crackers 2 plums

Special Occasion Menus for Fall and Winter

★ ★ ★

Tailgate Party
*Party Meal in a Bowl with
assorted fresh vegetables
*Marinated Mexican Chicken Sandwich
*Tailgate Salad
fresh Cortland apples (stick one in
your pocket for the game)

Halloween
*Mexican Corn Main Dish
*Herbed Corn Bread
*Low-Fat Granola Apple Crisp

Oktoberfest
*Rouladen
*German Potato Salad
*German Red Cabbage
dark rye bread with margarine
*Fresh Fruit Soup

Thanksgiving Dinner
*Tarragon Turkey
*Fruit Stuffing
*Cranberry Salad
*Nutty Glazed Carrots
*Cranapple Bread
*Marinated Fruit on a Platter

Special Occasion Menus for Fall and Winter

★ ★ ★

Thanksgiving Brunch
*Dilly Cocktail
*Turkey Crepes
*Cold Sweet and Sour Vegetables
*Mountain Dew Fruit Salad
*Rolled Pumpkin Cheesecake

Holiday Cocktail Party
*Wrapped Carrots
*Nutty Mushrooms
*Popeye's Spinach Croquettes
*Chili Dip with Potato Skins
*Christmas Tree Canapes

Christmas Eve
*Savory Ham Balls
*Decorated Breadsticks
*Crunchy Broccoli Salad
*Lemon Citron Crisps

Christmas Day
*Marinated Loin of Pork
*Christmas Stuffing
*Baked Carrots and Sprouts
*Tangy Cabbage and Dried Fruit Salad
*Pumpkin Tofu Pie

Special Occasion Menus for Fall and Winter

★ ★ ★

New Year's Eve

*Jambalaya
*Sweet and Sour Cucumbers
wheat rolls with margarine
vanilla ice milk with creme de menthe topping

New Year's Day

*Halibut in a Sesame Crust
*Sweet Onion Soufflé
*Fruit Crunch for Sherbet

Sledding Party Potluck

*Cock-a-Leekie Soup
*Chunky Beef Chili
*Cathy's Cheese Pepper Bread
(Ask your friends to bring a vegetable tray)
chocolate frozen yogurt cones

Valentine's Day

*Romantic Chicken Marsala
*Green Beans with Garlic Dressing
*Fabulous French Bread
*Fruit Plate with Strawberry Dip

St. Patrick's Day

*Irish Potato Soup
*Honey LIme Salmon Fillets
fresh greens with
*Creamy Garlic Dressing
*Chocolate Espresso Angel Food Cake

Special Occasion Menus for Fall and Winter
★ ★ ★

Winter Dinner Party
*Tomato Pockets
*Stuffed Sole
*Broccoli Rice Casserole
*Autumn Buns
*Pear Melba

Bridge Club Desserts
*Chocolate Mousse
*Poppy Seed Bread
*Kiwi for Company
*Sharon B's Whole Wheat Apple Cake
*Oat Bran Apple Crisp
*Recipe is in this book. Check index for page numbers.

Black Bean and Cheese Nachos

Preparation time: 30 minutes
Yield: 8 servings - 6-8 nachos each

16-ounce can black beans in sauce
1 teaspoon chili powder
1/2 teaspoon cumin
2 green onions, diced
1/3 cup medium-hot thick and chunky
    salsa
4 cups baked tortilla chips (such as
    Highland Northern Lights)
4 ounces reduced-fat Monterey Jack
    cheese, grated

Preheat oven to 400°F. In a medium skillet, combine beans in sauce, chili powder, cumin, green onions, and salsa. Cook uncovered over medium heat for 10 minutes. Meanwhile, spread baked tortilla chips out on a large baking sheet. Spoon a small amount of bean mixture on each tortilla chip, then sprinkle cheese on top of beans. Bake for 15 minutes. Pass additional salsa as needed.

Calories per serving: 131
Fat: 4 g.
Cholesterol: 10 mg.
Sodium: 243 mg.

For exchange diets, count: 1 starch, 1 lean meat

Brewing the Best Coffee

Warm up a winter afternoon with coffee brewed with care.
Drip brewing time: 2 to 4 minutes
Yield: 1 cup of coffee

★ ★ ★

2 rounded tablespoons ground coffee
(1 standard coffee measure)
6 ounces cold tap water

Use freshly drawn cold tap water. Water is 90 percent of coffee brewing success. If you don't care for the taste of tap water, use bottled water for coffee. Use the correct grind of coffee for your coffeemaker. Too fine a grind will cause overextraction and bitterness. Too coarse a grind will cause watery coffee. For drip brewers, the appropriate grind should allow the coffee to finish dripping in 2 to 4 minutes. Do not skimp on coffee by grinding it finer or using less coffee, or you will have a thin, bitter brew. Coffee can be kept warm over a burner for only about 20 minutes before the flavor loses its pleasantness. An airpot or vacuum server will keep coffee hot and delicious for much longer. Coffee holds its flavor best at 185°F. Never reheat coffee; make it fresh each time you serve it, and make only as much as you plan to drink.

Coffee has negligible nutrient content.

Chili Dip with Potato Skins
Preparation time: 40 minutes
Yield: 8 3/4-cup servings of dip and 1/2 potato

16-ounce can no-added-salt chili beans
1 cup plain yogurt
1 avocado, peeled and chopped
1/2 cup scallions, chopped
5-ounce can green chilies, chopped
1/2 cup diced fresh tomato
4 ounces shredded part-skim American
 cheese
Potato Skins:
4 potatoes
2 tablespoons margarine, melted
1 teaspoon chili powder

Preheat oven to 400°F. Scrub potatoes. Microwave for 6 minutes, turning after 3 minutes, or bake at 400°F. for 1 hour. Meanwhile, prepare dip: Combine beans, yogurt, and avocado in a blender. Process until smooth. Spread over a 9-inch round flat plate. Top with scallions, chilies, tomato, and cheese. Refrigerate. When potatoes are done, cut in half lengthwise and scoop out pulp. Cut skins lengthwise with sharp scissors, about 1-inch wide. Arrange skins on baking sheet, and brush with melted margarine and chili powder. Bake at 475°F. for 8 to 10 minutes. Serve hot with dip.

Calories per serving: 204
Fat: 5 g.
Cholesterol: 9 mg.
Sodium: 368 mg.

For exchange diets, count: 1 1/2 starch,
1 vegetable, 1 meat

Christmas Tree Canapés

Preparation time: 15 minutes
Yield: 8 servings

---

8 slices white bread
3 ounces reduced-calorie cream cheese,
    softened
2 tablespoons catsup
1 tablespoon horseradish
1/4 teaspoon garlic powder
1 dash cayenne pepper
1/4 cup chopped fresh parsley
6 ounces imitation crab, thawed and
    flaked

Using a Christmas tree cookie cutter, cut a Christmas tree shape out of each slice of bread. Reserve shapes and discard edges. Mix remaining ingredients into cream cheese. Spread this mixture evenly over Christmas tree-shaped bread. Place under preheated broiler until lightly browned. Serve immediately.

Calories per slice: 116
Fat: 3 g.
Cholesterol: 14 mg.
Sodium: 365 mg. (To reduce sodium, use low-
salt catsup.)

For exchange diets, count: 1 starch,
1/2 lean meat

Decorated Breadsticks

Preparation time: 25 minutes
Yield: 8 servings

---

1 tube soft breadstick dough
2 tablespoons chopped pimiento
2 tablespoons chopped green pepper

Preheat oven to 350°F. Unroll dough and separate into 8 strips. Twist each strip and place on an ungreased cookie sheet. Press edges down firmly. Carefully sprinkle strips on all sides with pimiento and green pepper. Bake for 15 to 18 minutes until golden brown.

Calories per breadstick: 103
Fat: 2 g.
Cholesterol: <5 mg.
Sodium: 230 mg.

For exchange diets, count: 1 starch, 1/2 fat

Appetizers and Beverages

Cocktail Meatballs

Preparation time: 35 minutes
Yield: 16 2-ounce servings

Meatballs:
2 pounds very lean ground beef or pork
1 beaten egg or 1/4 cup liquid egg
    substitute
1 small onion, diced fine
1/4 teaspoon garlic salt
1/4 teaspoon celery salt
1/2 teaspoon pepper

Sauce:
20-ounce can pineapple tidbits in juice
8-ounce can no-added-salt tomato sauce
2 tablespoons brown sugar
1/2 teaspoon minced garlic
1 cup catsup
1/3 cup all-fruit grape preserves

Preheat broiler. Combine ingredients for meatballs in a large mixing bowl. Form into small balls and place on a broiling rack that has been placed over a baking sheet. Broil meatballs for 20 minutes until done. Meanwhile, combine ingredients for the sauce in a medium saucepan, and simmer for 15 minutes. Transfer meatballs and sauce to a Crockpot or chafing dish for serving.

Calories per 2-ounce serving: 167
Fat: 6 g.
Cholesterol: 56 mg. with egg;
52 mg. with substitute
Sodium: 199 mg.

For exchange diets, count: 2 lean meat, 1 fruit

Cranberry Fizzy

*Throw this winter refresher together
with everyday ingredients.
Preparation time: 5 minutes
Yield: 8 1-cup servings*

12-ounce can cran-raspberry frozen
    concentrated juice
2 12-ounce cans water
2 12-ounce cans sugar-free lemon lime soft
    drink
1/2 cup crushed ice

Combine frozen juice concentrate and water in a large (2-quart)
pitcher. Stir to fully dissolve frozen juice. Pour in soft drink and
crushed ice just before serving. Serve in a large wine goblet or a
tall tumbler.

Calories per 1-cup serving: 123
Fat: 0
Cholesterol: 0
Sodium: 4 mg.

For exchange diets, count: 2 fruit

Appetizers and Beverages

Deviled Crab Dip

Preparation time: 10 minutes
Chilling time: 30 minutes; Yield: 8 1/3-cup servings

8-ounce package mock crab, shredded
1/2 cup finely chopped celery
1 green onion, finely chopped
1/4 cup reduced-fat mayonnaise
1/4 cup reduced-fat Thousand Island salad
    dressing
1/4 teaspoon celery seed
4 drops Tabasco sauce

Combine all ingredients for dip in a small mixing bowl. Cover
and chill at least 30 minutes before serving with reduced-fat
crackers (such as reduced-fat Wheat Thins) or breadsticks.

Calories per 1/3-cup serving: 80
Fat: 3 g.
Cholesterol: 41 mg.
Sodium: 146 mg.

For exchange diets, count: 2 lean meat

Dilly Cocktail

Preparation time: 5 minutes
Yield: 4 3/4-cup servings

---

4 lemon slices
24 ounces no-added-salt vegetable juice
1/2 teaspoon dill weed

Cut and twist lemon slices and secure them to edge of four wine glasses. Pour juice into wine glasses, and sprinkle with dill weed.

Calories per 3/4-cup serving: 37
Fat: 0
Cholesterol: 0
Sodium: 47 mg.

For exchange diets, count: 1 vegetable

Low-Fat Nachos

Preparation time: 15 minutes
Yield: 8 1/2-cup servings

4 cups baked tortilla chips (such as baked
    Tostitos)
8 ounces nonfat cheddar cheese, shredded
1/2 cup chunky salsa

Preheat oven to 400°F. Spread tortilla chips out over a large baking sheet. Sprinkle cheddar cheese over the top Carefully dot the salsa over the cheese. Bake for 10 minutes. Serve warm.

Calories per 1/2-cup serving: 55
Fat: 1 g.
Cholesterol: 1 mg.
Sodium: 256 mg.

For exchange diets, count: 1/2 starch

Nutty Mushrooms

Preparation time: 35 minutes
Yield: 4 5-mushroom servings

---

20 fresh mushrooms
2 tablespoons margarine
1/4 cup chopped onion
1/4 teaspoon garlic powder
1/4 cup Grape Nuts cereal
1 tablespoon chopped parsley
1/4 teaspoon pepper

Preheat oven to 350°F. Remove stems from mushrooms. Chop
stems and set aside. Melt margarine in a skillet. Mix in chopped
mushroom stems and onion, sautéing until onions are tender.
Stir in garlic powder, cereal, parsley, and pepper. Fill mushroom
caps. Bake for 20 minutes, and serve hot.

Calories per 5 mushrooms: 44
Fat: 3 g.
Cholesterol: 0
Sodium: 60 mg.

For exchange diets, count: 1 vegetable, 1/2 fat

Hot Chocolate Mix

Preparation time: 5 minutes
Yield: 4 1-cup servings

1 1/3 cups nonfat dry milk
1/4 cup cocoa
4 packets Equal sugar substitute
1 quart boiling water
1 teaspoon vanilla

Mix dry milk with cocoa and Equal in a 1 1/2 quart heat-proof container. Add the boiling water, and stir to mix. Stir in vanilla, and serve.

Calories per 1-cup serving: 100
Fat: 2 g.
Cholesterol: 7 mg.
Sodium: 35 mg.

For exchange diets, count: 1 skim milk

Low-Fat Popcorn
Preparation time: 5 minutes
Yield: 4 2-cup servings

1 tablespoon liquid vegetable oil or butter-
flavored popcorn oil
1/3 cup popping corn
Butter-flavored pump spray such as
I Can't Believe It's Not Butter

Combine oil and popping corn in the base of a corn popper. Pop as popcorn popper directs. Transfer to a serving bowl. Spray with butter-flavored spray; then salt and/or season as desired. This recipe works very well in a Presto microwave popper or it can be doubled for a Stir Crazy electric popper.

Calories per 2-cup serving: 92
Fat: 3 g.
Cholesterol: 0
Sodium: 0 mg.

For exchange diets, count: 1 starch

Party Meal in a Bowl

Preparation time: 45 minutes
Yield: 8 servings, 1/8 loaf bread & 3/4 cup dip

★ ★ ★

---

1 pound round loaf crusty bread, such as
 rye or Italian
2 10-ounce packages chopped, frozen
 spinach, thawed and squeezed dry
8-ounce package light cream cheese,
 softened to room temperature
3 tablespoons skim milk
1 tablespoon lemon juice
1/2 cup chopped pimiento
1/2 cup red onion, chopped
4 strips bacon, cooked, drained, and
 crumbled
1/2 teaspoon white pepper

For best results, allow loaf of bread to dry out 24 hours in the
open air. Remove 1 1/2-inch layer from top of loaf and chop into
1-inch cubes. Scoop out the remaining bread from the loaf, and
cut into cubes. Combine remaining ingredients in a mixing bowl,
and chill for 30 minutes. Serve the dip in the bread bowl and use
the cubes of bread as dippers.

Calories per serving: 249
Fat: 10 g.
Cholesterol: 24 mg.
Sodium: 479 mg.

For exchange diets, count: 1 1/2 starch,
2 vegetable, 2 fat

Popeye's Spinach Croquettes
Preparation time: 60 minutes
Yield: 8 servings, 4 pieces each

---

1 10-oz. package frozen chopped spinach
1 cup dry bread crumbs
1 beaten egg or 1/4 cup liquid egg
    substitute
1/4 cup minced onion
1/4 teaspoon garlic powder
1/4 cup margarine, melted
1/4 cup Parmesan cheese
1/8 teaspoon pepper

Cook spinach and drain well. Combine spinach with other ingredients. Form into 1-inch balls, and place on a lightly greased baking sheet. Place in freezer for 20 minutes or until firm. Bake at 325°F. for 25 to 30 minutes.

Calories per serving: 147
Fat: 8 g.
Cholesterol: 22 mg.
Sodium: 247 mg.

For exchange diets, count: 1 starch, 1 1/2 fat

Three-Minute Bean Dip

Three minutes to prepare and three minutes to warm up!
Preparation time: 6 minutes
Yield: 8 1/3-cup servings

Nonstick cooking spray
16-ounce can fat-free refried beans with
green chilies
1/2 cup chunky salsa
8 ounces fat-free cheddar cheese,
shredded
1 tablespoon dried parsley

Spread beans over the bottom of a 7 by 11-inch baking dish that
has been sprayed with cooking spray. Carefully dot the salsa
over the beans. Sprinkle the cheese over the salsa and the parsley over the cheese. Microwave on 70 percent power for 3 minutes. Serve with baked tortilla chips.

Calories per 1/3-cup serving: 85
Fat: 1 g.
Cholesterol: 1 mg.
Sodium: 447 mg. (To reduce sodium, substitute
fresh chopped peppers, tomatoes, and onions
for the salsa.)

For exchange diets, count: 1 starch

Tomato Pockets

Preparation time: 15 minutes
Yield: 8 2-piece servings

---

16 cherry tomatoes, cleaned
1/4 cup chopped celery
1 cup chopped cooked chicken pieces
1 tablespoon chopped pimiento
1 tablespoon chopped almonds
1/4 cup light mayonnaise
16 toothpicks

Use a sharp knife to cut off the top 1/4 of each tomato. Set the tops aside. Scoop out the inside and discard. Combine remaining ingredients and stuff inside. Replace the tomato tops, and secure with toothpicks.

Calories per serving: 78
Fat: 4 g.
Cholesterol: 20 mg.
Sodium: 43 mg.

For exchange diets, count: 1 vegetable, 1 fat

Wrapped Carrots

Preparation time: 15 minutes
Yield: 4 servings, 4 pieces each

---

4 medium carrots, cleaned and peeled
1/2 cup light mayonnaise
2 tablespoons dry buttermilk salad
    dressing mix
16 slices thinly sliced lean turkey
    or dried beef
16 toothpicks

Cut the carrots into 4 pieces. Combine the mayonnaise and dressing mix. Dip each piece of carrot into the dressing, and roll up in slices of turkey or dried beef. Secure with a toothpick.

Calories per 4-piece serving: 111
Fat: 8 g.
Cholesterol: 21 mg.
Sodium: 141 mg. (using turkey)

For exchange diets, count: 1 vegetable,
1 lean meat, 1 fat

Soups and Stews

Beefy Mushroom and Barley Soup

Preparation time: 45 minutes
Yield: 8 servings, 1-cup each

---

1 pound lean stew beef, cubed
6 cups water
2 1/2 cups sliced mushrooms
1/2 cup chopped onion
2 tablespoons margarine
1/3 cup flour
2 cups skim milk
1/2 cup quick pearl barley
1 tablespoon dry sherry
2 teaspoons Worcestershire sauce
1 tablespoon dried parsley
1/4 teaspoon pepper

In a 2-quart kettle, simmer stew beef in water for 15 minutes. In skillet, sauté mushrooms and onion in margarine. Stir in flour, and gradually add milk, stirring until thick. Transfer this to the kettle, and stir to blend. Stir in barley and seasonings. Simmer for 15 minutes. This may be prepared and frozen for later use.

Calories per 1-cup serving: 253
Fat: 9 g.
Cholesterol: 29 mg.
Sodium: 126 mg.

For exchange diets, count: 3 lean meat,
1 1/2 starch

California Blend Cream Soup
Preparation time: 20 minutes
Yield: 4 1 1/2 cup-servings

★ ★ ★

1 cup chopped onion
1 tablespoon margarine
2 teaspoons dried parsley
10 ounces frozen California blend
    vegetables (carrots, broccoli, and
    cauliflower, or use vegetable of choice)
14 ounces no-added-salt chicken broth
2 tablespoons flour
1/4 teaspoon pepper
1 cup skim milk
1/4 teaspoon grated lemon peel
1/4 cup (or 2 ounces) soft cheddar cheese
    spread (such as Cheez Whiz)

In a 2-quart stockpot, sauté onion in margarine. Add parsley, vegetables, and broth. In shaker container, combine flour and pepper with milk. Slowly whisk the milk into the vegetables and broth. Heat just until boiling. Add lemon peel and cheese. Reduce heat. Do not allow milk-based soups to come to a rolling boil or they will lose their creamy consistency.

Calories per 1 1/2-cup serving: 137
Fat: 6 g.
Cholesterol: 12 mg.
Sodium: 298 mg.

For exchange diets, count: 1 skim milk, 1 fat

Chicken and Rice Soup
Preparation time: 40 minutes
Yield: 8 1 1/2-cup servings

2 quarts no-added-salt chicken broth
2 cups diced cooked chicken
1/4 teaspoon salt
1/2 cup celery
2 scallions, chopped
2 carrots, peeled and sliced thin
3 whole cloves
1/2 teaspoon nutmeg
1 teaspoon dried parsley
1 bay leaf
1 cup frozen peas
1 cup sliced fresh mushrooms
1/2 cup quick rice (dry)

Combine all ingredients in a 4-quart stockpot. Bring to a boil, reduce heat, and simmer for 30 minutes. Remove bay leaf before serving.

Calories per 1 1/2-cup serving: 135
Fat: 2 g.
Cholesterol: 45 mg.
Sodium: 102 mg.

For exchange diets, count: 1 1/2 lean meat,
2 vegetable

Note: Instead of using canned chicken broth, you can make your own by stewing a chicken and removing the fat from the stock.

Chunky Beef Chili

Preparation time: 20 minutes
Yield: 8 1 1/2-cup servings

1 cup chopped onion
1/2 cup chopped green pepper
1/4 cup chopped celery
1 tablespoon vegetable oil
1 pound stew beef, cubed, trimmed, and
    browned
16-ounce can no-added-salt tomatoes
8-ounce can no-added-salt tomato sauce
1/2 teaspoon thyme
1/4 teaspoon garlic powder
1/2 teaspoon sugar
1/4 teaspoon oregano
1 tablespoon chili powder
15-ounce can chili beans

Sauté onion, pepper, and celery in oil in a 3-quart stockpot. When
vegetables are tender, add cooked meat and all remaining ingredients. Bring to a boil, reduce heat, and simmer for 20 minutes.

Calories per 1 1/2-cup serving: 208
Fat: 7 g.
Cholesterol: 15 mg.
Sodium: 37 mg.

For exchange diets, count: 2 lean meat, 1 starch

Cock-a-Leekie Soup

Preparation time: 60 minutes
Yield: 4 2-cup servings

1 pound uncooked chicken pieces
2 quarts no-added-salt chicken broth
1/2 cup barley
1/4 teaspoon salt (optional)
1 bay leaf
1 tablespoon dried parsley
1/4 teaspoon ground cloves
6 leeks (1 pound), sliced
1 tea bag
6 peppercorns

In a 3-quart soup kettle, simmer chicken pieces in broth for 20 minutes. (Or simmer a 3-pound whole chicken in 2 quarts water, then debone the meat and save the broth. Be sure to remove the fat from the top of the reserved broth.) Add barley, salt, bay leaf, parsley, cloves, and leeks to the chicken and broth. Remove the tea from the bag and tie peppercorns securely inside. Add this to soup, and bring to a boil. Reduce heat to simmer, and cook for 30 to 45 minutes more. Remove peppercorns and bay leaf before serving.

Calories per 2-cup serving: 318
Fat: 6 g.
Cholesterol: 65 mg.
Sodium: 213 mg. with salt; 97 mg. without salt

For exchange diets, count: 4 lean meat, 1 starch,
1 vegetable

Irish Potato Soup

Preparation time: 25 minutes
Yield: 4 1-cup servings

---

4 medium potatoes, peeled and cubed fine
1/4 cup chopped onion
1/4 cup chopped celery
1/4 cup grated carrots
1/2 cup no-added-salt chicken broth
1/4 teaspoon salt (optional)
1/4 cup flour
1 tablespoon margarine, melted
2 cups skim milk
Fresh parsley

In a 2-quart kettle or microwave dish, steam vegetables with broth and optional salt until tender. Combine flour, margarine, and milk in shaker container. Stir into vegetables, bring to a boil, and reduce to simmer for 5 minutes. Ladle into bowls, and garnish with fresh parsley.

Calories per 1-cup serving: 186
Fat: 4 g.
Cholesterol: 4 mg.
Sodium: 236 mg. with salt; 113 mg. without salt

For exchange diets, count: 2 starch, 1 fat

Soups and Stews

Fresh Tomato Soup
Make this in the fall and freeze it for winter days.
Preparation time: 30 minutes
Yield: 8 1-cup servings

6 large fresh tomatoes, stemmed, peeled,
  and quartered
1 large carrot, peeled and cut into chunks
1 medium onion, cut into quarters
1 green pepper, stemmed, seeded, and cut
  into wedges
2 ribs celery, cleaned and cut into chunks
1 tablespoon sugar
1/4 teaspoon salt
1/2 teaspoon pepper
2 teaspoons dried basil (optional)
1 teaspoon dried oregano (optional)

Chop tomatoes to desired consistency in a food processor or
blender. Add the other vegetables one at a time, and continue to
chop to desired consistency. Transfer the mixture to a stockpot,
add sugar and seasonings, and heat to boiling. Reduce heat, and
continue to simmer uncovered for 15 minutes. This soup can be
frozen in plastic or glass containers.

Calories per 1-cup serving: 32
Fat: 0
Cholesterol: 0
Sodium: 84 mg.

For exchange diets, count: 1 vegetable

Soups and Stews

Michigan Bean Soup

Preparation time: 35 minutes using canned beans
Yield: 8 1-cup servings

1 1/2 cups dry or 24-ounce can navy beans
6 cups water
1 cup chopped onions
8 ounces lean ham, cubed
1/4 teaspoon garlic powder
1 tablespoon margarine
2 cups celery, chopped
1 cup carrots, diced
2 whole cloves
2 bay leaves
4 cups no-added-salt beef or chicken broth
1/4 teaspoon pepper
2 tablespoons cider vinegar

If using dry beans, place beans and water in a one-gallon kettle, and soak overnight. Pour off the water, and drain beans in a colander. Sauté onion, ham, and garlic powder in margarine until onion is tender. Combine all ingredients except vinegar in the kettle. Simmer for 4 hours with dried beans or 20 minutes with canned beans. Add vinegar just before serving. This may be prepared and frozen for later thawing and reheating.

Calories per 1-cup serving: 210; Fat: 4 g.
Cholesterol: 31 mg.; Sodium: 292 mg.

For exchange diets, count: 2 starch,
1 1/2 lean meat

Speed Alert: If dry beans are used, allow overnight soaking and then 4 1/2 hours cooking time.

Microwave Minestrone

Preparation time: 30 minutes
Yield: 4 1 1/2-cup servings

1/2 cup chopped onion
1/2 cup chopped celery
1/4 teaspoon garlic powder
1/4 cup water
16 ounces no-added-salt chunky tomatoes
1 cup linguini
1 cup sliced cabbage
1 1/2 teaspoons low-sodium beef bouillon
    powder
1/2 teaspoon basil
1/2 teaspoon oregano
1 1/2 cups water
1/2 pound fully cooked turkey sausage,
    sliced thin

Place onion, celery, garlic powder, and 1/4 cup water in a 3-quart microwave dish. Cover and microwave on high power for 3 minutes. Add remaining ingredients except sausage, stirring to blend. Cover and microwave on high power for 15 minutes, or until the noodles are tender, stirring twice. Stir in sausage. Cover and let stand for 10 minutes.

Calories per 1 1/2-cup serving: 227
Fat: 3 g.
Cholesterol: 40 mg.
Sodium: 61 mg.

For exchange diets, count: 2 vegetable,
1 starch, 2 lean meat

Pumpkin Soup

Preparation time: 30 minutes
Yield: 4 1 1/2-cup servings

---

1 tablespoon margarine
1 cup chopped onion
1/2 cup sliced celery
1/4 teaspoon garlic powder
3 cups no-added-salt chicken broth
1/4 teaspoon salt
1/2 teaspoon white pepper
16-ounce can solid pack pumpkin
1 cup evaporated skim milk
2 scallions, finely chopped

Melt margarine in a 2-quart saucepan. Add onion, celery, and garlic powder, and cook until vegetables are soft. Add broth, salt, and pepper, and simmer for 15 minutes. Stir in pumpkin and milk. Cook for 5 minutes. Pour into a blender, and process on low speed about 30 seconds until creamy. Ladle into soup bowls, and top with chopped scallions.

Calories per 1 1/2-cup serving: 120
Fat: <1 g.
Cholesterol: 2 mg.
Sodium: 215 mg.

For exchange diets, count: 1 starch, 2 vegetable

Shopper's Chili

Put this in the Crockpot while you go shopping.
Preparation time: 4 to 8 hours in Crockpot
Yield: 8 1 1/2-cup servings

---

1 1/2 pounds lean ground beef
1/4 teaspoon garlic powder
28-ounce can no-added-salt tomatoes,
   undrained
2 medium onions, chopped
1 medium green pepper, diced
15-ounce can no-added-salt tomato sauce
1 1/2 cups water
1/4 cup chili powder
1 stalk celery, diced
1 1/2 teaspoons pepper
1/2 teaspoon salt (optional)
1 bay leaf
15-ounce can red kidney beans, drained
   and rinsed

Brown meat in microwave or skillet. Drain well, and transfer to a Crockpot or slow cooker. Add all remaining ingredients, and slow cook 4 to 8 hours, uncovered. Remove bay leaf before serving.

Calories per 1 1/2-cup serving: 275
Fat: 11 g.
Cholesterol: 63 mg.
Sodium: 428 mg. with salt; 306 mg. without salt

For exchange diets, count: 3 lean meat,
1 vegetable, 1 starch

Speed Alert: Recipe requires 4 to 8 hours.

Spicy Chicken Stew

Preparation time: 30 minutes
Yield: 4 1 1/2-cup servings

8 ounces diced chicken pieces
1 onion, chopped
1 tablespoon vegetable oil
2 tablespoons chili powder
16-ounce can no-added-salt tomatoes
4-ounce can chopped green chilies
1 cup water
16-ounce can black beans
6 ounces frozen whole kernel corn
1 tablespoon dried parsley
1/4 teaspoon salt, optional

Sauté chicken pieces and onion in oil in a Dutch oven until chicken is browned. Add all remaining ingredients, and bring to a boil. Reduce heat to simmer, and cook 15 more minutes. This recipe can be prepared and frozen for later. Thaw, reheat, and serve.

Calories per 1 1/2-cup serving: 330
Fat: 2 g.
Cholesterol: 32 mg.
Sodium: 195 mg. with salt; 81 mg. without salt

For exchange diets, count: 2 lean meat,
2 vegetable, 2 starch

Smoky Bean Soup

Preparation time: 10 minutes
Cooking time: 20 minutes or up to 2 hours
Yield: 8 1-cup servings

16-ounce can white beans, drained and
   rinsed
16-ounce can pinto beans, drained and
   rinsed
16-ounce can kidney beans, drained and
   rinsed
28-ounce can no-added-salt stewed
   tomatoes
8-ounce jar chunky salsa
4 ounces cooked lean Canadian bacon,
   diced
1 teaspoon liquid smoke flavoring

Combine all ingredients in a stockpot. Bring mixture to a boil,
then cover and reduce heat. Simmer for a minimum of 20 minutes or up to 2 hours.

Calories per 1-cup serving: 204
Fat: 2 g.
Cholesterol: 14 mg.
Sodium: 650 mg. (To reduce sodium, use cooked
lean roast beef instead of Canadian bacon and
reduce salsa to 4 ounces.)

For exchange diets, count: 2 starch,
1 vegetable, 1 very lean meat

Vegetable Chowder with Bacon

Preparation time: 30 minutes
Yield: 4 1 1/2-cup servings

★ ★ ★

6 slices bacon
16-oz. can no-added-salt chicken broth
2 cups finely chopped potatoes
1 cup shredded carrots
1/2 cup chopped onion
1/2 teaspoon curry powder
1/8 teaspoon pepper
12-ounce can evaporated skim milk

Broil bacon until crisp, then crumble and set aside. Meanwhile, in a 3-quart kettle, combine broth and vegetables. Steam vegetables until tender. Stir in curry powder, pepper, bacon, and milk. Heat through, about 10 minutes over medium heat. Do not boil!

Calories per 1 1/2-cup serving: 243
Fat: 5 g.
Cholesterol: 11 mg.
Sodium: 304 mg.

For exchange diets, count: 1 vegetable,
2 starch, 1 fat

Autumn Morning Buns

Preparation time: 50 minutes
Yield: 12 buns

★ ★ ★

Nonstick cooking spray
1/2 cup chopped almonds
1/2 cup brown sugar, divided
1/2 cup vegetable oil
1 teaspoon light corn syrup
1 cup flour
1 cup whole wheat flour
1 tablespoon baking powder
1 teaspoon cinnamon
1/4 teaspoon salt
2 eggs or 1/2 cup liquid egg substitute
1 cup skim milk
1 teaspoon vanilla
1/4 teaspoon almond extract
1/2 teaspoon grated orange peel
1/4 cup dates

Preheat oven to 375°F. Spray 12 muffin cups with cooking spray. Sprinkle almonds evenly into muffin cups. Sprinkle 2 tablespoons brown sugar over almonds. In a mixing bowl, beat vegetable oil, remaining 6 tablespoons of brown sugar, and corn syrup together. Sift dry ingredients together. In a small mixing bowl, beat eggs, milk, vanilla, and almond extract together. Add dry ingredients and egg mixture alternately with sugar mixture, beating well after each addition. Fold in orange peel and dates. Pour into prepared muffin cups. Bake for 20 to 25 minutes until browned on top. Cool for 5 minutes only, then invert muffin tin onto plate, and allow buns to fall gently out. The tops of the buns will be crusty.

Breads

Calories per bun: 184
Fat: 4 g.
Cholesterol: 46 mg. with egg;
17 mg. with substitute
Sodium: 70 mg.

For exchange diets, count: 2 starch, 1 fat

Cathy's Cheese Pepper Bread

Cathy Carlyle gets the compliments for this recipe.
Preparation time: 2 hours
Yield: 16 slices

★ ★ ★

Nonstick cooking spray
1 package (quick type) active dry yeast
1/4 cup hot tap water
1 1/3 cups flour
2 tablespoons sugar
1/8 teaspoon salt
1/4 teaspoon baking soda
1 cup nonfat cottage cheese
1 egg or 1/4 cup liquid egg substitute
1 cup flour
1 cup shredded part-skim (or light)
  American cheese
1/2 teaspoon coarse ground pepper

Spray two 1-pound coffee cans or 1 loaf pan with cooking spray. In large mixing bowl, dissolve yeast in hot water. Add 1 1/3 cups flour, sugar, salt, soda, cottage cheese, and egg. Blend with an electric mixer 1/2 minute on low speed, scraping bowl constantly, then 2 minutes on high speed, scraping bowl occasionally. Stir in 1 cup flour, cheese, and pepper. Blend well. Pour batter in pans, and let rise 45 minutes. Preheat oven to 350°F. Bake 40 minutes or until golden brown. Cool 5 minutes. Remove from pans, and cool on rack.

Calories per 1-slice serving: 97; Fat: 2 g.
Cholesterol: 29 mg. with egg; 18 with substitute;
Sodium: 242 mg.

For exchange diets, count: 1 starch, 1 lean meat

Cranapple Bread

Preparation time: 55 minutes
Yield: 12 slices

Nonstick cooking spray
1 cup fresh or frozen cranberries, chopped
    fine
1/4 cup sugar
1 3/4 cups flour
1/3 cup sugar
1 tablespoon baking powder
3/4 teaspoon cinnamon
1/4 teaspoon allspice
1/2 teaspoon salt
1 egg, beaten, or 1/4 cup liquid egg
    substitute
1/3 cup vegetable oil
1 cup applesauce
1/4 cup chopped walnuts

Preheat oven to 350°F. Sprinkle chopped cranberries with 1/4 cup sugar, and set aside. Combine dry ingredients in a mixing bowl. Beat egg, oil, and applesauce together in a separate bowl. Add to dry ingredients, stirring well. Gently fold in nuts and cranberry mixture. Spray a large loaf pan with cooking spray; pour batter into the pan. Bake 35 minutes or until toothpick inserted in center comes out clean.

Calories per 1-slice serving: 166
Fat: 7 g.
Cholesterol: 14 mg. with egg; 0 with substitute
Sodium: 259

For exchange diets, count: 1 1/2 starch, 1 fat

Breads

Fancy Applesauce Bran Muffins

Preparation time: 40 minutes
Yield: 24 muffins

Nonstick cooking spray
3 cups All Bran cereal
2 cups skim milk
1 cup unsweetened applesauce
2 eggs or 1/2 cup liquid egg substitute
1/3 cup vegetable oil
2 1/2 cups flour
4 teaspoons baking powder
1/2 teaspoon salt
3/4 cup brown sugar
1 tablespoon cinnamon
1 teaspoon grated lemon peel
Topping:
2 tablespoons margarine
1/4 cup brown sugar

Preheat oven to 375°F. In a large mixing bowl, combine cereal, milk, and applesauce; allow to sit 10 minutes. Beat in eggs and oil. In a separate bowl, stir together all remaining dry ingredients. Fold dry ingredients into cereal mixture, just until moistened. Spoon into 24 muffin tins sprayed with cooking spray. Combine margarine and brown sugar for topping, and sprinkle on top of muffins. Bake for 15 to 18 minutes.

Calories per muffin: 154
Fat: 5 g.
Cholesterol: 23 mg.
Sodium: 175 mg.

For exchange diets, count: 1/2 fruit, 1 starch,
1 fat

Fred's Fantastic Baked Donuts

*My son talked me into this donut experiment
one cold afternoon. They were a hit!*
Preparation time: 30 minutes
Bread machine time: 1 hour and 40 minutes
Rising time: 30 minutes
Baking time: 15 minutes
Yield: 16 donuts

Dough:
3/4 cup skim milk
2 tablespoons water
1 egg or 1/4 cup liquid egg substitute
2 3/4 cups bread flour
1/4 cup sugar
1/2 teaspoon salt
1/2 teaspoon nutmeg
1 1/2 teaspoons bread machine yeast
1 tablespoon soft margarine
Nonstick cooking spray
Glaze:
1/2 cup powdered sugar
1/2 teaspoon vanilla
Hot water

Combine dough ingredients in order listed in a bread machine
pan. Program machine for "dough" method. Dough will be ready
in about 1 1/2 to 2 hours. Remove dough from the pan, and roll
out on a floured surface. Use a donut cutter to cut donuts. Place
donuts and holes on a baking sheet that has been sprayed with
cooking spray. Allow to rise in a warm place for 30 to 45 minutes.
Preheat oven to 350°F. Bake donuts for 12 to 15 minutes or until
they're golden brown. Cool on a wire rack. Prepare glaze when

Continued on next page.

Fred's Fantastic Baked Donuts
(continued)

---

donuts are cool to the touch. Combine powdered sugar and vanilla in a mixing bowl. Add hot tap water a couple drops at a time to produce a thin glaze. Pour glaze over the donuts, and allow the donuts to dry.

Calories per donut: 116
Fat: 1 g.
Cholesterol: 13 mg. with egg;
1 mg. with substitute
Sodium: 165 mg.

For exchange diets, count: 1 1/2 starch

Breads

Herbed Corn Bread
Preparation time: 35 minutes
Yield: 8 squares

---

8 1/2-ounce box corn bread mix
1/4 cup nonfat cottage cheese
2 tablespoons dried parsley
2 tablespoons dried chopped chives
1 teaspoon sage

Preheat oven to 350°F. Spray an 8-inch baking pan with non-stick cooking spray. Prepare mix according to package directions. Stir in cottage cheese, parsley, chives, and sage. Pour batter into an 8-inch square pan. Bake for 25 minutes or until lightly browned. Cool and cut into 8 squares.

Calories per square: 118
Fat: 3 g.
Cholesterol: 1 mg.
Sodium: 300 mg.

For exchange diets, count: 1 starch, 1 fat

Serving suggestion: Dot each square of hot corn bread with 1 tablespoon maple syrup or honey.

Calories: 50
Fat: 0
Cholesterol: 0
Sodium: 8 mg.

For exchange diets, count: 1 fruit

Orange-Glazed Coffee Cake

Preparation time: 10 minutes
Bread machine time: 1 hour and 40 minutes
Rising time: 30 minutes
Baking time: 20 minutes
Yield: 16 slices

★ ★ ★

Dough:
3/4 cup water
2 tablespoons frozen orange juice
  concentrate
1/4 cup nonfat ricotta cheese
1 egg
3 cups bread flour
1/4 cup sugar
1/2 teaspoon salt
1/2 teaspoon finely grated orange rind
1 1/2 teaspoons bread machine yeast
1 tablespoon soft margarine
Nonstick cooking spray
Glaze:
1/2 cup powdered sugar
1/2 teaspoon vanilla
Orange juice

Combine dough ingredients in order listed in a bread machine
pan. Program machine for "dough" method. Dough will be ready
in about 1 1/2 to 2 hours. Remove dough from the pan, and roll out
into a 9-inch circle on a floured surface. Transfer rolled dough to
a 9-inch round baking pan that has been sprayed with cooking
spray. Allow to rise in a warm place for 30 to 45 minutes. Preheat
oven to 350°F. Bake for 20 to 22 minutes or until the top is golden
brown. Cool on a wire rack. Prepare glaze when cake is cool to the
touch. Combine powdered sugar and vanilla in a mixing bowl.

Breads

Add orange juice a couple drops at a time to produce a thin glaze. Pour over the coffee cake, and cut into 16 slices.

Calories per slice: 116
Fat: 1 g.
Cholesterol: 13 mg. with egg;
1 mg. with substitute
Sodium: 165 mg.

For exchange diets, count: 1 1/2 starch

Pineapple Nut Bread

Preparation time: 65 minutes
Yield: 12 slices

Nonstick cooking spray
2 cups flour
3/4 cup sugar
2 teaspoons baking powder
1/2 teaspoon baking soda
1/2 teaspoon mace
1/4 teaspoon salt
1 egg or 1/4 cup liquid egg substitute
8-ounce can juice-pack crushed pineapple
1/2 cup nonfat sour cream
2 tablespoons vegetable oil
2 tablespoons chopped pecans or walnuts

Preheat oven to 350°F. Combine flour, sugar, baking powder, soda, mace, and salt in a large mixing bowl; mix well. In a medium bowl, beat egg well. Add pineapple with juice, sour cream, and oil. Stir to mix. Add pineapple mixture to the dry ingredients, and mix just until moist. Spoon batter into a loaf pan that has been sprayed with cooking spray. Sprinkle nuts over the top of the batter. Bake for 45 to 50 minutes or until a wooden pick inserted into the center comes out clean. Cool in the pan for several minutes, then remove to a wire rack to cool.

Calories per slice: 182 ; Fat: 3 g.
Cholesterol: 14 mg. with egg;
1 mg. with substitute
Sodium: 207 mg.

For exchange diets, count: 1 1/2 starch, 1 fruit

Poppy Seed Bread

My dear neighbor, Diane Tisue, invented this.
Preparation time: 65 minutes
Yield: 2 loaves, 18 slices each

★ ★ ★

3 cups flour
1/2 teaspoon salt
1 1/2 teaspoons baking powder
1 1/2 cups sugar or substitute
2 teaspoons vanilla
1 1/2 cups skim milk
3/4 cup vegetable oil
1/2 cup frozen orange juice concentrate,
   thawed
2 tablespoons poppy seeds
3 eggs or 3/4 cup liquid egg substitute
1 1/2 teaspoons almond extract
2 tablespoons powdered sugar
1 tablespoon finely grated orange peel

Preheat oven to 350°F. Spray 2 loaf pans with nonstick cooking spray. Put all ingredients except powdered sugar and orange peel into a bowl. Beat for 2 minutes. Divide dough between 2 loaf pans, and bake for 55 minutes. Remove from pans, and sprinkle with powdered sugar and orange peel while warm.

Calories per slice: 125
Fat: 5 g.
Cholesterol: 14 mg. with egg; 0 with substitute
Sodium: 31 mg.

For exchange diets, count: 1 starch, 1 fat

Sour Cream Banana Bread

Preparation time: 65 minutes
Yield: 16 slices

★ ★ ★

Nonstick cooking spray
8-ounce carton nonfat sour cream
3/4 cup sugar
2 tablespoons soft margarine
3 large very ripe bananas, mashed
2 eggs or 1/2 cup liquid egg substitute
1 tablespoon finely grated lemon rind
    (optional, but recommended)
2 tablespoons lemon juice (may substitute
    banana flavoring)
2 1/2 cups flour
1 1/2 teaspoons baking powder
1/2 teaspoon baking soda
1/4 teaspoon salt

Preheat oven to 350°F. In a medium mixing bowl, combine sour cream, sugar, and margarine until blended. Stir in banana, eggs, lemon rind, and lemon juice. Mix to blend. Sift together flour, baking powder, soda, and salt in a large bowl. Add banana mixture to the dry ingredients, and stir just until moist. Pour batter into a 9-inch loaf pan that has been sprayed with cooking spray. Bake for 45 to 50 minutes or until a wooden pick inserted into the center of the bread comes out clean. Cool for 5 minutes, then remove from pan and cool on a wire rack.

Calories per slice: 168; Fat: 2 g.
Cholesterol: 27 mg. with egg;
1 mg. with substitute
Sodium: 160 mg.

For exchange diets, count: 1 starch, 1 1/2 fruit

Cauliflower Salad for Everyone

Preparation time: 35 minutes
Yield: 8 1 1/4-cup servings

★ ★ ★

1 large head cauliflower, cleaned,
    stemmed, and cut into small florets
2 ribs celery, diced fine
2 green onions, diced fine
8 large radishes, sliced thin
2 tablespoons sunflower seeds
Dressing:
1/2 cup reduced-fat mayonnaise (may use
    nonfat)
2 tablespoons white or rice wine vinegar
1 tablespoon sugar or sugar substitute
1/4 teaspoon salt
1/2 teaspoon white pepper
1/4 cup freshly grated Parmesan cheese
1/2 teaspoon minced garlic

Combine ingredients for the salad in a large bowl. Mix together
ingredients for the dressing in a small bowl. Pour dressing over
the salad, and refrigerate at least 20 minutes or up to 4 hours to
allow flavors to blend.

Calories per 1 1/4-cup serving: 97;
61 calories with nonfat mayonnaise
Fat: 6 g.; 2 g. with nonfat mayonnaise
Cholesterol: 2 mg.
Sodium: 253 mg.

For exchange diets, count: 2 vegetable, 1 fat

Salads

Cold Sweet 'n Sour Vegetables

Preparation time: 45 minutes
Yield: 8 3/4-cup servings

★ ★ ★

2 cups celery, chopped very fine
1 large onion, chopped fine
20-ounce package frozen mixed
   vegetables, thawed and drained
Dressing:
3/4 cup sugar or equivalent in substitute
1/2 cup vinegar
1 tablespoon flour
1 tablespoon prepared mustard

Combine celery, onion, and vegetables in a 2-quart bowl. Combine dressing ingredients in a small saucepan. Bring to a boil, and boil for 1 minute. Cool for 10 minutes. Pour over the vegetables, and chill. This salad keeps very well in the refrigerator for up to a week.

Calories per 3/4-cup serving:
132 with sugar; 60 with substitute
Fat: 1 g.
Cholesterol: 0
Sodium: 31 mg.

For exchange diets, count: 2 vegetable, 1 fruit
If using sugar substitute, count 2 vegetable, 0 fruit.

Important: If using Equal brand sugar substitute, do not cook; add Equal to the cooled dressing.

Salads

Cranberry Salad

Preparation time: 2 hours, 15 minutes
Yield: 8 1/2-cup servings

3-ounce package sugar-free raspberry
    gelatin
3-ounce package sugar-free lemon gelatin
1 1/4 cups boiling water
1 cup chopped cranberries
1 cup finely chopped apples
1 cup finely chopped celery
1/2 cup sugar-free lemon lime soft drink
    (7-Up, Sprite, Squirt, and Slice are good
    choices)
1 tablespoon grated lemon peel

In a 2-quart mixing bowl, dissolve gelatin in boiling water. Stir in all remaining ingredients, and chill in a 6-cup mold or a 1 1/2-quart pan until firm. Cut, and serve on a bed of greens.

Calories per 1/2-cup serving: 28
Fat: 0
Cholesterol: 0
Sodium: 50 mg.

For exchange diets, count: 1/2 fruit

Speed Alert: This recipe requires 2 hours for gelatin to set.

Creamy Garlic Salad Dressing
Preparation time: 10 minutes
Yield: 1 1/2 cups total or 12 2-tablespoon servings

---

1 cup light mayonnaise or salad dressing
1 tablespoon instant minced garlic or 1 1/2
   teaspoons garlic powder
2 tablespoons Dijon mustard
1/4 cup sugar or equivalent in substitute
1/2 teaspoon dill seed

Combine all ingredients in blender, and process until smooth.
This will keep in the refrigerator for 2 weeks.

Calories per 2-tablespoon serving:
75 with sugar; 60 with sugar substitute
Fat: 5 g.
Cholesterol: 7 mg.
Sodium: 126 mg.

For exchange diets, count: 1 fat

Crunchy Broccoli Salad

Preparation time: 15 minutes
Yield: 8 1-cup servings

★ ★ ★

1 large bunch of fresh broccoli, chopped
    into bite-sized pieces
1 small red onion, sliced thin
4 strips bacon, broiled crisp and crumbled
1/2 cup raisins
1/2 cup chopped walnuts
Dressing:
1/3 cup light mayonnaise
1/2 cup plain nonfat yogurt
1/4 cup sugar or substitute
2 tablespoons vinegar

Mix together broccoli, onion, bacon, raisins, and walnuts in a salad bowl. These ingredients will keep covered in the refrigerator for 4 days. Combine ingredients for dressing in shaker container. Pour over broccoli just before serving. Toss and serve.

Calories per 1-cup serving: 178 with sugar;
154 with sugar substitute
Fat: 4 g.
Cholesterol: 14 mg.
Sodium: 135 mg.

For exchange diets, count: 3 vegetable,
1/2 starch, 1 1/2 fat
With sugar substitute, count: 3 vegetable,
1 1/2 fat

Mountain Dew Fruit Salad

*Kids think they're getting something special
with this salad made with a soft drink.
Preparation time: 30 minutes
Yield: 8 1-cup servings*

2 apples, cored, quartered, and sliced thin
2 cups grapes
8-ounce can pineapple tidbits in juice
2 large bananas, peeled and sliced
12-ounce can diet Mountain Dew soft
   drink

Combine fruits in a salad bowl. Pour soft drink over the fruits.
Cover and chill at least 20 minutes or up to 4 hours. Use a slotted spoon or ladle to serve into fruit bowls.

Calories per 1-cup serving: 60
Fat: 0
Cholesterol: 0
Sodium: 1 mg.

For exchange diets, count: 1 fruit

Salads

Sweet and Sour Apple Coleslaw

Preparation time: 45 minutes
Yield: 8 3/4-cup servings

★ ★ ★

16-ounce bag shredded cabbage and
    carrots
1 large Granny Smith apple, cored,
    halved, and shredded
1 green onion, diced
Dressing:
2 tablespoons vegetable oil
2 tablespoons white vinegar
1/4 teaspoon salt
1/4 teaspoon pepper
2 tablespoons sugar or equivalent sugar
    substitute
1 tablespoon water
2 tablespoons lemon juice
1 teaspoon dill weed

In a salad bowl, combine cabbage and carrots, apple, and onion.
In a shaker container, mix ingredients for the dressing. Pour
dressing over salad, toss, and chill at least 30 minutes to allow
flavors to blend. This salad keeps well for 48 hours.

Calories per 3/4-cup serving: 74;
62 calories with sugar substitute
Fat: 4 g.
Cholesterol: 0
Sodium: 79 mg.

For exchange diets, count: 1 vegetable, 1 fat

Tangy Cabbage and Dried Fruit Salad

Preparation time: 30 minutes
Yield: 8 3/4-cup servings

1/4 cup light mayonnaise
1/4 cup skim milk
2 teaspoons lemon juice
1/8 teaspoon salt
1/8 teaspoon pepper
4 cups shredded cabbage
20 dates, cut unto pieces
1 ounce toasted slivered almonds

In a salad bowl, blend mayonnaise, milk, lemon juice, salt, and pepper. Add cabbage and dates; toss. Chill for 20 minutes. Sprinkle with almonds, and serve.

Calories per 3/4-cup serving: 131
Fat: 7 g.
Cholesterol: 2 mg.
Sodium: 74 mg.

For exchange diets, count: 1 vegetable, 1 fruit,
1 fat

Italian Garden Salad

Preparation time: 1 hour, 15 minutes
Yield: 8 2-cup servings

1 small head cauliflower, cut in pieces
1/2 pound broccoli, cut in pieces
2 ribs celery, cut into 1/4-inch slices
1/2 pound sliced mushrooms
1/2 red onion, sliced thin
1 green pepper, chopped fine
2 carrots, shredded

Dressing:
1/4 cup vegetable oil
1/2 cup lemon juice
1/3 cup Parmesan cheese
1 teaspoon oregano
1/4 teaspoon garlic powder
1 teaspoon basil
1/4 teaspoon salt, optional
1/2 teaspoon sugar

Layer the vegetables in a 9 by 13-inch pan. Combine ingredients for dressing in a shaker container and pour over vegetables. The salad is best if allowed to marinate for at least an hour. This keeps well covered and refrigerated for 3 days.

Calories per 2-cup serving: 125
Fat: 9 g.
Cholesterol: 5 mg.
Sodium: 204 mg. with salt; 143 mg. without salt

For exchange diets, count: 2 vegetable, 2 fat

Sweet and Sour Cucumbers

Preparation time: 15 minutes
Yield: 4 1-cup servings

★ ★ ★

1/2 cup sugar or equivalent in sugar
    substitute
1/3 cup vinegar
1/4 teaspoon garlic powder
1/8 teaspoon celery seed
Dash salt
4 medium cucumbers, sliced thin
1 medium onion, peeled and chopped

Combine the first five ingredients in a salad bowl. Stir to mix. Add sliced onions and cucumbers to dressing. Toss and serve. This keeps well refrigerated for 3 days. Serve with a slotted spoon.

Calories per 1-cup serving: 40 with sugar; 24
with sugar substitute
Fat: 0
Cholesterol: 0
Sodium: 231 mg.

For exchange diets, count: 1 vegetable

Tailgate Salad

Preparation time: 60 minutes
Yield: 8 3/4-cup servings

---

4 large potatoes, peeled
1 cup frozen cut green beans
3/4 cup feta cheese
1/4 cup sliced olives
1/3 cup sliced red onion
1/4 cup chopped green pepper
3/4 cup sliced radishes

Dressing:
3 tablespoons vegetable oil
2 teaspoons basil
1 teaspoon tarragon
2 tablespoons white wine vinegar
2 teaspoons lemon juice
1/4 teaspoon garlic powder
1/8 teaspoon cayenne (optional)
1/4 teaspoon salt (optional)

In a 3-quart saucepan, cook potatoes in boiling water for 20 minutes. Add beans, and cook 5 minutes more. Drain and cool. Chop the potatoes into 1/2-inch cubes. In a large salad bowl, combine cubed potatoes, beans, cheese, olives, onion, and pepper. Combine ingredients for dressing in a shaker container, and pour over salad, tossing to mix. Chill for 1/2 hour before serving. Add radishes just before serving. This keeps well in the refrigerator for up to 3 days.

Calories per 3/4-cup serving: 200
Fat: 8 g.; Cholesterol: 6 mg.
Sodium: 185 mg with salt; 124 mg. without salt

For exchange diets, count: 2 starch, 1 1/2 fat

Baked Potato Burrito

Preparation time: 45 minutes
Yield: 8 servings

4 potatoes
1 tablespoon vegetable oil
1 cup chopped onions
1/2 teaspoon garlic powder
2 teaspoons chili powder
2 teaspoons cumin
1/2 teaspoon oregano
1/2 teaspoon pepper
1/4 teaspoon salt
1 pound lean hamburger
1 tablespoon tomato paste
1/2 cup salsa
1 ounce part-skim cheddar cheese,
    shredded
3 cups shredded lettuce
3 tomatoes, cubed

Bake potatoes in microwave (8 to 12 minutes on high power, turning once during cooking). Cool, then slice in half lengthwise. Scoop out half the pulp from each piece and set aside. Meanwhile, heat oil over medium heat in a large skillet. Add onions, and sauté 5 minutes. Add spices, and cook 1 minute. Add hamburger, and cook until browned. Pour mixture into a colander and drain off all fat, pressing meat to promote draining. Stir in reserved potato pulp, tomato paste, and salsa. Stuff the potato shells with prepared meat filling. Place on a baking sheet, and cover with cheese. Broil 6 to 8 minutes until cheese is melted. Serve with lettuce and tomatoes on the side.

Calories per potato half: 232
Fat: 6 g.
Cholesterol: 36 mg.
Sodium: 238 mg.

For exchange diets, count 1 1/2 lean meat,
1 starch, 3 vegetable

Bean 'n Bacon Casserole
Preparation time: 30 minutes
Yield: 8 1 1/2-cup servings

8 slices bacon, broiled and crumbled
1/3 cup sugar
2 tablespoons cornstarch
3/4 cup vinegar
1/2 cup water
16-ounce can no-added-salt green beans
16-ounce can lima beans
16-ounce can wax beans
15-ounce can kidney beans
15-ounce can garbanzo beans

Combine sugar, cornstarch, vinegar, and water with whisk in a medium-sized skillet. Cook and stir to boiling. Drain all the beans well. Add the beans to the skillet, just stirring to mix. Simmer for 20 minutes. Stir in crumbled bacon, and serve. This casserole can be prepared and frozen for later use.

Calories per 1 1/2-cup serving: 255
Fat: 4 g.
Cholesterol: 6 mg.
Sodium: 411 mg.

For exchange diets, count: 1 1/2 starch,
1 vegetable, 2 lean meat

Main-Dish Salads and Casseroles

Chestnut Chicken and Rice

Preparation time: 50 minutes
Yield: 4 servings, 1 chicken breast + 3/4 cup rice each

10-ounce can reduced-fat cream of
    mushroom soup
1 cup no-added-salt chicken or vegetable
    broth or water
3/4 cup instant rice, dry
1 teaspoon rosemary
8-ounce can sliced water chestnuts,
    drained
4 skinless, boneless chicken breast halves
1/4 teaspoon paprika
1/4 teaspoon white pepper

Preheat oven to 375°F. In a 2-quart shallow baking dish, mix
soup, broth, or water, rice, rosemary, and water chestnuts. Place
chicken on rice mixture, and sprinkle with paprika and pepper.
Cover and bake for 40 minutes.

Calories per serving: 296
Fat: 3 g.
Cholesterol: 73 mg.
Sodium: 121 mg.

For exchange diets, count: 2 starch,
4 very lean meat

Chili Cheese Brunch Bake

Preparation time: 55 minutes
Yield: 8 servings, 1 square each

Nonstick cooking spray
2 4-ounce cans chopped green chilies,
    drained
14-ounce can Mexican style chopped
    tomatoes
2 cups nonfat cheddar cheese, shredded
1 cup reduced-fat baking mix such as
    Bisquick
1/2 cup nonfat sour cream
3 eggs or 3/4 cup liquid egg substitute

Preheat oven to 375°F. Spray an 11 by 7-inch baking dish with
cooking spray. Spread chilies over the bottom of the dish. Sprinkle with tomatoes and cheese. Beat remaining ingredients with
a wire whisk or hand beater until smooth, then pour over the
top. Bake for 35 to 40 minutes or until a knife inserted into the
center comes out clean. Remove from the oven and allow to rest
5 minutes before slicing into 8 squares.

Calories per serving: 160
Fat: 3 g.
Cholesterol: 85 mg. with eggs;
6 mg. with substitute
Sodium: 313 mg.

For exchange diets, count: 1 starch,
1 vegetable, 2 very lean meat

Eight Minute Fat-Free Baked Potato Supper

Preparation time: 10 minutes
Yield: 4 servings, 1 potato each

---

4 medium baking potatoes, scrubbed clean
1/4 cup hot tap water
Toppings:
8 ounces fat-free ham, diced
4 ounces fat-free cheddar cheese,
    shredded
2 green onions, diced
1/2 cup fat-free sour cream

Place potatoes in a microwave steamer (I prefer the one sold by Tupperware). Sprinkle water over the top, cover, and microwave for 4 minutes. Turn potatoes over, and microwave another 4 minutes. Time will need to be increased to 6 to 8 minutes per side for large potatoes. Remove potatoes from steamer, cut in half, and serve with toppings.

Calories per 1-potato serving: 280
Fat: 1 g.
Cholesterol: 22 mg.
Sodium: 478 mg.

For exchange diets, count: 2 starch,
3 very lean meat

Fettuccini Low-Fat Alfredo

Preparation time: 30 minutes
Yield: 8 1-cup servings

8 ounces fettuccini
4 cups vegetables cut into bite-sized pieces
  (such as broccoli, carrots, red pepper,
  pea pods, zucchini, mushrooms, and
  onions)
1 tablespoon water
1 teaspoon margarine
1/4 teaspoon garlic powder
1 cup part-skim ricotta cheese
2 tablespoons Parmesan cheese
2 tablespoons skim milk
1 egg or 1/4 cup liquid egg substitute
1/4 teaspoon salt (optional)
1/2 teaspoon oregano
1/8 teaspoon pepper

Cook fettuccini according to package directions. Meanwhile, microwave vegetables in a covered dish with 1 tablespoon water for 3 minutes. At the same time, melt margarine in a saucepan, and add garlic powder. Stir to mix. Blend in cheeses, milk, egg, and seasonings. Bring to a boil, reduce heat to low, and cook for 3 minutes. Transfer this sauce to a blender, and blend smooth. Drain noodles and vegetables well. Transfer to serving bowl. Pour sauce over noodles and vegetables, and toss gently.

Calories per 1-cup serving: 200; Fat: 6 g.
Cholesterol: 43 mg. with egg; 11 mg. with substitute
Sodium: 137 mg. with salt; 75 mg. without salt

For exchange diets, count: 1 skim milk, 1 starch, 1 fat

Harvest Casserole with Wild Rice

Preparation time: 45 minutes if microwaved
Yield: 8 1 1/4-cup servings

1 pound lean ground pork
1 medium onion, chopped
1 medium pepper, chopped
8 ounces mushrooms, sliced
1 cup celery, chopped
2 cups wild rice
11-oz. can Campbell's Special Request
    cream of mushroom soup
15-ounce can no-added-salt chicken broth
3-oz. jar chopped pimiento
1 teaspoon parsley
2 teaspoons marjoram
1 teaspoon thyme
1/2 teaspoon pepper

Brown pork in a large skillet, and drain. Add onion, pepper, mushrooms, and celery; cook until vegetables are tender. Add uncooked wild rice, soup, broth, pimiento, and seasonings. Mix well, then pour into a 3-quart casserole and cover. Bake 1 3/4 hours at 325°F. or microwave at 70 percent power for 30 minutes, stirring twice during the cooking period. This recipe can be doubled and frozen for later use.

Calories per 1 1/4-cup serving: 313
Fat: 12 g.
Cholesterol: 42 mg.
Sodium: 210 mg.

For exchange diets, count: 2 lean meat,
2 starch, 1 fat

Main-Dish Salads and Casseroles

Hoppin' John

Preparation time: 50 minutes
Yield: 8 1-cup servings

---

1 cup dried black-eyed peas or 16-ounce
   can precooked black-eyed peas
1 medium onion, chopped
3/4 cup chopped celery
1 bay leaf
3 cups water
1/2 teaspoon black pepper
1 cup uncooked rice
2 cups cubed lean cooked ham

In a 3-quart saucepan, combine dried peas, onion, celery, bay leaf, water, and pepper. Simmer for 2 hours until peas are tender. If using precooked peas, reduce water to 1 1/2 cups and simmer 15 minutes. Stir in rice, and simmer for 30 minutes more. Stir in ham just before serving, warming through. Remove bay leaf. This may be frozen and reheated for later use.

Calories per 1-cup serving: 156
Fat: 6 g.
Cholesterol: 14 mg.
Sodium: 588 mg. (To reduce sodium content, use
a reduced-sodium ham or substitute lean roast
beef or pork.)

For exchange diets, count: 1 starch,
1 vegetable, 1 lean meat

Marinated Mexican Chicken Sandwich
Preparation time: 15 minutes
Yield: 4 servings, 1 sandwich each

★ ★ ★

---

4 chicken breasts
1/2 teaspoon chili powder
1/4 teaspoon cumin
1/8 teaspoon cayenne pepper
4 hamburger rolls, split
Mexican dressing:
2 tablespoons nonfat mayonnaise
2 tablespoons chunky salsa
3/4 teaspoon finely grated lime peel
1/4 teaspoon ground pepper

Rub chili powder, cumin, and cayenne pepper into raw chicken breasts. Broil or grill for 4 to 6 minutes on each side under medium flame or over medium-high heat. Meanwhile, mix together ingredients for Mexican dressing, and spread over rolls. Place broiled chicken breasts into the rolls and serve with shredded lettuce on the side.

Calories per sandwich: 276
Fat: 5 g.
Cholesterol: 73 mg.
Sodium: 408 mg. (To reduce sodium, reduce salsa.)

For exchange diets, count: 1 1/2 starch,
4 very lean meat

Mary's Cream Soup Substitute

Preparation time: 15 minutes
Yield: equivalent of 10 cans of soup

---

2 cups nonfat dried milk
3/4 cup cornstarch
1/4 cup chicken or beef bouillon particles
2 tablespoons dried minced onion
1 teaspoon thyme
1 teaspoon basil
1/2 teaspoon pepper

Mix ingredients together, and store in a covered container. To use, mix 1 1/4 cups cold water with 1/3 cup of mix in a small saucepan. Add 1 teaspoon margarine. Cook until thickened. Substitute for a 15-ounce can of cream soup in casserole recipes.

Calories per 1/3-cup mix: 94
Fat: <1 g.
Cholesterol: 3 mg.
Sodium: 112 mg. (To reduce sodium, use low-sodium bouillon.)

For exchange diets, count: 1 starch

Main-Dish Salads and Casseroles

Mexican Corn Main Dish

Preparation time: 35 minutes if microwaved
Yield: 8 3/4-cup servings

★ ★ ★

Nonstick cooking spray
1 pound lean ground beef
4 ears fresh corn or 10-ounce package
    frozen corn, thawed
1/2 cup nonfat yogurt
1 egg or 1/4 cup liquid egg substitute
1 cup shredded mozzarella cheese
1/2 cup cornmeal
7-ounce can diced green chilies
1/4 teaspoon garlic powder
1/4 teaspoon salt (optional)
Chopped fresh parsley (optional)

Preheat oven to 350°F. Brown ground beef; drain well. Spray a
3-quart casserole dish with cooking spray. Cut fresh corn off the
cob. Put yogurt and egg in blender. Puree well. Combine this
with corn, browned meat, and all other ingredients in casserole
dish. Sprinkle fresh parsley over the top as a garnish. Bake for
50 minutes or microwave on high for 20 minutes. This casserole
is done when the center is firm and the top is lightly browned.
This may be assembled, frozen, and thawed for later baking.

Calories per 3/4-cup serving: 187
Fat: 5 g.
Cholesterol: 40 mg. with egg;
8 mg. with substitute
Sodium: 172 mg. with salt;
109 mg. without

For exchange diets, count: 2 lean meat, 1 starch

Main-Dish Salads and Casseroles

Pizza Rounds

Preparation time: 45 minutes
Rising time: 1 hour
Yield: 8 servings

1-pound loaf frozen bread dough
1/2 cup no-added-salt tomato sauce
1/2 teaspoon basil
1/2 teaspoon oregano
1/4 teaspoon garlic
1/4 teaspoon fennel
3/4 cup shredded mozzarella cheese
1/4 cup Parmesan cheese
8 ounces shredded roast beef
1/2 cup onion, chopped

Preheat oven to 375°F. Cover dough and allow to thaw at room temperature until pliable. Roll dough on a lightly floured board into a 12-inch square. Spread with tomato sauce, sprinkle with seasonings, and layer remaining ingredients. Roll dough up tightly in jelly-roll fashion, pinching the edges to seal. Cut roll into 8 pieces, and place in muffin tins sprayed with cooking spray. Let rise until double in bulk—about an hour. Bake for 18 minutes or until browned. Remove from pan and serve. These may be baked and frozen for later use. If frozen, rewarm for 45 seconds to 1 minute in the microwave before serving.

Calories per round: 234
Fat: 5 g.
Cholesterol: 28 mg.
Sodium: 377 mg.

For exchange diets, count: 1 1/2 starch,
2 lean meat

Pork Tortilla Pizza

Preparation time: 20 minutes
Yield: 4 servings, 1 tortilla pizza each

★ ★ ★

1/2 pound lean ground pork
1 medium onion, chopped
1 teaspoon dried oregano
1/4 teaspoon salt
4 large flour tortillas
Butter-flavored spray such as I Can't
    Believe It's Not Butter
1 medium fresh tomato, seeded and
    chopped
1 tablespoon fresh basil
1 cup nonfat mozzarella cheese, shredded
1/4 cup grated Parmesan cheese

Preheat oven to 400°F. In a medium skillet over medium-high heat, brown pork with onion until meat is no longer pink. Pour off drippings, then stir in oregano and salt. Spray tortillas with butter-flavored spray. Bake tortillas for 3 minutes. Remove from oven, and spoon pork mixture evenly over the top of each tortilla. Top with tomato, basil and cheeses. Return tortillas to the oven for 10 more minutes or until the cheese is melted and the tortillas are lightly browned.

Calories per serving: 289
Fat: 8 g.
Cholesterol: 52 mg.
Sodium: 459 mg.

For exchange diets, count: 1 1/2 starch,
1 vegetable, 4 very lean meat

Savory Black Bean Casserole

Preparation time: 30 minutes if microwaved
Yield: 8 1-cup servings

Nonstick cooking spray
2 16-ounce cans black beans
2 large onions, chopped fine
3 long ribs celery, diced
1 large carrot, cleaned and shredded
1/2 teaspoon minced garlic
1 tablespoon dried parsley
1/2 teaspoon ground pepper
1/2 teaspoon dried oregano
2 bay leaves
Dash of cayenne pepper
Garnish:
Fat-free sour cream

Preheat oven to 375°F. Combine all ingredients in a casserole dish that has been sprayed with cooking spray. Cover and bake for 45 minutes. Or microwave on 70 percent power for 18 to 20 minutes until vegetables are tender. Serve with sour cream on the side.

Calories per 1-cup serving: 169
Fat: 1 g.
Cholesterol: 0
Sodium: 499 mg.

For exchange diets, count: 2 starch, 1 lean meat

Spinach and Bacon Crunch

Preparation time: 40 minutes if microwaved
Yield: 4 wedges

★ ★ ★

Nonstick cooking spray
8 ounces fresh mushrooms, sliced thin
2 strips bacon
1/2 cup part-skim ricotta cheese
5 ounces evaporated skim milk
2 beaten eggs or 1/2 cup liquid egg
  substitute
1 teaspoon onion powder
2 teaspoons lemon juice
1/4 teaspoon pepper
10 ounces frozen spinach, thawed and
  squeezed dry
1 tablespoon margarine
3 cups Corn or Rice Chex cereal, crushed
  fine
1/4 teaspoon garlic powder

Preheat oven to 350°F. (Recipe can also be microwaved if you prefer.) Spray a 2-quart round baking dish (soufflé dish works best) with cooking spray. Spray a skillet with cooking spray. Sauté the mushrooms in the skillet until tender. Remove mushrooms, and cook bacon until crisp. Drain bacon, blot with paper towel, and crumble. Next, put the ricotta cheese in a blender, and blend until smooth. In a mixing bowl, mix cheese, milk, eggs, bacon, mushrooms, onion powder, lemon juice, pepper, and spinach until blended. Melt margarine in skillet. Add the crushed cereal and garlic powder, tossing to coat. Sprinkle this

Continued on next page

Spinach and Bacon Crunch
(continued)

over the spinach mixture. Bake 30 to 40 minutes until the mixture is bubbly, or microwave on high power for 12 to 15 minutes.

Calories per wedge: 270
Fat: 7 g.
Cholesterol: 100 mg. with egg;
12 mg. with substitute
Sodium: 426 mg.

For exchange diets, count: 2 lean meat, 2 starch

Main-Dish Salads and Casseroles

Taco Casserole

Preparation time: 40 minutes
Yield: 8 1-cup servings

Nonstick cooking spray
15-ounce can kidney beans, processed
   smooth in blender
1 pound lean ground beef, browned and
   drained
1/2 teaspoon garlic powder
1/2 teaspoon cumin
1/4 teaspoon cayenne pepper (optional)
8 ounces no-added-salt tomato sauce
1/4 cup chopped onion
1/4 cup chopped green pepper
4 medium flour tortillas, cut into triangles
2 ounces part-skim American cheese,
   grated
Garnish:
Chili powder

Preheat oven to 375°F. Spray a 9 x 13-inch dish or two 8 x 8-inch baking dishes with cooking spray. Spread processed beans onto bottom of prepared pan. Combine browned meat with garlic powder, cumin, cayenne pepper, and tomato sauce. Spread over beans. Top with onion, green pepper, tortilla triangles, and cheese. Sprinkle chili powder on top. Bake for 30 minutes or microwave for 20 to 22 minutes on medium-high power. Remove from oven and let stand for 5 minutes. Serve with chopped lettuce and tomato. This may be assembled and frozen for later baking.

Calories per 1-cup serving: 246; Fat: 7 g.
Cholesterol: 19 mg.; Sodium: 192 mg.

For exchange diets, count: 1 starch, 2 vegetable, 2 lean meat

Tuna and Noodle Casserole
Preparation time: 40 minutes
Yield: 4 1 1/2-cup servings

★ ★ ★

Nonstick cooking spray
4 ounces noodles of choice
1/2 cup green onion, chopped fine
4 ounces fresh mushrooms, sliced thin
1 tablespoon margarine
8-ounce can sliced water chestnuts,
    drained
5-ounce can water-packed tuna, drained
1 cup plain low-fat yogurt
1 tablespoon flour
1/4 teaspoon marjoram
1/4 teaspoon thyme
1/4 teaspoon salt (optional)
1/2 teaspoon white pepper
1 tablespoon lemon juice
1/2 cup chow mein noodles

Preheat oven to 350°F. Cook noodles according to package directions. Do not overcook. Meanwhile, sauté onions and mushrooms in margarine. Combine cooked noodles, vegetables, and tuna in an 8-inch square baking dish sprayed with cooking spray. Combine yogurt, flour, marjoram, thyme, salt, pepper, and lemon juice. Fold into the tuna mixture. Top with chow mein noodles. Bake for 30 minutes or microwave for 18 to 20 minutes until bubbly. This recipe can be assembled, frozen, and cooked later. To serve later, defrost in microwave for 15 minutes, then bake for 30 minutes or microwave on high power 18 to 20 minutes.

Main-Dish Salads and Casseroles

Calories per 1 1/2-cup serving: 299
Fat: 7 g.
Cholesterol: 16 mg.
Sodium: 186 mg. with salt; 62 mg. without salt

For exchange diets, count: 3 lean meat, 3 starch

Main-Dish Salads and Casseroles

Tuna Stuffed Manicotti

Preparation time: 25 minutes if microwaved
Yield: 4 servings, 2 shells each

Nonstick cooking spray
8 manicotti shells
2 5-ounce cans water-packed tuna,
    drained
1/2 cup nonfat cottage cheese
1 tablespoon dried parsley
1/4 cup diced onions
1 teaspoon lemon juice
1/4 teaspoon dill weed
Sauce:
1/2 cup nonfat cottage cheese, blended
    smooth
1/2 cup plain nonfat yogurt
1/4 teaspoon dill weed
1/8 teaspoon garlic powder
Topping:
2 tablespoons Parmesan cheese

Cook manicotti according to package directions. Drain and cool.
Preheat oven to 350°F. Combine tuna, cottage cheese, parsley,
onions, lemon juice, and dill weed in a small mixing bowl. Stuff
manicotti shells with tuna mixture, and place seam side down
in a 7 by 11-inch baking dish sprayed with cooking spray. Combine ingredients for the sauce, and spoon over manicotti. Sprinkle with Parmesan cheese. Bake for 30 minutes or microwave
for 8 minutes on high power.

Calories per serving: 285; Fat: 3 g.
Cholesterol: 76 mg.; Sodium: 327 mg.

For exchange diets, count: 2 lean meat, 1 starch, 1 skim milk

Turkey and Mushroom Tetrazzini

Preparation time: 35 minutes
Yield: 4 1 1/2-cup servings

Nonstick cooking spray
3 ounces spaghetti
1 teaspoon margarine
8 ounces fresh mushrooms, sliced thin
2 teaspoons margarine
2 tablespoons flour
1/8 teaspoon salt
1/4 teaspoon pepper
1 cup no-added-salt chicken broth
1/2 cup skim milk
1 tablespoon sherry
1 cup cooked turkey, cut into chunks
1/4 cup Parmesan cheese

Cook spaghetti according to package directions, and drain. Preheat oven to 350°F. In a Dutch oven, sauté mushrooms in 1 teaspoon margarine. Remove to a 2-quart casserole dish sprayed with cooking spray. Melt 2 teaspoons margarine over medium heat, and add flour, salt, pepper, broth, and milk, stirring until mixture thickens. Add the milk mixture, cooked spaghetti, mushrooms, sherry, and turkey to the casserole dish. Stir. Sprinkle with Parmesan cheese. Bake for 30 minutes or microwave for 14 minutes on high power.

Calories per 1 1/2-cup serving: 269
Fat: 9 g.
Cholesterol: 48 mg.
Sodium: 239 mg.

For exchange diets, count: 1 1/2 starch,
3 lean meat

Turkey Crepes

Preparation time: 50 minutes
Yield: 8 crepes

Crepes:
2/3 cup skim milk
2/3 cup flour
1 egg or 1/4 cup liquid egg substitute
1 tablespoon margarine, melted
1 teaspoon vegetable oil

Blend milk, flour, egg, and margarine until smooth with rotary beater. Pour oil into a 6-inch skillet, and heat over medium heat, tipping to cover the pan. Add 2 tablespoons batter to skillet and cook until the bottom is browned. Turn over to brown the other side. Place crepes between layers of wax paper on a plate.

Filling:
Nonstick cooking spray
2 tablespoons onion, diced
2 tablespoons celery, diced
1 tablespoon margarine
1/4 cup flour
Dash black pepper
1 2/3 cups skim milk
1/4 cup orange juice concentrate
2 teaspoons dried parsley
1 1/2 cups chopped cooked turkey
3/4 cup seedless green grapes

Sauté onion and celery in margarine until tender. Add flour and pepper, then gradually stir in milk, stirring until thick. Add the juice concentrate and parsley. Pour half of this sauce into a pitcher. Add the turkey and grapes to the remaining half of the sauce. Stir. Use the turkey mixture to fill crepes, rolling up and placing seam side down in a 7 by 11-inch baking pan sprayed with cooking spray. Pour reserved sauce over the crepes, and bake 20 minutes at 350°F. or microwave for 10 minutes on high power.

Calories per crepe: 207
Fat: 5 g.
Cholesterol: 41 mg. with egg;
20 mg. with substitute
Sodium: 115 mg.

For exchange diets, count: 2 lean meat,
1 starch, 1 vegetable

Turkey Salad à l'Orange

Preparation time: 20 minutes
Yield: 4 1-cup servings

---

1 1/2 cups cooked turkey, cut into small
    pieces
1 cup sliced celery
1 tablespoon red onion, diced fine
1 orange, peeled and cut into 1/2-inch
    pieces
Dressing:
3 tablespoons orange juice concentrate
1 teaspoon vegetable oil
1 tablespoon sugar
1 tablespoon vinegar
1/8 teaspoon dry mustard
Dash Tabasco sauce (optional)
2 tablespoons light mayonnaise or salad
    dressing

Combine first four ingredients for salad in a salad bowl. In a
shaker container, combine all ingredients except mayonnaise for
the dressing. When well blended, use a whisk to blend in the
mayonnaise. Pour over salad, and serve on a bed of fresh greens.

Calories per 1-cup serving: 222
Fat: 7 g.
Cholesterol: 69 mg.
Sodium: 122 mg.

For exchange diets, count: 2 lean meat,
1/2 starch, 1 fruit

Main-Dish Salads and Casseroles

Two Step Stuffed Peppers

Preparation time: 50 minutes
Yield: 4 servings, 1 stuffed pepper each

1 package cheddar broccoli rice and sauce
    mix
2 cups no-added-salt vegetable broth
4 large red or yellow peppers
1/2 pound cooked roast turkey, diced (may
    use cooked chicken or roast pork)
4 tablespoons shredded reduced-fat
    cheddar cheese

Preheat oven to 375°F. Prepare rice and sauce with broth according to package directions. Meanwhile, wash and seed peppers. Add turkey to the broccoli mixture, then stuff peppers with the broccoli mixture. Bake for 30 minutes. Sprinkle with cheese during the last 10 minutes of baking.

Calories per serving: 228
Fat: 4 g.
Cholesterol: 41 mg.
Sodium: 648 mg. (To reduced sodium,
use just half of rice sauce mix.)

For exchange diets, count: 1 1/2 starch,
1 vegetable, 2 very lean meat

Vegetable Enchiladas

Preparation time: 25 minutes if microwaved
Yield: 4 servings, 1 tortilla each

Nonstick cooking spray
1 cup tomato chunks
1/2 cup shredded zucchini
1/2 cup shredded carrots
1/3 cup chopped green pepper
1/4 cup chopped onion
1 cup shredded part-skim Monterey Jack
   cheese
1/2 cup part-skim ricotta cheese
1/2 teaspoon chili powder
1/4 teaspoon cumin
4 flour tortillas
1/2 cup chunky salsa

Preheat oven to 350°F. (Recipe can be microwaved if you prefer.) Combine tomato, zucchini, carrots, pepper, and onion in a 1-quart baking dish. Cover and steam for 4 minutes in the microwave. Meanwhile, combine the cheeses, chili powder, and cumin. Spread the cheese mixture over the tortillas. Spoon vegetable mixture on top. Roll up the tortillas, and place seam side down in an 8-inch square baking dish sprayed with cooking spray. Pour the salsa over the top, and bake for 25 minutes or microwave for 7 minutes on high power until bubbly.

Calories per serving: 251
Fat: 9 g.
Cholesterol: 26 mg.
Sodium: 348 mg.

For exchange diets, count: 2 starch, 1 lean meat, 1 fat

Almond Chicken with Vegetables

Preparation time: 20 minutes
Yield: 4 servings (4 ounces chicken & 1/2 cup vegetables)

2 chicken breasts, boned and skinned
1 tablespoon cornstarch
2 tablespoons sherry
2 tablespoons vegetable oil
1/2 cup diced sweet red pepper
1/2 cup sliced green onions
1/4 cup sliced water chestnuts
8-ounce can pineapple chunks in juice,
    drained, with liquid reserved
3 tablespoons slivered almonds
Sauce:
1 1/2 tablespoons sherry
1 teaspoon sesame or vegetable oil
1 teaspoon sugar
1/4 cup low-sodium chicken broth
1 1/2 tablespoons reduced-sodium soy
    sauce
1 teaspoon cornstarch
1 teaspoon reserved pineapple juice

Cube chicken. Mix 1 tablespoon cornstarch and 2 tablespoons sherry together, and pour over chicken. Set aside. Heat oil in a wok or heavy skillet. Add chicken, and stir-fry until lightly browned. Add pepper, onion, and water chestnuts. Stir-fry 2 minutes. Meanwhile, combine ingredients for the sauce in a measuring cup or bowl. Add pineapple, almonds, and sauce mixture to the pan. Cook 2 more minutes or until sauce is thickened and smooth.

Continued on next page

Almond Chicken with Vegetables
(continued)

Calories per serving: 326
Fat: 13 g.
Cholesterol: 67 mg.
Sodium: 299 mg.

For exchange diets, count: 3 lean meat, 1 fat,
1 fruit, 2 vegetable

Basil or Tarragon Flavored Oil for Stir-Fry

Preparation time: 20 minutes
Standing time: 24 hours
Yield: 16 tablespoons or 1 cup

★ ★ ★

---

1 cup packed fresh basil or tarragon
   leaves
1 cup soybean oil

Blanch basil or tarragon in boiling water for 1 minute. Immediately place in ice water; drain and dry thoroughly. Place oil in a 1-cup glass measure. Microwave on high power for 30 seconds. Transfer drained herbs into a food processor. Puree basil or tarragon while slowly adding warm oil. Remove from food processor, and allow to stand at room temperature for 24 hours or overnight. Strain oil through a very fine strainer or cheesecloth into a pouring container. Cover and refrigerate. Use with chicken and salmon recipes. This keeps 3 months in the refrigerator.

Calories per 1-tablespoon serving: 120
Fat: 14 g.
Cholesterol: 0
Sodium: 0

For exchange diets, count: 3 fat

Chicken Breast Midwest

Preparation time: 60 minutes
Yield: 4 1 1/2-cup servings

★ ★ ★

1 cup apple juice
1 tablespoon vegetable oil
1 tablespoon brown sugar
1 tablespoon light soy sauce
3 tablespoons lemon juice
2 teaspoons dried parsley
1/4 teaspoon garlic powder
1/4 teaspoon peppercorns
1 teaspoon Worcestershire sauce
1 bay leaf
4 skinless chicken breasts
2 cups julienne carrots
2 cups julienne zucchini
2 cups julienne yellow squash
1 tablespoon vegetable oil

In a small mixing bowl, prepare a marinade of apple juice, oil, brown sugar, soy sauce, lemon juice, parsley, garlic, peppercorns, Worcestershire sauce, and bay leaf. Place chicken breasts in marinade, cover with plastic wrap, and refrigerate at least 30 minutes. Remove chicken from bowl, and broil for 14 to 18 minutes, turning once. Meanwhile, steam the carrots, zucchini, and squash with 1 tablespoon oil and 2 tablespoons leftover marinade in a covered dish for 4 to 6 minutes in the microwave. Arrange the steamed vegetables on a serving platter, and place the broiled chicken breasts on top.

Calories per 1 1/2-cup serving: 395; Fat: 12 g.
Cholesterol: 96 mg.; Sodium: 404 mg.

For exchange diets, count: 4 lean meat, 2 starch, 1 vegetable

Chicken Cacciatore
Preparation time: 20 minutes
Yield: 4 1-cup servings

---

1 pound skinned, boned chicken, cut into
  strips
1/2 cup chopped onion
1 medium green pepper, cut into strips
1 tablespoon vegetable oil
16-ounce can no-added-salt whole
  tomatoes
8-ounce can no-added-salt tomato sauce
1/2 teaspoon oregano
1/2 teaspoon basil
1 cup quick rice

Sauté chicken, onion, and pepper in oil. Stir in tomatoes, sauce, and seasonings; bring to a boil. Stir in rice. Cover. Reduce heat to low, and cook for 10 minutes. This may be prepared and frozen for later use. Defrost 10 minutes in microwave, then heat 10 to 15 minutes on high power.

Calories per 1-cup serving: 339
Fat: 6 g.
Cholesterol: 68 mg.
Sodium: 104 mg.

For exchange diets, count: 3 lean meat,
2 starch, 2 vegetable

Chicken Stroganoff

Preparation time: 30 minutes if microwaved
Yield: 4 4-ounce servings

Nonstick cooking spray
2 whole chicken breasts, split, boned, and
　　skinned
1/4 teaspoon garlic powder
1/4 teaspoon white pepper
1/2 cup Campbell's Special Request cream
　　of mushroom soup
1 cup plain yogurt
6-ounce can sliced mushrooms, drained
2 tablespoons sherry
1/4 cup Parmesan cheese

Preheat oven to 350°F. Spray an 8 by 11-inch casserole dish with cooking spray. Place chicken breasts in casserole. Do not overlap. Sprinkle with garlic powder and pepper. Combine soup, yogurt, mushrooms, and sherry, and pour over chicken. Sprinkle cheese over all. Bake for 50 minutes or microwave covered on high power for 18 minutes or until chicken is tender. Serve with your favorite cooked noodles.

Calories per 4 ounces of stroganoff and 1/2
chicken breast (not including noodles): 202
Fat: 6 g.
Cholesterol: 63 mg.
Sodium: 133 mg.

For exchange diets, count: 3 lean meat,
1/2 skim milk

Cumin or Curry Flavored Oil for Stir-Fry
Yield: 16 tablespoons or 1 cup

★ ★ ★

1 cup soybean oil
2 tablespoons ground cumin or
    4 teaspoons curry powder

Place oil in a 1-cup glass measure. Microwave on high power for 30 seconds. Combine cumin or curry powder with oil. Allow to stand at room temperature about 24 hours or overnight. Strain oil through a very fine strainer or cheesecloth into a pouring container. Cover and refrigerate. Use with Mexican and Indian poultry and seafood recipes, beans, rice, or corn. This keeps 3 months in the refrigerator.

Calories per 1-tablespoon serving: 120
Fat: 14 g.
Cholesterol: 0
Sodium: 0

For exchange diets, count: 3 fat

Terrific Tuna Melt
Preparation time: 20 minutes
Yield: 4 servings, 1 sandwich each

★ ★ ★

11-ounce can waterpack tuna, drained
1 tablespoon dried onion flakes
1 rib celery, chopped very fine
1/3 cup fat-free mayonnaise or fat-fee
    Thousand Island salad dressing
1 teaspoon dill weed, optional
4 hamburger rolls
4 1-ounce slices fat-free American cheese
Garnish:
Dill pickle spears

Combine tuna, onion, celery, mayonnaise, and optional dill weed
in a small bowl. Divide tuna mixture among the bottom halves
of the 4 rolls. Top each with a slice of cheese. Place under broiler
for 5 minutes or until cheese is melted. Place top half of bun on
the sandwich and garnish with a dill pickle.

Calories per serving: 245
Fat: 3 g.
Cholesterol: 24 mg.
Sodium: 817 mg.

For exchange diets, count: 2 starch,
3 very lean meat

Fish and Potato Bake

Preparation time: 25 minutes if microwaved
Yield: 4 1 1/2-cup servings

★ ★ ★

---

1 onion, chopped
2 green peppers, cut in 1/2-inch strips
1/4 teaspoon garlic powder
1 tablespoon vegetable oil
15-ounce can Italian-style stewed
    tomatoes
1/4 teaspoon pepper
16-ounce can new potatoes, drained and
    sliced
1 pound white fish fillets, cut into chunks

Preheat oven to 375°F. (Recipe can be microwaved if you prefer.) Sauté onion, green pepper, and garlic powder in oil in a skillet for 5 minutes. Add tomatoes and pepper; cover, and simmer for 5 minutes. Spread 3 tablespoons of tomato/vegetable sauce over bottom of an 8-inch square casserole dish. Layer with potatoes and fish, then pour remaining sauce over the top. Bake for 25 minutes or until fish is flaky, or microwave on high power for 12 to 14 minutes.

Calories per serving: 240
Fat: 6 g.
Cholesterol: 77 mg.
Sodium: 263 mg.

For exchange diets, count: 3 lean meat, 1 starch

Garlic or Chili Flavored Oil for Stir-Fry

Yield: 16 tablespoons or 1 cup

---

1 cup soybean oil
8 large garlic cloves, peeled or
  2 tablespoons dried Chinese hot chilies

Place oil in a small saucepan, and add garlic or chilies. Heat over medium heat until garlic or chilies are golden brown, about 12 minutes for garlic and 6 minutes for chilies. Cool at room temperature for 4 hours, then strain oil through a very fine strainer or cheesecloth into a pouring container. Cover and refrigerate. Use with chicken, seafood, vegetable, pasta, and rice recipes. This keeps 3 months in the refrigerator.

Calories per 1-tablespoon serving: 120
Fat: 14 g.
Cholesterol: 0
Sodium: 0

For exchange diets, count: 3 fat

Jambalaya

Preparation time: 35 minutes
Yield: 8 1 1/2-cup servings

★ ★ ★

---

2 tablespoons oil
1 large green pepper, diced
2 medium onions, chopped
1/2 teaspoon garlic powder
1/2 cup cubed cooked lean ham
2 cups quick rice
2 1-pound, 12-ounce cans no-added-salt
  tomatoes
1 teaspoon hot pepper sauce
1/2 teaspoon pepper
1 teaspoon basil
1/2 teaspoon thyme
1 1/2 pounds peeled and deveined shrimp
  (For economy meal, substitute chunks
  of white fish, such as cod or haddock.)

Heat oil in a 4-quart Dutch oven. Sauté pepper, onion, and garlic. Add ham; sauté until brown. Stir in all remaining ingredients except for shrimp. Simmer for 20 minutes. Add shrimp or
fish, and cook for 5 minutes or until shrimp is pink or fish is tender and flaky. This can be prepared and frozen for later use.
Defrost for 10 minutes in microwave, then cook on high power
for 10 to 15 minutes.

Calories per 1 1/2-cup serving: 292
Fat: 5 g.
Cholesterol: 136 mg.
Sodium: 209 mg.

For exchange diets, count: 1 1/2 starch,
2 vegetable, 2 lean meat

Pineapple Chicken
Marinating time: 30 minutes to 24 hours
Preparation time: 55 minutes
Yield: 4 4-ounce servings

Nonstick cooking spray
4 chicken breasts, skinned, boned, and
    pounded
1/3 cup reduced-fat Italian salad dressing
20-ounce can crushed pineapple, drained,
    with liquid reserved
2 tablespoons brown sugar
1/2 teaspoon ginger
1/3 cup chopped green pepper
1/4 cup slivered almonds
1 tablespoon cornstarch

Marinate chicken breasts in salad dressing, pineapple juice, brown sugar, and ginger in the refrigerator for at least 30 minutes or up to 24 hours. Preheat oven to 375°F. In a small bowl, combine crushed pineapple, green pepper, and almonds. Remove chicken from marinade, and spoon pineapple mixture evenly on top of breasts. Roll them up, secure with a toothpick, and place seam side down in a baking dish sprayed with cooking spray. Pour 1/4 cup of marinade over the chicken. Cover and bake for 35 minutes or microwave on 70 percent power for 14 minutes until chicken is tender. Remove chicken to a platter. In a small pan, combine remaining marinade and chicken dish drippings with cornstarch, and cook for 2 minutes until thick. Pour over chicken.

Calories per 4-ounce serving: 276; Fat: 8 g.
Cholesterol: 69 mg.; Sodium: 183 mg.

For exchange diets, count: 3 lean meat, 1 starch, 1 fruit

Quick Italian White Fish Bake

Preparation time: 45 minutes
Yield: 4 4-ounce servings

---

1 pound frozen white fish fillets, such as
   cod, orange roughy, or halibut
1 cup chunky no-added-salt spaghetti
   sauce
1/4 cup grated Parmesan cheese

Preheat oven to 425°F. Place fish fillets close together in a shallow baking dish. Pour spaghetti sauce over the fish. Cover and bake for 30 minutes. Uncover and sprinkle with cheese. Return to the oven for 5 to 10 more minutes until cheese is melted. Serve with pasta or rice.

Calories per 4-ounce serving: 167
Fat: 5 g.
Cholesterol: 51 mg.
Sodium: 171 mg.

For exchange diets count: 3 very lean meat,
1 vegetable, 1 fat

Quick Mexican White Fish Bake

Preparation time: 45 minutes
Yield: 4 4-ounce servings

1 pound frozen white fish fillets, such as
  cod, orange roughy, or halibut
1 cup chunky salsa
1/4 cup grated fat-free mozzarella cheese

Preheat oven to 425°F. Place fish fillets close together in a shallow baking dish. Pour salsa over the fish. Cover and bake for 30 minutes. Uncover and sprinkle with cheese. Return to the oven for 5 to 10 more minutes until cheese is melted. Serve with corn, beans, or rice.

Calories per 4-ounce serving: 167
Fat: 5 g.
Cholesterol: 51 mg.
Sodium: 653 mg. (To reduce sodium,
use no-added-salt Mexican-flavored chunky
tomatoes instead of salsa.)

For exchange diets count: 3 very lean meat,
1 vegetable, 1 fat

Roast Venison in the Crockpot

Preparation time: Marinate overnight, 8 hours in crockpot.
Yield: 8 4-ounce servings

---

2 pounds venison
Cold water to cover meat
2 tablespoons flour
1 tablespoon vegetable oil
1/2 teaspoon garlic powder
1 large onion, sliced
2 tablespoons brown sugar
1 teaspoon mustard
1 tablespoon Worcestershire sauce
1/4 cup lemon juice
16-ounce can no-added-salt tomatoes
Marinade:
1/2 cup vinegar
1/2 teaspoon garlic powder
2 tablespoons salt

To make marinade, mix vinegar, garlic powder, and salt together. Place meat in a deep flat pan. Pour cold water over meat, and add vinegar mixture. Marinate overnight. Remove meat from marinade, and drain well. Roll meat in flour and brown in oil in a skillet. Transfer browned meat to the crockpot. Add all remaining ingredients, and cook on low for 8 hours. This makes an excellent leftover.

Calories per 4-ounce serving: 291; Fat: 10 g.
Cholesterol: 65 mg.; Sodium: 86 mg.

For exchange diets, count: 3 lean meat, 1 1/2 starch

Speed Alert: For best results, this recipe should be marinated overnight.

Romantic Chicken Marsala
Preparation time: 25 minutes
Yield: 4 8-ounce servings

1/4 cup chopped onion
1/2 cup chopped celery
1 cup sliced mushrooms
1 tablespoon liquid margarine
1 pound skinless diced chicken pieces
1/4 teaspoon sage
1/2 cup white wine
1 tablespoon flour
1 cup skim milk
1/4 teaspoon salt, optional
1/4 teaspoon white pepper

In a saucepan, sauté onion, celery, and mushrooms in margarine until tender. Add chicken and sage, and cook for 5 more minutes. Add wine, and cook for 10 more minutes, allowing liquid to evaporate. Combine flour and milk in a shaker container. Slowly stir into sauce, cooking 3 minutes or until thick. Stir in salt and pepper. Serve over thick noodles.

Calories per 1-cup serving (noodles not included): 219
Fat: 7 g.
Cholesterol: 80 mg.
Sodium: 299 mg. with salt; 177 mg. without salt

For exchange diets, count: 3 lean meat,
2 vegetable

Salmon in a Horseradish Crust

Preparation time: 45 minutes
Yield: 4 4-ounce servings

2 tablespoons chopped fresh parsley
1 teaspoon minced garlic
1/4 cup creamy horseradish
1 pound frozen salmon, cut into 4 fillets

Preheat oven to 425°F. In a small bowl, combine parsley, garlic, and horseradish. Arrange fillets close together in a shallow baking dish. Spread horseradish over the top of the fillets. Bake, covered, for 30 to 35 minutes, until fish is flaky. Serve with boiled potatoes.

Calories per 4-ounce serving: 163
Fat: 8 g.
Cholesterol: 54 mg.
Sodium: 129 mg.

For exchange diets, count: 3 lean meat

Sesame Coated Halibut

Preparation time: 45 minutes
Yield: 4 4-ounce servings

---

2 tablespoons reduced-fat mayonnaise
2 tablespoons sesame seeds
1 teaspoon lemon pepper seasoning
1 pound frozen halibut, cut into 4 fillets

Preheat oven to 425°F. In a small bowl, combine mayonnaise, sesame seeds, and lemon pepper. Arrange fillets close together in a shallow baking dish. Spread mayonnaise over the top of the fillets. Bake, covered, for 30 to 35 minutes, until fish is flaky. Serve with baked potatoes.

Calories per 4-ounce serving: 202
Fat: 12 g.
Cholesterol: 99 mg.
Sodium: 99 mg.

For exchange diets, count: 3 1/2 lean meat

Seafood Scampi

Preparation time: 15 minutes
Yield: 4 1 1/2-cup servings

---

1 pound shrimp, mock crab, or cod
1 onion, chopped
1/2 teaspoon garlic powder
1 tablespoon liquid margarine
8 ounces no-added-salt chicken broth
1 teaspoon no-added-salt chicken bouillon
1 tablespoon flour
1 red pepper, chopped
1 tablespoon lemon juice
1/4 teaspoon salt, optional
1 1/2 cups quick rice
1/4 cup fresh chopped parsley

Sauté seafood, onion, and garlic powder in margarine in a large skillet until seafood turns white. Combine broth, bouillon, and flour in a shaker container. Stir into seafood mixture. Add pepper, lemon juice, and optional salt. Bring to a boil. Stir in rice and parsley. Cover. Remove from heat and let stand for 5 minutes. Serve.

Calories per 1 1/2-cup serving: 266
Fat: 4 g.
Cholesterol: 43 mg.
Sodium: 495 mg. with salt; 373 mg. without salt

For exchange diets, count: 2 lean meat,
1 1/2 starch, 1 vegetable

Stuffed Sole
Preparation time: 30 minutes
Yield: 4 4-ounce servings

1 cup sliced mushrooms
1/2 cup sliced green onions
1 tablespoon vegetable oil
3/4 cup oatmeal or bread crumbs
1 egg or 1/4 cup liquid egg substitute
1/4 teaspoon salt, optional
1 tablespoon lemon juice
1/2 teaspoon marjoram
1 tablespoon lemon juice
1 pound sole, flounder, orange roughy, or
    cod fillets
Paprika

Preheat oven to 375°F. (Recipe can be microwaved if you prefer.)
Sauté mushrooms and onions in oil for 3 minutes. Add oatmeal
or bread crumbs, egg, salt, 1 tablespoon lemon juice, and marjoram. Spread stuffing mixture on the fillets, spreading to within
1/2 inch of the edge. Roll up fillets, and secure with a toothpick.
Place seam side down in an 8-inch square baking dish. Sprinkle
with the remaining 1 tablespoon of lemon juice, and dust with
paprika. Bake for 20 minutes or microwave for 8 minutes, just
until the fish flakes easily with a fork.

Calories per 4-ounce serving: 260
Fat: 11 g.
Cholesterol: 114 mg. with egg;
50 mg. with substitute
Sodium: 263 mg. with salt; 141 mg. without salt

For exchange diets, count: 3 lean meat, 1 starch

Tarragon Turkey

Yield: 8 to 10 servings from an 8-pound turkey

★ ★ ★

Turkeys are best roasted on a rack at 325°F. An 8 to 12 pound turkey requires 4 hours; allow for 4 1/2 hours for a 12 to 16 pound bird. Cover the turkey loosely with foil for a beautiful browned appearance. Roast with breast down because the juices keep the white meat moist. Allow the roasted bird to sit 15 minutes at room temperature before carving. Serve a 3 to 5 ounce portion of turkey with this sauce on the side:

Sauce:

Preparation time: 10 minutes for sauce
Yield: 8 3-tablespoon servings or 1 1/2 cups

1 tablespoon vegetable oil
2 tablespoons finely diced onion
1/4 cup white wine
2 tablespoons tarragon wine vinegar
1 cup plain yogurt
2 tablespoons Dijon mustard
1/8 teaspoon crushed dried tarragon
1/2 teaspoon sugar

Heat oil in a saucepan; add onion, and sauté. Stir in wine and vinegar, and simmer for 3 minutes, reducing volume. Reduce heat, and fold in yogurt, mustard, tarragon, and sugar. Keep sauce warm on low heat or prepare ahead of time and chill. Microwave the sauce in a glass pitcher for 1 1/2 minutes just before serving.

Calories per 3 tablespoons of sauce: 32; Fat: 2 g.
Cholesterol: <1 mg.; Sodium: 87 mg.

For exchange diets, count: 1/2 skim milk

Turkey Fillets Marinated Three Ways

Preparation time: 10 minutes
Marinating time: 4 hours to overnight
Broiling time: 15 minutes
Yield: 4 4-ounce servings

1 pound turkey breast fillets
Pineapple garlic marinade:
1 cup pineapple juice
2/3 cup dry sherry
2 tablespoons brown sugar
1/2 teaspoon dried rosemary leaves
1 clove garlic, crushed
Spicy tomato basil marinade:
1 cup chunky tomatoes
4 sun-dried tomato halves, chopped fine
1 tablespoon dried basil
1/4 teaspoon cayenne pepper
2 tablespoons Dijon mustard
2 tablespoons honey
1 teaspoon minced garlic
Orange-mustard marinade:
1 cup orange juice
3 tablespoons reduced-sodium soy sauce
2 tablespoons honey
1 tablespoon Dijon mustard
1 teaspoon chopped fresh gingerroot
1/2 teaspoon minced garlic

Combine ingredients for the marinade in a shallow baking dish.
Place the turkey fillets in the marinade, and spoon the liquid
over all sides of the fillets. Cover and refrigerate at least 4 hours
or up to overnight. Grill or broil the turkey fillets for 6 to 8 minutes on each side.

Poultry, Fish and Game

Calories per 4-ounce serving: 176
Fat: 4 g.
Cholesterol: 73 mg.
Sodium: 53 mg. for pineapple garlic, 151 mg. for
spicy tomato, 537 mg. for orange-mustard

For exchange diets, count: 3 very lean meat, 1
fruit

Speed Alert: Requires at least 4 hours to marinate.

Leftover Turkey, Kabob Style

Preparation time: 30 minutes
Yield: 4 servings

4 medium yams or sweet potatoes
2 tablespoons water
8 ounces pineapple chunks, in juice
1 teaspoon cornstarch
1/2 teaspoon cinnamon
1/4 teaspoon dry mustard
1/8 teaspoon ground cloves
1/2 cup jellied cranberry sauce
3/4 pound roast turkey, cut into chunks
4 small canned onions

Cut off woody stem of yams. Place yams in a covered microwave baking dish with water. Microwave for 10 minutes on high power until tender. Cool the yams long enough to be able to peel and quarter them. Meanwhile, drain pineapple, and combine juice in a small saucepan with cornstarch, cinnamon, mustard, cloves, and cranberry sauce. Heat until thick and bubbly. On 4 skewers, thread turkey, yam, pineapple chunks, and onions. Broil for 8 minutes, brushing with sauce on both sides before and during broiling. Pass remaining sauce at the table.

Calories per serving: 393
Fat: 6 g.
Cholesterol: 70 mg.
Sodium: 195 mg.

For exchange diets, count: 2 1/2 starch, 1 fat,
3 lean meat

Turkey with Orange Raisin Sauce

Preparation time: 10 minutes for sauce
Yield: 8 1/3-cup servings (for a 10-pound turkey)

3 tablespoons margarine
1/4 cup minced onion
1/2 cup raisins
1/2 cup orange juice
1/4 cup honey
1 tablespoon grated orange peel
1 Tbsp. corn starch
1/2 cup water

Prepare and start a 10 to 12 pound turkey roasting. (See page 000 for directions on roasting turkeys.) To prepare sauce, melt margarine in a small saucepan. Add onion, and sauté until tender. Stir in raisins, orange juice, honey, and orange peel. Using a wire whisk, stir in cornstarch and water. Cook over medium heat just until boiling, then reduce heat and cook for 3 more minutes. Pour 1 cup of sauce over turkey 1/2 hour before it is done, leaving the bird uncovered to produce a brown glaze. Pass remaining sauce at the table.

Calories per 1/3-cup
of sauce: 155
Fat: 6 g.
Cholesterol: 0
Sodium: 27 mg.

Calories per 3-ounce
serving of turkey: 165
Fat: 9 g.
Cholesterol: 51 mg.
Sodium: 63 mg.

For exchange diets, count: 1 1/2
fruit and 1 fat for 1/3 cup of sauce

For exchange diets, count: 3 lean
meat for 3 ounces of turkey

Speed Alert: Preparation time depends on size of turkey.

Apple Glazed Pork Kabobs

Preparation time: 30 minutes
Yield: 4 4-ounce servings

1 pound boneless pork loin
2 tablespoons lemon juice
1/4 teaspoon salt (optional)
Apple Glaze:
1/3 cup apple jelly
1 tablespoon lemon juice
1/8 teaspoon cinnamon
1 tablespoon margarine, melted

Trim pork, and cut into 1-inch cubes. Sprinkle lemon juice and salt over pork in a shallow pan. In a glass measuring cup, mix jelly, lemon juice, cinnamon, and margarine. Thread pork cubes onto skewers, and baste with glaze. Grill or broil kabobs for 10 to 12 minutes, turning and basting two more times.

Calories per 4-ounce serving: 310
Fat: 12 g.
Cholesterol: 92 mg.
Sodium: 214 mg. with salt; 146 mg. without salt

For exchange diets, count: 4 lean meat
and 1 starch

Brushed Beef Roast

Preparation time: 10 minutes
Marinating time: 3 to 8 hours
Broiling time: 15 minutes
Yield: 8 slices

★ ★ ★

1/4 cup liquid margarine
2 tablespoons red wine
1/4 cup minced onion
2 tablespoons lemon juice
1/2 teaspoon oregano
1/4 teaspoon marjoram
1/4 teaspoon thyme
1/4 teaspoon pepper
1/4 teaspoon garlic powder
2 pounds flank steak, 2 inches thick

Melt margarine, and mix in wine, onion, lemon juice, and spices. Transfer marinade to a plastic bag; place flank steak in bag. Seal. Turn the bag to coat the meat, and let this marinate in the refrigerator for 3 to 8 hours. Remove the meat from the bag, and place on a broiling pan or rack. Brush the surface of the meat with marinade, and broil for 6 minutes. Turn and brush other side of steak with remaining marinade. Broil 8 more minutes. Slice and serve.

Calories per slice: 205
Fat: 11 g.
Cholesterol: 72 mg.; Sodium: 84 mg.

For exchange diets, count: 4 lean meat

Speed Alert: Requires at least 3 hours to marinate.

Iowa Beef Stroganoff

Preparation time: 40 minutes
Yield: 6 servings

1 pound top round steak
1/4 teaspoon freshly ground black pepper
4-oz. can mushrooms, sliced thin
2 tablespoons oil
1 onion, sliced
3 tablespoons flour
3 cups low-sodium beef broth
2 tablespoons no-added-salt tomato paste
1 teaspoon dry mustard
1/4 teaspoon oregano
1/4 teaspoon dill weed
1 tablespoon sherry
1/3 cup low-fat yogurt

Remove all visible fat from meat, and cut into thin strips, about 2 inches long. Sprinkle with pepper. In a heavy skillet, sauté mushrooms in oil until tender. Remove from skillet, and sauté onions in the same oil until brown. Remove from skillet. Brown meat quickly in skillet; remove and set aside. Blend the flour into the oil in the skillet. Gradually add the broth, stirring constantly until smooth and thick. Add the tomato paste, mustard, oregano, dill weed, and sherry. Blend well. Combine the sauce with the meat, mushrooms, and onions in skillet. Simmer for 20 minutes, stirring occasionally. Blend in the yogurt just before serving. Serve with rice or noodles.

Calories per 1-cup serving: 197; Fat: 8 g.
Cholesterol: 49 mg.; Sodium: 56 mg.

For exchange diets, count: 3 lean meat, 1 vegetable

London Broil

Preparation time: 5 minutes
Marinating time: 8 hours
Yield: 4 3-ounce servings

1 pound flank steak
1 envelope Italian salad dressing mix
1/4 cup red wine
2 tablespoons vegetable oil

Score flank steak 1/8 inch deep in criss cross pattern on both sides. Place meat in a shallow pan. Combine the dressing mix with the wine and oil in a shaker container. Pour over the meat, and marinate covered in the refrigerator 8 hours or overnight. Broil or grill the meat to desired doneness, and discard remaining marinade.

Calories per 3-ounce serving: 194
Fat: 10 g.
Cholesterol: 69 mg.
Sodium: 233 mg.

For exchange diets, count: 3 lean meat

Speed Alert: Requires 8 hours to marinate

Low-Fat Breakfast Sausage
Preparation time: 10 minutes
Chilling time: 8 to 24 hours
Yield: 8 2-ounce servings

1 pound lean ground beef or pork
1/2 teaspoon salt
3/4 teaspoon black pepper
1 teaspoon sage
1/4 teaspoon sugar
1 tablespoon water

Combine all ingredients in a mixing bowl. Cover and chill overnight to allow flavors to blend. Shape into patties or links. Cook over medium heat in a nonstick skillet until beef is no longer pink.

Calories per 2-ounce serving: 84
Fat: 3 g.
Cholesterol: 33 mg.
Sodium: 161 mg.

For exchange diets, count: 2 very lean meat

Speed Alert: This recipe requires 8 to 24 hours chilling time.

Low-Fat Italian Sausage

Preparation time: 10 minutes
Chilling time: 8 to 24 hours
Yield: 8 2-ounce servings

1 pound lean ground beef or pork
1 tablespoon paprika
2 teaspoons dried sage
1 1/2 teaspoons fennel
1/2 teaspoon salt
1/2 teaspoon cayenne
1/2 teaspoon black pepper
1 tablespoon water

Combine all ingredients in a mixing bowl. Cover and chill overnight to allow flavors to blend. Shape into patties or links. Cook over medium heat in a nonstick skillet until beef is no longer pink.

Calories per 2-ounce serving: 84
Fat: 3 g.
Cholesterol: 33 mg.
Sodium: 161 mg.

For exchange diets, count: 2 very lean meat

Speed Alert: This recipe requires 8 to 24 hours chilling time.

Marinated Loin of Pork

Preparation time: 5 minutes
Marinating time: 3 hours
Roasting and cooling time: 2 hours, 10 minutes
Yield: 8 4-ounce servings

2 pounds pork loin, trimmed
1 can light beer
1/2 cup apple juice
1 teaspoon thyme
1 tablespoon brown sugar
1/2 teaspoon black pepper

Combine ingredients for marinade in a shaker container. Pour over the pork loin in a shallow pan. Cover and refrigerate for 3 hours. Preheat oven to 400°F. Drain marinade and save. Roast meat for 20 minutes. Reduce heat to 325°F. and continue roasting for 1 1/2 hours. Pour some reserved marinade over the meat at 30 minute intervals. Meat is well done when thermometer registers 170°F. Allow meat to cool for 20 minutes before slicing.

Calories per 4-ounce serving: 197
Fat: 7 g.
Cholesterol: 54 mg.
Sodium: 47 mg.

For exchange diets, count: 3 lean meat, 1/2 fruit

Speed Alert: This recipe requires 3 hours to marinate and 2 hours to cook.

Red Meats

Old-Fashioned Swiss Steak

Preparation time: 20 minutes
Cooking or baking time: 1 hour, 30 minutes
Yield: 4 4-ounce servings

1/4 cup flour
1/4 teaspoon salt
1/4 teaspoon black pepper
1 pound top round steak, well trimmed
    and cut into 4 portions
Nonstick cooking spray
1 large onion, sliced
1 cup no-added-salt beef broth
1 teaspoon dried parsley

Combine flour, salt, and pepper in a plastic bag. Add round steak to the bag, and shake to coat. Spray a heavy nonstick skillet with cooking spray. Heat over medium heat. Add round steak. Brown both sides of the steak. Top with sliced onion. Add broth and parsley, and reduce heat to medium-low. Cook on the stovetop for 1 1/2 hours or transfer to the oven and bake at 350°F. for 1 1/2 hours.

Calories per 4-ounce serving: 190
Fat: 7 g.
Cholesterol: 66 mg.
Sodium: 190 mg.

For exchange diets, count: 3 lean meat,
1/2 starch

Speed Alert: This recipe takes about 2 hours.

Rouladen

Preparation time: 15 minutes
Baking time: 1 hour
Yield: 4 4-ounce servings

1 large onion, chopped fine
2 strips bacon, diced fine
4 minute steaks, 4 ounces each
2 teaspoons Dijon mustard
1/2 teaspoon salt, optional
1 large pickle, cut into four thin strips
1 1/2 cups no-added-salt beef broth,
   divided
4 peppercorns
1 bay leaf
1 tablespoon cornstarch

In a small skillet, cook onion and bacon until bacon is crisp.
Drain well. In the meantime, pound steaks flat, then spread
with mustard and sprinkle with salt. Sprinkle with bacon and
onion mixture, and place one strip of pickle down the center of
each steak. Roll the steaks up, and secure with a toothpick or
string. Brown the steaks in the skillet. Transfer the steaks to a
Dutch oven. Pour 1 cup broth, peppercorns, and bay leaf over
steaks, and cover. Bake for 1 hour at 350° F. Just before the meat
is done, mix the cornstarch with the remaining 1/2 cup of broth.
Add it to the meat juices, and stir until thick. Remove bay leaf,
and serve as a sauce over the steak rolls.

Calories per 4-ounce serving: 238
Fat: 12 g.
Cholesterol: 65 mg.
Sodium: 346 mg. with salt; 285 mg. without

For exchange diets, count: 4 lean meat, 1 vegetable

Savory Ham Balls

Preparation time: 20 minutes
Baking time: 1 hour, 30 minutes
Yield: 12 servings, 2 ham balls each

---

1 pound ground lean ham
1 pound ground lean fresh pork
1/2 cup graham cracker crumbs
1 egg or 1/4 cup liquid egg substitute
3/4 cup skim milk
Sauce:
8 ounces no-added-salt tomato sauce
1/4 cup red wine vinegar
1/4 cup brown sugar
1/2 teaspoon dry mustard

Preheat oven to 325°F. Combine ham, pork, cracker crumbs, egg, and milk in a mixing bowl. Shape by 1/3 cupfuls into balls, and arrange in a 9 by 13-inch baking dish. Bake covered for 1 hour. Combine all ingredients for sauce. Remove meat from oven and pour off all drippings. Pour sauce over the ham balls, and bake for 30 minutes more.

Calories per serving: 170
Fat: 6 g.
Cholesterol: 69 mg. with egg;
55 mg. with substitute
Sodium: 72 mg.

For exchange diets, count: 2 1/2 lean meat,
1/2 fruit

Speed Alert: This recipe requires about 2 hours.

Spicy Orange Pork Loin

Preparation time: 15 minutes
Marinating time: 1 to 24 hours
Baking time: 1 hour, 30 minutes
Yield: 4 4-ounce servings

1 pound boneless pork loin
2 navel oranges, cut into 1/2-inch thick
  rounds
1 teaspoon dried thyme
Marinade:
6 ounces frozen orange juice concentrate,
  thawed
1/4 cup balsamic vinegar
2 teaspoons dried thyme
1 teaspoon minced dried garlic
1 teaspoon black pepper

Trim and tie pork roast if needed. Pierce the roast with a fork
several times. Rub the orange flesh and juice over the meat. Rub
1 teaspoon thyme into the meat. In a shallow pan, combine
ingredients for the marinade. Place pork in the pan, and spoon
marinade over the meat. Place oranges into the marinade as
well. Marinate for at least 1 hour or up to 24 hours. Remove the
pork from the marinade, and grill 5 inches from the heat for 1 to
1 1/2 hours or until a meat thermometer registers 165°F.

Calories per 4-ounce serving: 166
Fat: 6 g.
Cholesterol: 41 mg.
Sodium: 33 mg.

For exchange diets, count: 2 lean meat, 1 fruit

Speed Alert: This recipe requires at least 2 hours, 45 minutes.

Tex-Mex Pork Loaf
Preparation time: 60 minutes
Yield: 4 3-ounce servings

★ ★ ★

1 pound lean ground pork
1/4 cup dried bread crumbs
1/3 cup chopped onion
1/4 cup skim milk
1 1/2 teaspoons chili powder
1/2 teaspoon cumin
1/2 teaspoon oregano
1/4 teaspoon garlic powder
1/4 teaspoon black pepper
1/8 teaspoon salt, optional

Preheat oven to 350°F. Combine pork, crumbs, onion, milk, and seasonings in a large bowl, mixing lightly. Shape into a 6 by 3 by 3-inch loaf. Place loaf on a rack in a shallow roasting pan. Bake for 45 to 55 minutes. Remove from oven and allow to stand for 5 minutes. Slice and serve.

Calories per 3-ounce serving: 244
Fat: 11 g.
Cholesterol: 81 mg.
Sodium: 213 mg. with salt; 152 mg. without salt

For exchange diets, count: 3 lean meat, 1 starch

Traditional Pot Roast

Preparation time: 10 minutes
Marinating time: 12 to 24 hours
Cooking time: 3 to 6 hours
Yield: 8 3-ounce meat and 3/4-cup vegetable servings

---

2 pounds boneless chuck roast, trimmed
2 cups no-added-salt beef broth
1/2 cup red wine
1/2 teaspoon garlic powder
1/2 cup chopped onion
1 tablespoon Dijon mustard
2 teaspoons Worcestershire sauce
1 teaspoon thyme
4 potatoes, peeled and quartered
6 medium carrots, peeled and chunked

Place chuck roast in a glass dish. Combine broth, wine, garlic powder, onion, mustard, Worcestershire sauce, and thyme in a shaker container, and pour over the meat. Cover. Marinate in refrigerator for 12 to 24 hours. Place meat and marinade in Dutch oven or Crockpot. Add potatoes and carrots. Simmer in Dutch oven for 3 hours or cook in Crockpot until tender, about 3 to 6 hours. The marinade tenderizes the chuck cut. The marinade is unnecessary if you are working with a tender cut, such as loin.

Calories per serving: 261
Fat: 9 g.
Cholesterol: 85 mg.
Sodium: 128 mg.

For exchange diets, count: 3 lean meat, 1/2 starch, 2 vegetable

---

Speed Alert: This recipe marinates for 12 to 24 hours and cooks for 3 to 6 hours.

Apple Stuffing

Preparation time: 65 minutes
Yield: 8 1-cup servings

Nonstick cooking spray
2 cups bread crumbs
4 cups chopped apples
1 small onion, chopped
3 stalks celery, chopped
1/4 cup raisins
1/2 cup apple juice
2 tablespoons brown sugar
1/4 teaspoon salt
1 teaspoon cinnamon
2 tablespoons liquid margarine, melted

Preheat oven to 350°F. Combine crumbs, apple, onion, celery, and raisins in a 3-quart baking pan that has been sprayed with cooking spray. In a small mixing bowl, combine remaining ingredients, stirring to blend. Pour liquid over bread mixture, and toss to coat. Cover and bake for 45 minutes. Uncover and bake 10 more minutes to promote crusting.

Calories per 1-cup serving: 169
Fat: 1 g.
Cholesterol: 0
Sodium: 265 mg.

For exchange diets, count: 1 fruit, 1 1/2 starch

Baked Carrots and Sprouts

Preparation time: 20 minutes if microwaved
Yield: 8 1-cup servings

2 cups fresh Brussels sprouts
3 cups sliced fresh carrots
2 tablespoons water
1/2 cup chopped onion
2 tablespoons liquid margarine
1/4 cup flour
1 teaspoon dill weed
3 cups skim milk
1/3 cup chopped fresh parsley

Steam Brussels sprouts and carrots with 2 tablespoons of water in a covered dish in the microwave for 5 minutes. Drain off water. Meanwhile, sauté onion in margarine in a medium-sized skillet. Stir in flour and dill weed, then gradually stir in milk. Cook until thick. Pour sauce over vegetables, and top with fresh parsley. Microwave for 12 minutes uncovered on high power or bake uncovered for 30 minutes at 350°F.

Calories per 1-cup serving: 108
Fat: 4 g.
Cholesterol: 1 mg.
Sodium: 227 mg.

For exchange diets, count: 1/2 starch,
1 vegetable, 1 fat

Broccoli Rice Casserole
Preparation time: 45 minutes
Yield: 4 1 1/2-cup servings

1/2 cup chopped onion
1/2 cup diced celery
1/2 pound fresh mushrooms, sliced
2 tablespoons margarine
2 10-ounce packages chopped broccoli
1 cup quick rice, uncooked
2 ounces light American cheese, shredded
Cream Soup Substitute:
2 cups instant nonfat dry milk
3/4 cup cornstarch
1/4 cup low-sodium chicken bouillon
    particles
2 tablespoons dried onion flakes
1 teaspoon basil
1 teaspoon thyme
1/2 teaspoon white or black pepper
(Yield is 9 cups of mix. Use 1/3 cup with
1 1/4 cups water as a substitute for
canned soups in casseroles. Store in a
covered container.)

Preheat oven to 350°. (Recipe can also be microwaved if you prefer.) In a nonstick skillet, sauté onion, celery, and sliced mushrooms in margarine until tender. Using 1 large or two small casserole dishes, combine sautéed vegetables with broccoli, rice, and cheese. Combine 2/3 cup Cream Soup Substitute with 2 1/2 cups water in a shaker container. Add to the other ingredients, and mix well. Bake for 30 minutes or microwave on high power for 15 to 18 minutes, until mixture is bubbly.

Continued on next page.

Broccoli Rice Casserole
(continued)

Calories per 1 1/2-cup serving: 132
Fat: 5 g.
Cholesterol: 4 mg.
Sodium: 302 mg.

For exchange diets, count: 1 starch,
1 vegetable, 1 fat

Vegetables and Starches

Carolyn's Veggie Pilaf

My friend and fellow Stephen leader,
Carolyn Hoffmann, found this treat.
Preparation time: 30 minutes
Yield: 8 1-cup servings

★ ★ ★

Nonstick cooking spray
1 quart no-added-salt chicken broth
1 cup barley
1/2 cup wild rice
4 cups chopped fresh veggies of choice
    (carrots, onions, peppers, celery,
    zucchini, broccoli, yellow squash)
1 tablespoon dried oregano
1 tablespoon dried basil
1/2 teaspoon black pepper
1/4 cup fresh lemon juice

Bring broth to a boil in a medium saucepan. Add barley and wild rice, and cook covered over medium heat for 20 minutes. Meanwhile, chop vegetables. Drain barley and rice well, then transfer to a large nonstick skillet that has been sprayed with cooking spray. Add vegetables, oregano, basil, pepper, and lemon juice, and stir-fry over medium-high heat for 8 minutes until veggies are tender crisp.

Calories per 1-cup serving: 103
Fat: 0
Cholesterol: 0
Sodium: 23 mg.

For exchange diets, count: 1 starch, 1 vegetable

Christmas Stuffing

Preparation time: 60 minutes
Yield: 12 3/4-cup servings

★ ★ ★

Nonstick cooking spray
4 cups fresh bread crumbs
1/2 cup skim milk
1/2 cup diced onion
1 tablespoon margarine, melted
1/2 pound turkey sausage, browned and
    drained
3/4 cup chopped celery
1/4 cup raisins
1/4 cup cranberries
1 teaspoon sage

Preheat oven to 350°F. Combine all ingredients in a mixing bowl, and toss to mix thoroughly. Spray a 2-quart casserole dish with cooking spray, and put the stuffing in the casserole. Cover and bake for 45 minutes. Add additional water if the mixture becomes dry while baking. Remove cover, and brown the top for 10 more minutes.

Calories per 3/4-cup serving: 177
Fat: 5 g.
Cholesterol: 14 mg.
Sodium: 186 mg.

For exchange diets, count: 1 lean meat, 1/2 fruit,
1 starch, 1/2 fat

Fruit Stuffing
Preparation time: 60 minutes
Yield: 8 3/4-cup servings

1 cup chopped cranberries
2 tablespoons sugar
12 slices raisin bread, cut into cubes
2 tablespoons margarine
2 teaspoons grated orange peel
1/8 teaspoon salt
2 tablespoons orange juice

Preheat oven to 325°F. Combine all ingredients in a mixing bowl, stirring to moisten the bread. Stuff turkey loosely, and roast, or add 1 cup no-added-salt chicken or turkey broth, then stir and transfer to a casserole dish that has been sprayed with cooking spray. Bake for 45 minutes, removing the cover the last ten minutes to brown.

Calories per 3/4-cup serving: 141
Fat: 4 g.
Cholesterol: 0
Sodium: 203 mg.

For exchange diets, count: 1 starch, 1 fat

German Potato Salad

Preparation time: 40 minutes
Yield: 8 1/2-cup servings

4 large potatoes, boiled, peeled, and diced
3 strips bacon, diced, fried crisp, and
   drained well
4 green onions, diced
Dressing:
1/4 teaspoon pepper
1 tablespoon oil
2 tablespoons vinegar
1/2 teaspoon sugar
1/4 teaspoon salt

Combine potatoes, bacon, and onions in a bowl. Combine the
dressing ingredients in a shaker jar. Just before serving, pour
dressing over the potatoes, and toss. Serve at room temperature.
Recipe is for 8 servings. It works well to use half of the potato
mixture and half of the dressing for 2 meals of 4 servings each.

Calories per 1/2-cup serving: 94
Fat: 3 g.
Cholesterol: 2 mg.
Sodium: 92 mg.

For exchange diets, count: 1 starch, 1/2 fat

German Red Cabbage

Preparation time: 25 minutes
Yield: 8 1-cup servings

★ ★ ★

---

1 head red cabbage
1 cup water
1/2 cup chopped onion
1 small apple, chopped
3 bay leaves
1/4 cup vinegar
2 tablespoons brown sugar
4 slices bacon, broiled crisp and crumbled

Coarsely shred cabbage, and place in 3-quart saucepan with water, onion, apple, and bay leaves. Bring to a boil, and cook for 12 to 15 minutes. Drain in a colander, and remove bay leaves. Transfer to a serving bowl, and add vinegar, sugar, and bacon. Mix well, and serve immediately.

Calories per 1-cup serving: 92
Fat: 2 g.
Cholesterol: 3 mg.
Sodium: 70 mg.

For exchange diets, count: 2 vegetable, 1 fat

Green Beans with Garlic Dressing

Preparation time: 25 minutes
Yield: 4 1-cup servings

4 cups fresh or fresh frozen green beans
1/2 cup reduced-calorie French dressing
1/2 teaspoon garlic powder
2 tablespoons minced onion
1/4 teaspoon oregano

Cook beans until tender. Meanwhile, combine dressing, garlic, onion, and oregano in a shaker container. Transfer beans to a serving bowl. Toss beans and dressing. Serve immediately.

Calories per 1-cup serving: 71
Fat: 1 g.
Cholesterol: <1 mg.
Sodium: 150 mg.

For exchange diets, count: 3 vegetable

Garlic Cheese Potatoes

Preparation time: 30 minutes
Yield: 8 3/4-cup servings

★ ★ ★

---

4 large Yukon Gold potatoes, peeled and
   cut into cubes
1/2 cup nonfat cottage cheese
1/2 cup nonfat evaporated milk
2 teaspoons minced garlic
1/2 teaspoon salt

In a medium saucepan, cover potatoes with cold water, and
bring to a boil. Cook for 15 minutes until potatoes are tender.
Meanwhile, combine cottage cheese, milk, garlic, and salt in a
blender, and process smooth. Drain potatoes and return them to
the saucepan. Add cheese mixture to the potatoes, and beat the
potato and cheese mixture until fluffy with an electric mixer.

Calories per 3/4-cup serving: 92
Fat: 0
Cholesterol: 1 mg.
Sodium: 153 mg.

For exchange diets, count: 1 starch

Herbed Peppers and Potatoes

Preparation time: 20 minutes
Yield: 8 3/4-cup servings

1 tablespoon soft margarine
1/4 teaspoon salt
1/4 teaspoon garlic powder
1/4 teaspoon thyme leaves
1/8 teaspoon pepper
6 large potatoes, washed, quartered, and
  cut into wedges
1 red pepper, seeded and diced
1 green pepper, seeded and diced

Place margarine in a 2-quart microwave-safe casserole dish. Microwave on high power for 30 seconds. Add all remaining ingredients, and toss to mix. Cover and microwave on high power for 8 minutes, stopping cooking twice to stir the mixture.

Calories per 3/4-cup serving: 119
Fat: 1 g.
Cholesterol: 0
Sodium: 85 mg.

For exchange diets, count: 1 vegetable, 1 starch

Oven Roasted Fall Vegetable Medley

Preparation time: 1 hour, 10 minutes
Yield: 8 1-cup servings

---

6 parsnips, peeled, halved lengthwise,
  then cut into chunks
3 large carrots, scrubbed clean and cut
  into chunks
1 large red onion, peeled and sliced thin
1 teaspoon minced garlic
1 tablespoon dried rosemary
1 tablespoon dried thyme
1 tablespoon olive oil
Salt and pepper as desired

Preheat oven to 400°F. Mix vegetables and spices together in a large roasting pan. Dot mixture with olive oil, and roast uncovered for 1 hour. Stir twice during baking. Add salt and pepper if desired.

Calories per 1-cup serving: 112
Fat: 2 g.
Cholesterol: 0
Sodium: 19 mg. without salt

For exchange diets, count: 1 vegetable, 1 starch

Rhonda's Stuffed Squash

Rhonda Walters shares this low-fat treat for fall.
Preparation time: 50 minutes
Yield: 8 1/2-squash servings

1/2 pound ground pork
2 ribs celery, finely chopped
2 green onions, chopped
1 green pepper, seeded and diced
1 teaspoon dried thyme
1 teaspoon marjoram
1/3 cup fat-free Parmesan cheese
1 cup nonfat sour cream
4 acorn squash, washed, cut in half, and
   seeded

Preheat oven to 375°F. In a medium skillet, brown pork with celery, onions, and pepper for 8 minutes over high heat. Drain well. Return pork to the pan and mix in spices, Parmesan cheese, and sour cream. Meanwhile, place squash halves in the microwave, and cook on high power for 10 minutes. Place squash on a baking pan, stuff with pork mixture, and bake for 30 minutes or until the squash is tender.

Calories per 1/2-squash serving: 183
Fat: 4 g.
Cholesterol: 21 mg.
Sodium: 76 mg.

For exchange diets, count: 1 lean meat,
1 vegetable, 1 1/2 starch

Rice Creole

Preparation time: 30 minutes
Yield: 4 1-cup servings

3 cups no-added-salt tomato juice
1/2 cup quick rice
1/4 teaspoon salt (optional)
1/4 teaspoon pepper
1/4 cup chopped onion
1/4 cup chopped celery
2 slices bacon, broiled crisp and crumbled

Combine all ingredients in a 2-quart baking dish. Microwave for 20 minutes on medium power until the mixture has thickened. Serve in bowls as a side dish. May simmer uncovered on stove-top for 35 minutes, instead of using microwave method, if you prefer.

Calories per 1-cup serving: 125
Fat: 2 g.
Cholesterol: 3 mg.
Sodium: 180 mg. with salt; 58 mg. without salt

For exchange diets, count: 1 vegetable, 1 starch

Sweet Onion Soufflé

Preparation time: 65 minutes
Yield: 8 3/4-cup servings

Nonstick cooking spray
1 tablespoon soft margarine
3 medium sweet or yellow onions, thinly
    sliced
3 eggs or 3/4 cup egg substitute
1 cup evaporated skim milk
1 cup nonfat sour cream
1/4 teaspoon salt
1/4 teaspoon pepper
4 ounces nonfat cheddar cheese, shredded
1 green onion, diced

Preheat oven to 450°F. In a large skillet, melt margarine over
medium heat. Add onion, and cook for 5 minutes. In a large mixing bowl, beat eggs with milk and sour cream. Stir in salt, pepper, and cheese. Fold in cooked onions. Transfer to a soufflé dish
that has been sprayed with cooking spray. Sprinkle green onion
on top. Bake for 10 minutes, then reduce temperature to 350°F.
and continue baking for 30 more minutes. Remove soufflé from
the oven, and let stand for 10 minutes before serving.

Calories per 3/4-cup serving: 82
Fat: 1 g.
Cholesterol: 65 mg.
3 mg. with egg substitute
Sodium: 140 mg.

For exchange diets, count: 1 starch

Anita's Pretty Fruit Cups

*This recipe comes from a cook
for all seasons, Anita Schmelzer.
Preparation time: 2 hours
Yield: 4 1-cup servings*

---

1 cup boiling water
3 ounces reduced-calorie lemon gelatin
3 ounces frozen orange juice concentrate
1 medium banana, sliced
1/2 cup mandarin orange slices
1/2 cup crushed pineapple, drained

Pour boiling water over gelatin in a medium bowl. Stir to dissolve gelatin. Add orange juice concentrate. Stir to mix, then refrigerate for 1/2 hour until partially set. Fold in bananas, oranges, and pineapple. Pour into 4 tall glass dessert dishes. Chill until set.

Calories per serving: 105
Fat: 0
Cholesterol: 0
Sodium: 3 mg.

For exchange diets, count: 2 fruit

Speed Alert: This recipe requires 2 hours for gelatin to set.

Apple Pie with Crumb Topping
Preparation time: 50 minutes
Yield: 10 slices

★ ★ ★

6 Golden Delicious apples, peeled, cored,
and sliced thin
1/4 cup sugar
1 teaspoon cinnamon
1/4 teaspoon nutmeg
1/4 teaspoon salt
1 9-inch prepared shortbread pie crust
Topping:
1/2 cup brown sugar
1/2 cup flour
1/2 teaspoon ground nutmeg
3 tablespoons soft margarine

Preheat oven to 400°F. Combine apples with sugar and spices in
a mixing bowl. Pour into the shortbread crust. In a small mixing
bowl, mix the ingredients for the topping until they are crumbly.
Sprinkle crumb topping evenly over the apples. Bake for 35 minutes or until filling is bubbly, then transfer to a wire rack to cool.

Calories per slice: 233
Fat: 6 g.
Cholesterol: 0 mg.
Sodium: 165 mg.

For exchange diets, count: 2 fruit, 1 starch, 1 fat

Desserts

Buttermilk Lemon Pie in the Microwave

Preparation time: 20 minutes
Chilling time: 3 hours
Yield: 10 slices ·

★ ★ ★

1 9-inch reduced-fat prepared graham
   cracker crust
Filling:
1 1/2 cups sugar
3 tablespoons cornstarch
2 cups buttermilk
4 eggs or 1 cup liquid egg substitute
1/2 cup fresh squeezed lemon juice
1 tablespoon finely grated lemon peel
Garnish:
Sliced strawberries or peaches

Combine ingredients for the filling in order given in a large mixing bowl, beating well with an electric mixer after each addition. Microwave on high power for 12 minutes, or until mixture is thickened, stopping to stir twice during cooking. Pour into the pie crust, and chill for 3 hours. Garnish the top of the pie with berries or peaches.

Calories per slice: 245
Fat: 5 g.
Cholesterol: 87 mg. with egg;
2 mg. with substitute
Sodium: 213 mg.

For exchange diets, count: 1 starch, 1 skim milk,
1 fruit, 1/2 fat

Speed Alert: This recipe requires 3 hours for chilling.

Chocolate Espresso Angel Food Cake
Preparation time: 55 minutes
Yield: 12 servings

1/4 cup slivered almonds
1 two-step angel food cake mix
Water
3 tablespoons unsweetened cocoa
2 teaspoons instant espresso granules

Preheat oven to 375°F. Sprinkle almonds in the bottom of the angel food cake pan. Beat egg white mixture (first step of the mix) with water according to package directions until egg whites form stiff peaks. Mix envelope of flour (second step) with cocoa and espresso in a mixing bowl. Carefully fold the dry ingredients into the egg whites according to package directions. Bake for 35 minutes. Cool the cake upside down until cool to the touch, then remove from the pan using a narrow metal spatula to loosen the cake from the sides of the pan.

Calories per serving: 157
Fat: 2 g.
Cholesterol: 0
Sodium: 258 mg.

For exchange diets, count: 2 starch

Double Chocolate Chip Cookies

Preparation time: 30 minutes
Yield: 36 cookies

★ ★ ★

1/4 cup soft margarine
1/4 cup nonfat cream cheese
1/3 cup sugar
1/2 cup brown sugar
1 tablespoon vanilla
1 cup flour
1/2 cup unsweetened cocoa
1/4 teaspoon salt
1/4 cup reduced-fat chocolate chips

Preheat oven to 350°F. In a medium mixing bowl, cream margarine, cream cheese, sugar, and brown sugar. Beat in vanilla. In a small mixing bowl, stir together flour, cocoa, and salt. Mix the dry ingredients with the margarine and sugar mixture. Fold in chocolate chips. Form dough into small balls, and place on 2 nonstick cookie sheets. Dip the bottom of a glass into sugar, and use to press down each cookie. Bake for 8 minutes until the cookies are slightly puffed up. Remove from the oven and allow to cool on the sheet for 5 minutes before transferring to a wire rack to cool completely.

Calories per cookie: 55
Fat: 1 g.
Cholesterol: 0
Sodium: 24

For exchange diets, count: 1 fruit

Desserts

Fat-Free Tapioca

Preparation time: 15 minutes
Cooling time: 2 hours
Yield: 6 servings

---

3 tablespoons instant tapioca
2 cups skim milk
1/4 cup liquid egg substitute
3 tablespoons sugar
1 egg white
2 tablespoons sugar
1 teaspoon vanilla or almond flavoring
Garnish:
Chocolate thin mint candy

In a medium saucepan, mix together tapioca, milk, egg substitute, and 3 tablespoons of sugar. Let stand for 5 minutes. Meanwhile, beat egg white in a small bowl with electric mixer on high speed until foamy. Gradually add remaining 2 tablespoons sugar, beating until soft peaks form. Set aside. Cook tapioca and milk mixture over medium heat until mixture comes to a full boil. Then remove from the heat, and fold in egg white mixture and vanilla. Cool for 20 minutes at room temperature or in the refrigerator, then stir again, and portion into 6 dessert dishes Refrigerate at least 1 1/2 hours before serving. Garnish with a chocolate thin mint candy.

Calories per 1/2-cup serving: 97
Fat: 0
Cholesterol: 0
Sodium: 60 mg.

For exchange diets, count: 1 fruit, 1/2 skim milk

Speed Alert: This recipe requires 2 hours to chill.

Fresh Fruit Soup

Preparation time: 45 minutes
Yield: 8 1-cup servings

---

3 tablespoons minute tapioca
2 tablespoons sugar or substitute
1 cup water
6 ounces frozen orange juice concentrate
16 ounces frozen strawberries without
    sugar
1 small can mandarin oranges

Combine tapioca, sugar, and water in a saucepan, and allow to stand for 5 minutes. Then cook until clear. (If using sugar substitute, add to tapioca after cooking.) Add juice concentrate, strawberries, and oranges. Chill for 30 minutes. This dessert keeps well covered and refrigerated for 3 days.

Calories per 1-cup serving: 144
132 with sugar substitute
Fat: <1 g.
Cholesterol: 0
Sodium: 4 mg.

For exchange diets, count: 2 fruit

Fruit Crunch for Ice Milk and Sherbet
Preparation time: 60 minutes
Yield: 8 servings, 2 tablespoons each

---

1 tablespoon margarine
1 cup wheat germ
2 tablespoons sugar
1/2 teaspoon cinnamon
1 tablespoon grated orange or lemon rind

Preheat oven to 200°F. Melt margarine and pour in bottom of a pie pan. Add wheat germ, sugar, cinnamon, and rind. Mix well, and bake for 45 minutes, stirring twice during baking. Store cooled crunch mix in a covered container. Serve over sherbet or ice milk.

Calories per 2-tablespoon serving: 78
Fat: 3 g.
Cholesterol: 0
Sodium: 17 mg.

For exchange diets, count: 1/2 starch, 1/2 fat

Fruit Plate with Strawberry Dip

Preparation time: 20 minutes
Yield: 4 1/2-cup servings

---

1 1/2 cups low-fat cottage cheese
1/3 cup sugar or equivalent sugar
   substitute
1 teaspoon almond flavoring
1/2 cup diced strawberries, drained

Assorted fruits for dipping such as: chunks of pineapple or bananas, or wedges of peaches, apples, kiwifruit, or pears. Combine cottage cheese, sugar or substitute, almond flavoring, and berries in a blender. Process smooth. Transfer to a small, pretty serving bowl. Place bowl on a large plate with fruit selections around the bowl.

Calories per 1/2-cup serving of dip with sugar: 150;
with sugar substitute: 86
Fat: 2 g.
Cholesterol: 7 mg.
Sodium: 344 mg.

For exchange diets, count: 1/2 fruit,
1 1/2 skim milk (using sugar)
With sugar substitute, count: 1/2 fruit,
1/2 skim milk

Kiwi for Company

Preparation time: 30 minutes
Yield: 8 1-cup servings

---

6 kiwifruits, peeled and sliced
8 ounces pineapple chunks in juice
3 bananas, sliced diagonally
1 cup sliced grapes
Dressing:
1 1/2 teaspoons grated orange peel
1/2 teaspoon ginger
1 cup nonfat yogurt
1/4 cup light mayonnaise
2 tablespoons honey

In a large salad bowl, gently mix kiwifruit, pineapple and juice, bananas, and grapes. Cover and refrigerate for 20 minutes, allowing flavors to blend. Combine ingredients for dressing with a whisk in a small mixing bowl. Pour dressing over fruits just before serving. This dessert can be used as a leftover for up to 48 hours.

Calories per 1-cup serving: 153
Fat: 3 g.
Cholesterol: 3 mg.
Sodium: 45 mg.

For exchange diets, count: 2 fruit, 1 fat

Lemon Citron Crisps
Preparation time: 60 minutes
Yield: 72 cookies

3 cups flour
2 teaspoons baking powder
2 tablespoons cinnamon
1 teaspoon cloves
1/2 teaspoon nutmeg
1 cup thinly sliced citron
Grated peel of 1 lemon
4 eggs or 1 cup liquid egg substitute
2 cups sugar

Sift all dry ingredients together. Stir in citron and lemon peel, and set aside. Using an electric mixer and a large mixing bowl, beat eggs and sugar together until very thick. Fold in dry ingredients. Chill dough 30 minutes. Preheat oven to 350°. Roll out dough on floured board. Cut into 72 2-inch by 2-inch squares or Christmas shapes. Bake on greased cookie sheets for 15 minutes. These cookies freeze well. The dough can also be refrigerated for up to 10 days and baked as needed.

Calories per cookie: 51
Fat: <1 g.
Cholesterol: 20 mg. with egg;
0 with substitute
Sodium: 14 mg.

For exchange diets, count: 1/2 starch

Lemon Custard Sauce for Fruit or Cake

Preparation time: 15 minutes
Cooling time: 2 hours
Yield: 8 1/3-cup servings

1/2 cup water
1 cup skim milk
1 package lemon instant pie filling
1 tablespoon finely grated lemon
1 cup nonfat refrigerated lemon yogurt

Mix first 4 ingredients together in a saucepan, and cook over medium heat, stirring constantly until boiling. Boil for 3 minutes, stirring constantly. Remove from heat, and cool to room temperature. Fold in yogurt. Refrigerate at least 1 1/2 hours before serving as a topping for fresh fruit desserts or low-fat cake.

Calories per 1/3-cup serving: 108
Fat: 0
Cholesterol: 0
Sodium: 84 mg.

For exchange diets, count: 1 1/2 skim milk

Speed Alert: This recipe requires 2 hours for cooling.

Low-Fat Chocolate Chip Bars

Preparation time: 35 minutes
Yield: 12 servings

★ ★ ★

---

1 tube refrigerated reduced-fat chocolate
   chip cookie dough
1 cup crisped rice cereal

Preheat oven to 350°F. Remove dough from packaging, and place
in a mixing bowl. Microwave on 50 percent power for 1 minute
to soften the dough. Fold in crisped rice cereal, and pat into an
11 by 7-inch baking pan. Bake for 20 to 24 minutes until golden.
Cool to room temperature, then cut and serve.

Calories per serving: 54
Fat: 22g.
Cholesterol: 2 mg.
Sodium: 66mg.

For exchange diets, count: 1 fruit

Desserts

Low-Fat Granola Apple Crisp

Preparation time: 1 hour
Yield: 8 servings

---

4 tablespoons brown sugar
1 tablespoon flour
2 tablespoons orange juice
1 teaspoon orange peel
1 teaspoon almond extract
1 1/2 teaspoons cinnamon
6 Golden Delicious apples, peeled, cored,
   and sliced thin
1 1/2 cups low-fat granola

Preheat oven to 350°F. In an 8-inch square baking dish, mix together first 6 ingredients in order given, stirring to mix after each addition. Layer apples on top of mixture. Top with granola, and bake for 40 minutes until the apples are tender when pierced with a fork.

Calories per serving: 130
Fat: 1 gm.
Cholesterol: 0
Sodium: 13 mg.

For exchange diets, count: 1 fruit, 1 starch

Desserts

Marinated Fruit on a Platter

Preparation time: 30 minutes
Chilling time: 1 1/2 hours
Yield: 8 3/4-cup servings

---

1 firm banana, peeled and cut into 1 1/2-
   inch chunks
1 Golden Delicious apple, quartered
1 red Delicious apple, quartered
1 Granny Smith apple, quartered
4 pineapple rings
2 fresh oranges, peeled and sliced into
   rings
1 kiwifruit, peeled and sliced
Poppy seed garnish
Marinade:
1 cup white wine
1 tablespoon grenadine
1 can sugar-free 7 Up
2 tablespoons lemon juice
1/2 cup pineapple juice

Combine ingredients for marinade in a 2-quart bowl. Add prepared fruit. Cover and refrigerate for 1 1/2 hours. Remove fruit
to a platter, and sprinkle with poppy seeds.

Calories per 3/4-cup serving: 60
Fat: 0
Cholesterol: 0
Sodium: 25 mg.

For exchange diets, count: 1 fruit

Speed Alert: This recipe requires 1 1/2 hours chilling time.

Oatmeal Crunch Apple Crisp

Preparation time: 45 minutes if microwaved
Yield: 12 1/2-cup servings

★ ★ ★

8 medium apples suited for baking, such
    as McIntosh, Rome, or Jonathans
1 tablespoon lemon juice
Topping:
1/4 cup oatmeal
1/2 cup bran flakes, crushed fine
1/2 cup brown sugar
1/3 cup whole wheat flour
1/3 cup margarine
2 teaspoons cinnamon

Preheat oven to 375°F. (Recipe can also be microwaved if you
prefer.) Core and finely slice apples into an 8 by 11-inch baking
dish. Sprinkle with lemon juice. Combine ingredients for topping
in a 1-quart bowl, using a pastry blender to make a crumbly mixture. Sprinkle the topping over apples. Bake for 45 minutes or
microwave for 18 to 22 minutes until apples are tender.

Calories per 1/2-cup serving: 158
Fat: 6 g.
Cholesterol: 0
Sodium: 69 mg.

For exchange diets, count: 1 fruit, 1 fat, 1 starch

Pear Melba Dessert

Preparation time: 30 minutes
Yield: 4 servings

4 ripe pears
Lemon juice
3 ounces reduced-calorie cream cheese,
    well chilled
2 tablespoons slivered almonds
10-ounce package frozen raspberries
2 tablespoons sugar or equivalent sugar
    substitute
1 tablespoon cornstarch
1/4 cup red wine

Halve and core pears. Peel, if desired. Brush the exposed pear flesh with lemon juice. Arrange 2 pear halves on each of four dessert plates or put all the pear halves on a large serving platter. Shape cream cheese into 8 balls, and dip balls in almonds. Place the cheese balls almond side up in the center of the pear halves, then refrigerate. Combine all remaining ingredients in a saucepan and cook until clear, whisking thick. Chill for 15 minutes in the refrigerator, and serve warm over stuffed pears.

Calories per 2 pear halves: 188
Fat: 8 g.
Cholesterol: 16 mg.
Sodium: 86 mg.

For exchange diets, count: 1 fruit, 1 1/2 fat,
1 starch

Perfect Raspberry Chiffon

Preparation time: 2 1/2 hours
Yield: 8 1/2-cup servings

10-ounce package sweetened frozen
   raspberries
1 tablespoon unflavored gelatin
1/2 cup lukewarm water
4 tablespoons sugar
1 tablespoon flour
2 tablespoons lemon juice
1/3 cup ice water
1/3 cup nonfat dry milk powder
1 tablespoon lemon juice
2 tablespoons sugar

Chill the beaters of an electric mixer and a bowl. Thaw berries
and drain, reserving juice, and saving 8 firm berries for garnish.
Soften gelatin in water. In a saucepan, combine 4 tablespoons
sugar with the flour. Add reserved raspberry juice and softened
gelatin. Stir and heat slowly until sugar is dissolved. Remove
from heat, and add 2 tablespoons lemon juice and the berries.
Cook until thick and syrupy, but not set. In the chilled bowl,
combine ice water and milk powder. Beat until soft peaks form
(3 to 4 minutes). Add 1 tablespoon lemon juice, and beat another
3 to 4 minutes until stiff. Fold in 2 tablespoons sugar, blending
well on low speed. Fold mixture into raspberry gelatin mixture.
Spoon into 8 stemmed glasses, and chill until firm, about 1 1/2
hours. Garnish each serving with a reserved whole berry.

Calories per 1/2-cup serving: 97; Fat: <1 g.
Cholesterol: 1 mg.; Sodium: 28 mg.

For exchange diets, count: 1 1/2 fruit

Pie Crust for All Seasons

Preparation time: 55 minutes
Yield: 1 9-inch crust, 8 slices

★ ★ ★

Nonstick cooking spray
3 egg whites at room temperature
1 cup sugar
1 1/2 teaspoons vanilla
14 squares soda crackers, crushed to
  fine crumbs
1/2 teaspoon baking soda
1/2 cup chopped walnuts

Preheat oven to 325°F. In a medium-sized mixing bowl, beat egg whites until frothy; then gradually add sugar until stiff peaks form. Fold in vanilla, cracker crumbs, soda, and walnuts. Spray a 9-inch pie pan with cooking spray, and transfer egg white mixture to the pan, spreading evenly over the bottom and sides. Bake for 45 minutes. Cool to room temperature, and fill with thickened fruit or skim milk-based puddings.

Calories per 1/8 crust: 143
Fat: 3 g.
Cholesterol: 0
Sodium: 129 mg.

For exchange diets, count: 2 starch

Desserts

Pumpkin Pie

Preparation time: 1 hour, 15 minutes
Yield: 8 slices

★ ★ ★

Crust:
1 1/2 cups (24 squares) graham cracker
    crumbs
1 tablespoon sugar
1 tablespoon melted margarine
Filling:
1 cup soft tofu
1 1/2 cups solid pack pumpkin
1/2 cup sugar
2 tablespoons cornstarch
1/2 cup skim milk
1 egg or 1/4 cup liquid egg substitute
3 teaspoons pumpkin pie spice
1/2 teaspoon salt

Preheat oven to 400°F. Mix ingredients for crust together in a 9-inch pie plate, and press evenly over the bottom and sides. Combine all ingredients for the filling in a blender or food processor until smooth. Pour into pie crust, and bake for 1 hour until set.

Calories per slice: 221
Fat: 7 g.
Cholesterol: 34 mg. with egg;
0 with substitute
Sodium: 147 mg.

For exchange diets, count: 1 fruit, 1 fat,
1/2 skim milk, 1 starch

Rolled Pumpkin Cheesecake

Preparation time: 3 hours
Yield: 18 slices

★ ★ ★

Nonstick cooking spray
3 eggs, slightly beaten, or 3/4 cup liquid
   egg substitute
1 cup sugar
2/3 cup canned pumpkin
3/4 cup flour
1 teaspoon baking powder
2 teaspoons cinnamon
1 teaspoon pumpkin pie spice
1/2 teaspoon salt
1/4 cup walnuts
Filling:
1/2 cup powdered sugar
8 ounces ricotta cheese
2 teaspoons vanilla

Preheat oven to 350°F. Spray a 10 by 15-inch jelly-roll pan with cooking spray, then place a large sheet of wax paper over bottom and sides of pan. In a medium-sized mixing bowl, beat eggs until foamy. Gradually add sugar and pumpkin, mixing well. Sift dry ingredients, and gradually add to pumpkin mixture. Stir in walnuts. Pour batter into prepared pan, and bake for 25 minutes, or just until an inserted toothpick comes out clean. Cool for 45 minutes. Remove cake from pan, tear off wax paper and roll cake in jelly-roll fashion in a towel. Meanwhile, strain liquid from the cheese by placing in a colander for 30 minutes. Using an electric mixer and a small mixing bowl, mix powdered sugar and vanilla into the curds of the ricotta cheese until smooth. Unroll cake and

Continued on next page.

Rolled Pumpkin Cheesecake
(continued)

spread cheese mixture evenly over the cake. Re-roll in jelly-roll
fashion, and cover with plastic wrap. Refrigerate at least 1 1/2
hours before serving. Slice and serve.

Calories per slice: 148
Fat: 3 g.
Cholesterol: 50 mg.
Sodium: 29 mg.

For exchange diets, count: 1 1/2 starch, 1/2 fat

Speed Alert: Recipe takes 3 hours.

Desserts

Sharon B's Whole Wheat Apple Cake

A wonderful baker and my childhood friend,
Sharon Buenger Holdiman gave this recipe to me.
Preparation time: 60 minutes
Yield: 8 servings

Nonstick cooking spray
1/2 cup whole wheat flour
1/2 cup white flour
2 tablespoons wheat germ
1 teaspoon soda
1/2 teaspoon cinnamon
1/4 teaspoon salt
1/4 teaspoon nutmeg
1/4 cup sugar
1/3 cup brown sugar
1/4 cup vegetable oil
1 egg or 1/4 cup liquid egg substitute
2 cups finely chopped peeled apples
1/2 teaspoon vanilla
Powdered sugar

Preheat oven to 350°F. Mix first 7 ingredients together in a small bowl. Set aside. In a medium-sized bowl, cream sugars and oil. Stir in egg, apples and vanilla. Fold in dry ingredients. Pour into an 8-inch square pan that has been sprayed with cooking spray. Bake for 30 minutes until golden brown. Dust with powdered sugar when cool. Serve with vanilla ice milk.

Calories per serving: 214; Fat: 8 g.
Cholesterol: 32 mg. with egg; 0 with substitute
Sodium: 174 mg.

For exchange diets, count: 2 starch, 1 1/2 fat

Tropical Fruit Upside Down Cake

Preparation time: 1 hour, 20 minutes
Yield: 24 servings

★ ★ ★

16-ounce can tropical fruit in juice,
    drained well
1 reduced-fat yellow cake mix
3 eggs or 3/4 cup liquid egg substitute
1 1/4 cups pineapple juice

Preheat oven to 350°F. Place drained fruit over the bottom of a
9 by 13-inch cake pan. In a large mixing bowl, beat cake mix,
eggs, and pineapple juice according to package directions. Pour
over the fruit, and bake for 40 to 45 minutes until cake tests
done with a wooden pick. Cool for 20 minutes, then place a serving plate over the top of the cake and turn upside down, so fruit
shows on the top.

Calories per serving: 110
Fat: 2 g.
Cholesterol: 27 mg. with egg; 0 with substitute
Sodium: 163 mg.

For exchange diets, count: 1 starch, 1/2 fruit

References

★ ★ ★

American Dietetic Association. *Exchange Lists for Meal Planning.* Chicago: American Dietetic Association. 1995.

American Dietetic Association. *Manual of Clinical Dietetics.* Chicago: American Dietetic Association. 1989.

American Dietetic Association. "Position on Fat Replacements." *Journal of the American Dietetic Association* 91:10, 1991, page 1288.

American Heart Association. *How to Read the New Food Label.* Dallas: American Heart Association. 1995.

American Heart Association Diet, *An Eating Plan for Healthy Americans.* Dallas: American Heart Association. 1988.

American Institute for Cancer Research *Dietary Guidelines to Lower Cancer Risk.* Washington, D.C.: American Institute for Cancer Research. 1996.

American Institute for Cancer *Research Newsletter.* "Pack It Up! Healthful Picnic Fare." Washington, D.C.: American Institute for Cancer Research. Summer, 1995.

American Institute for Cancer Research. *Healthy Eating Away from Home.* Washington, D.C.: American Institute for Cancer Research. 1996.

Dairy Council Digest. *The 1995 Dietary Guidelines.* Chicago: National Dairy Board. 67:2, 1996, page 7

Diet, Nutrition and Cancer Prevention: *The Good News.* National Institutes of Health, U.S. Department of Health and Human Services. 1987.

Franz, Marion. *Fast Food Facts.* Minneapolis: Chronimed Publishing. 1987.

Howe, John P. "Intake of Dietary Calcium to Reduce Incidence of Osteoporosis." *Report of the Council on Scientific Affairs to the American Medical Association.* 1995.

National Dairy Board. *Low-Fat Foods for Low-Cholesterol Diets.* Chicago: 1991.

National Live Stock and Meat Board. *Put Some Sizzle in a Healthy Diet.* Chicago. 1993.

Netzer, Corrine. *The Complete Book of Food Counts.* New York: Dell Publishing. 1988.

Oldways Preservation and Exchange Trust. *Mediterranean Diet Pyramid.* Cambridge, MA, 1996.

Pennington, Jean and Church, Helen. *Food Values.* New York: Harper and Row. 1980.

Procter and Gamble. *Canola Oil* Data on File, 1988.

Reeves, J.B. *Composition of Foods, Agriculture Handbook No. 8-4.* Washington, D.C. USDA, 1979.

Smith, Karen. *Sat. ...Fat, Keeping Track.* Iowa City, Iowa: Lipid Disorders Training Center, 1993.

Steinmuller, Patti. "Dietary Intervention in Cardiovascular Disease." *Diet Therapy,* USA. Iowa City, Iowa, 1993.

Willet, Walter et al. "Intake of Trans Fatty Acids and Risk of Coronary Heart Disease Among Women." *Lancet* 241:5. 1994, page 581.

United States Department of Agriculture. *Cholesterol Content of Eggs.* 1989.

United States Department of Agriculture and Food Marketing Institute. *The Food Guide Pyramid.* Hyattsville, MD. 1992.

Index

★ ★ ★

accompaniments, 66-68
activity, 23-24
Almond Chicken with Vegetables, 317-318
American Cancer Society, 3-4
American Heart Association, 6-7, 8
Anita's Pretty Fruit Cups, 371
Antipasto Salad, 103
appetizers, 83-91, 234, 236-239, 241, 243-244, 246-251
Apple Glazed Pork Kabobs, 342
Apple Pie with Crumb Topping, 372
Apple Stuffing, 355
apple cake, whole wheat, 393
apple crisp,
    low-fat granola, 384
    oatmeal crunch, 386
Apricot Muffins, 94
artichoke dip, crab and, 85
Asparagus Chef Salad, 125
Asparagus Vinaigrette, 104
Autumn Morning Buns, 266-267

bacon crunch, spinach and, 305-306
Baked Burrito, 126
Baked Carrots and Sprouts, 356
Baked Potato Burrito, 290-291
baked beans, summer, 194-195
baked potato supper, 295
bakery items, selecting, 32
baking items, selecting, 38-39
banana bread, sour cream, 278
banana split, brownie, 201
Barbecued Shrimp, 157
bars, low-fat chocolate chip, 383
Basil Flavored Oil for Stir-Fry, 319

Bayou Fish Stew, 127
Bean 'n Bacon Casserole, 292
Bean Casserole Olé, 128
bean casserole,
    fifteen minute, 136
    savory black, 304
bean dip, three-minute, 249
bean salad, lean, 113
bean soup,
    Michigan, 259
    smoky, 264
bean stir-fry, pork and black, 146
beans with garlic dressing, green, 364
beans, hoppin' John, 298
beef entrées, 177, 180-183, 343-347, 349-350, 354
beef kabobs, three pepper, 181
beef roast, brushed, 343
beef stroganoff, Iowa, 344
Beefy Mushroom and Barley Soup, 252
beverages, 92-93, 235, 240, 242, 245
Black Bean and Cheese Nachos, 234
Blue Cheese Dip for Veggies, 83
Blueberry and Pineapple Dessert Cups, 199
Blueberry Lemon Loaf, 95
bottled foods, selecting, 34
Bowtie Pasta Salad, 129
bran crunchies, oat, 214-215
bran muffins, applesauce, 270
breads, 94-102, 266-278
    selecting, 32
breadsticks, decorated, 238
breakfast menus, 78-79, 228-229

breakfasts, low-fat, 53-54
Brewing the Best Coffee, 235
Bridge Club Dieter's Treat, 200
Broccoli and Cheese Enchiladas, 130
Broccoli Rice Casserole, 357-358
broccoli salad, crunchy, 283
Broiled Salmon Steaks, 158
Broiled Tuna Basted with Pineapple
  Sauce, 159
Brownie Banana Split, 201
brownies, zucchini, 224
Brushed Beef Roast, 343
buns, autumn morning, 266-267
burrito, baked, 126
Buttermilk Lemon Pie in the
  Microwave, 373
buttermilk bread, summer herb, 102

cabbage,
  escalloped, 185
  German red, 363
Cajun Fish on the Grill, 160
cake,
  angel food, chocolate espresso,
    374
  lemon poke, 209
  tropical fruit upside down, 394
calcium-rich foods, 53
California Blend Cream Soup, 253
calories, fat and, 17, 25-26
canapés, Christmas tree, 237
cancer risks, reducing, 3-4
candy, selecting, 40
canned foods, selecting, 34-35
carbohydrate counting, 74
Carolyn's Veggie Pilaf, 359
Carrot Marinade, 105
carrots and sprouts, baked, 356
carrots, wrapped, 251
carry out food, selecting, 47-48
casseroles, 128, 133, 135, 142, 149,
  151, 155-156, 292-294, 297, 304,
  305-309, 357-358
Cathy's Cheese Pepper Bread, 268
Cauliflower Salad for Everyone, 279
cereals, selecting, 39-40
cheese ball, cheddar, 89

cheese pepper bread, Cathy's, 268
cheese supper bread, onion, 100
cheeseburgers, tortilla, 182
Cheesecake with Fruit Sauce, 203
cheesecake,
  coffee lovers', 202
  lemon with raspberry topping,
    206-207
  rolled pumpkin, 391-392
chef salad, asparagus, 125
Chestnut Chicken and Rice, 293
chestnut salad, chicken, 131
Chicken and Rice Soup, 254
Chicken Breast Midwest, 320
Chicken Cacciatore, 321
Chicken Chestnut Salad, 131
Chicken Divan, 161
Chicken Stroganoff, 322
chicken and rice, chestnut, 293
chicken casserole, make ahead
  cheesy, 142
chicken marinade, orange teriyaki,
  170
chicken marsala, 332
chicken salad, curried, 132
chicken sandwich, marinated
  Mexican, 299
chicken soup, cock-a-leekie, 256
chicken stew, spicy, 263
chicken with cheese, gourmet, 163
chicken with vegetables, almond,
  317-318
chicken,
  cornflake, 162
  lemon, 166
  pecan crusted, 171
  pineapple, 328
chiffon, perfect raspberry, 388
Chili Cheese Brunch Bake, 294
Chili Dip with Potato Skins, 236
Chili Flavored Oil for Stir-Fry, 326
chili,
  chunky beef, 255
  shopper's, 262
chilies, cornbread with, 96
Chinese foods, selecting, 35

Chocolate Espresso Angel Food
Cake, 374
chocolate mix, hot, 245
cholesterol risks, 6
cholesterol,
blood, 5-15
dietary, 13, 14 (table)
chowder with bacon, vegetable, 265
Christmas Stuffing, 360
Christmas Tree Canapés, 237
Chunky Beef Chili, 255
Cindy's Lasagna Salad, 140
Cock-a-Leekie Soup, 256
Cocktail Crab Dip, 84
Cocktail Meatballs, 239
cocktail, dilly, 242
cod, Mediterranean, 167
Coffee Lovers' Cheesecake, 202
coffee cake, orange-glazed, 274-275
coffee, brewing the best, 235
Cold Sweet 'n Sour Vegetables, 280
coleslaw,
easy fat-free, 109
sweet and sour apple, 285
Tex-Mex, 123
condiments, selecting, 34
cookies,
double chocolate chip, 375
selecting, 40
corn bread, herbed, 273
corn main dish, Mexican, 301
corn, scalloped, 192
Cornbread with Chilies, 96
Cornflake Chicken or Fish, 162
Crab and Artichoke Dip, 85
crab dip, deviled, 241
crab with vegetables, hot, 139
crackers, selecting, 40
Cranapple Bread, 269
Cranberry Fizz, 240
Cranberry Salad, 281
cream soup substitute, Mary's, 300
Creamy Cucumber Salad Dressing,
106
Creamy Garlic Salad Dressing, 282
Creamy Strawberry Squares, 204
crepes, turkey, 312-313

crisps, lemon citron, 381
crunch, fruit, for ice milk and
sherbet, 378
Crunchy Broccoli Salad, 283
crust, pie, 389
low-fat, 211
cucumber salad dressing, creamy,
106
Cucumbers with Honey Dressing,
107
cucumbers,
old-fashioned, 116
sweet and sour, 288
Cumin Flavored Oil for Stir-Fry, 323
Curried Chicken Salad, 132
Curry Flavored Oil for Stir-Fry, 323
custard sauce, lemon, 382

dairy products, selecting, 37-38
Decorated Breadsticks, 238
Deep Dish Pizza, 133
deli foods, selecting, 32
desserts, 68-70, 199-224, 372-394
Deviled Crab Dip, 241
diabetes, 71-74
Dietary Guidelines for Americans, 2-3
dietary fats, 12 (table), 18-20 (table)
Dilly Cocktail, 242
dinner menus, 76-77, 226-227
dip with potato skins, chili, 236
dip,
blue cheese, for veggies, 83
cocktail crab, 84
crab and artichoke, 85
deviled crab, 241
three-minute bean, 249
Double Chocolate Chip Cookies, 375
doughnuts, baked, 271-272
dressing,
honey, cucumbers with, 107
Italian, 118
pineapple in poppy seed, 216
salad,
creamy cucumber, 106
creamy garlic, 282

lemon and basil, 114
selecting, 34

Easter Salad, 108
Easy Fat-Free Coleslaw, 109
Easy Seafood Salad, 134
Eggplant and Tomato Parmesan, 184
Eggs for a Bunch, 135
Eight Minute Fat-Free Baked Potato Supper, 295
enchiladas,
broccoli and cheese, 130
vegetable, 316
entrée sauces, selecting, 36
Escalloped Cabbage, 185
exchanges, food, 71-73 (table)
exercise, 23-24
calorie expenditure (table)

Fabulous French Bread, 97
Fancy Applesauce Bran Muffins, 270
Fancy Marinated Tomatoes, 110
fast food, selecting, 43-45
fat consumption guidelines, 3
fat replacements, 29-30 (table)
fat,
calories and, 17, 25-26
dietary, 11-14, 18-20 (table)
saturated, 8-9 (table), 10, 11
types of, 11
Fat-Free Frozen Fruit Cups, 205
Fat-Free Tapioca, 376
Fettuccini Low-Fat Alfredo, 296
Fifteen Minute Bean Casserole for Potluck, 136
Fish and Potato Bake, 325
fish creole, white, 173
fish on the grill, cajun, 160
fish seasoning blends, 168-169
fish stew, bayou, 127
fish,
cornflake, 162
selecting, 33
Food Guide Pyramid, 4, 74
food exchanges, 71-73 (table)
food records, 21-22

Fred's Fantastic Baked Donuts, 271-272
French bread, fabulous, 97
Fresh Fruit Soup, 377
Fresh Mushroom Soup, 86
Fresh Spinach with Lemon and Garlic, 186
Fresh Tomato Soup, 258
frozen foods, selecting, 36-37
Fruit Crunch for Ice Milk and Sherbet, 378
Fruit Plate with Strawberry Dip, 379
Fruit Stuffing, 361
fruit cups,
Anita's pretty, 371
fat-free frozen, 205
fruit dip, lemon fluff, 88
fruit juices, selecting, 37
fruit on a platter, marinated, 385
fruit salad,
Mountain Dew, 284
tangy cabbage and dried, 286
fruit soup, fresh, 377

Garden Pizza, 137-138
garden salad, Italian, 287
Garlic Cheese Potatoes, 365
Garlic Flavored Oil for Stir-Fry, 326
gazpacho, my favorite, 90
German Potato Salad, 362
German Red Cabbage, 363
Glazed Lemon Muffins, 98
Gourmet Chicken with Cheese, 163
grains, selecting, 35
granola, homemade low-fat, 87
Green Bean and Dilly Stir-Fry, 187
Green Beans with Garlic Dressing, 364
Grilled Pork à l'Orange, 174
Grilled Vegetable Kabobs, 188
grilling, 56-56

halibut, sesame coated, 334
ham balls, savory, 351
Harvest Casserole with Wild Rice, 297

Hawaiian Pork, 176
Herbed Corn Bread, 273
Herbed Peppers and Potatoes, 366
Homemade Low-Fat Granola, 87
Honey Lime Salmon Fillets, 164
Honey of a Waldorf Salad, 111
honey dressing, cucumbers with, 107
Honeydew Whip, 208
Hoppin' John, 298
horseradish crust, salmon in a, 333
Hot Chocolate Mix, 245
Hot Crab with Vegetables, 139

Iowa Beef Stroganoff, 344
Irish Potato Soup, 257
Italian dressing, quick homemade, 118
Italian Garden Salad, 287
Italian Potato Salad, 189
Jambalaya, 327
Jelled Rhubarb Salad, 112

kabob style leftover turkey, 340
kabobs,
    apple glazed pork, 342
    grilled vegetable, 188
    three pepper beef, 181
kitchen gadgets, 41-43
Kiwi for Company, 380
Kiwi Orange Snapper, 165

lasagna casserole, zucchini, 155-156
lasagna salad, Cindy's 140
Layered Summer Salad, 141
Lean Bean Salad, 113
Leftover Turkey, Kabob Style, 340
legumes, selecting, 35
Lemon and Basil Salad Dressing, 114
Lemon Cheesecake with Fresh Raspberry Topping, 206-207
Lemon Chicken for Company, 166
Lemon Citron Crisps, 381
Lemon Custard Sauce for Fruit or Cake, 382
Lemon Fluff for Fresh Fruits, 88

Lemon Poke Cake, 209
Lemon Strawberry Supreme, 210
Lemon Zucchini, 190
lemon loaf, blueberry, 95
lipid profile, 6-7
London Broil, 345
Love My Cheddar Cheese Ball, 89
Low-Fat Breakfast Sausage, 346
Low-Fat Chocolate Chip Bars, 383
Low-Fat Granola Apple Crisp, 384
Low-Fat Italian Sausage, 347
Low-Fat Nachos, 243
Low-Fat Pie Crust, 211
Low-Fat Popcorn, 246
low-fat foods, selecting, 27-29, 31-41 (table)
lunch menus, 78-79, 228-229
lunches, bag, low-fat, 55-56

main-dish salads, 125, 129, 130-132, 134, 139-141, 143-145, 148, 150, 152, 298, 301, 314
Make Ahead Cheesy Chicken Casserole, 142
manicotti, tuna stuffed, 310
marinade,
    carrot, 105
    chicken, orange teriyaki, 170
Marinated Fruit on a Platter, 385
Marinated Loin of Pork, 348
Marinated Mexican Chicken Sandwich, 299
Marinated Mushroom Salad, 115
Marinated Pork Kabobs, 175
Mary's Cream Soup Substitute, 300
Meat Loaves Italiano, 177
meatballs, cocktail, 239
meats, 63-66
    selecting, 32-33
Mediterranean Cod, 167
Mediterranean Diet, 14-15
menus,
    breakfast, 78-79, 228-229
    dinner, 76-77, 226-227
    lunch, 78-79, 228-229
    quick, 57-70
    special occasion, 80-82, 230-233

Mexican Corn Main Dish, 301
Mexican Turkey Salad, 143-144
Michigan Bean Soup, 259
Microwave Minestrone, 260
Mile High Peach Pie, 212-213
minestrone, microwave, 260
molded salad, twenty calorie, 122
monounsaturated fat, 11
Mountain Dew Fruit Salad, 284
muffins,
    applesauce bran, 270
    apricot, 94
    glazed lemon, 98
    oat bran, 99
mushroom salad, marinated, 115
mushroom soup, fresh, 86
mushrooms, nutty, 244
mustard, salt-free, 179
My Favorite Gazpacho, 90

nachos,
    black bean and cheese, 234
    low-fat, 243
nut bread, pineapple, 276
Nutty Mushrooms, 244

Oat Bran Crunchies, 214-215
Oat Bran Muffins, 99
Oatmeal Crunch Apple Crisp, 386
Old-Fashioned Cucumbers, 116
Old-Fashioned Swiss Steak, 349
omelet, veggie baked, 154
Onion Cheese Supper Bread, 100
onion soufflé, sweet, 370
Orange Teriyaki Marinade for
    Chicken, 170
Orange-Glazed Coffee Cake, 274-275
Oven Roasted Fall Vegetable
    Medley, 367
Overnight Layered Spinach Salad,
    117

packaged dinners, selecting, 36
parfait, spring, 219
Party Meal in a Bowl, 247
Party Popcorn, 91
Party Potato Salad, 191

pasta salad,
    bowtie, 129
    salmon, 148
pasta sauces, selecting, 35-36
pasta, 58-59
    selecting, 35
peach pie, mile high, 212-213
Pear Melba Dessert, 387
Pecan Crusted Chicken, 171
peppers, two step stuffed, 315
Perfect Raspberry Chiffon, 388
picnic foods, low-fat, 54-55
Pie Crust of All Seasons, 389
pie crust, low-fat, 211
pie,
    apple, with crumb topping, 372
    buttermilk lemon, 373
    peach, mile high, 212-213
    pumpkin, 390
    strawberry, 220
pilaf, Carolyn's veggie, 359
Pineapple Chicken, 328
Pineapple in Poppy Seed Dressing,
    216
Pineapple Nut Bread, 276
pineapple dessert cups, blueberry
    and, 199
pineapple sauce, broiled tuna and,
    159
Pizza Rounds, 302
Pizza Salad, 145
pizza,
    deep dish, 133
    garden, 137-138
    pork tortilla, 303
polyunsaturated fat, 11
popcorn,
    low-fat, 246
    party, 91
Popeye's Spinach Croquettes, 248
Poppy Seed Bread, 277
Pork and Black Bean Stir-Fry, 146
Pork Tortilla Pizza, 303
pork à l'Orange, grilled, 174
pork entrées, 174-176, 178

pork kabobs,
  apple glazed, 342
  marinated, 175
pork loin,
  roast, 178
  spicy orange, 352
  Tex-Mex, 353
pork,
  Hawaiian, 176
  marinated loin of, 348
portion sizes, estimating, 10
pot roast, traditional, 354
potato salad,
  German, 362
  Italian, 189
  party, 191
potato skins, chili dip with, 236
potato soup, Irish, 257
potato supper, baked, 295
potatoes,
  garlic cheese, 365
  herbed peppers and, 366
poultry dishes, 161-163, 166, 171-
  172, 317-318, 320-322, 328, 332,
  337-341
poultry seasoning blends, 168-169
poultry, selecting, 33
produce, selecting, 33
Pumpkin Pie, 390
Pumpkin Soup, 261
pumpkin cheesecake, rolled, 391-392
punch for brunch, vitality, 93
punch, summer's here fruit, 92

Quiche Lorraine in a Fat-Free
  Crust, 147
Quick Homemade Italian Dressing,
  118
Quick Italian White Fish Bake, 329
Quick Mexican White Fish Bake,
  330

raspberry chiffon, perfect, 388
Red White and Blue Salad, 119
refrigerated products, selecting, 37-
  38
restaurant food, selecting, 43-46

Rhonda's Stuffed Squash, 368
Rhubarb Crunch, 217
Rhubarb Strawberry Crisp, 218
rhubarb muffins, strawberry, 101
rhubarb salad, jelled, 112
Rice Creole, 369
rice and vegetable salad, wild, 197
rice for picnics, wild, 198
Roast Pork Loin with Cumberland
  Sauce, 178
Roast Venison in the Crockpot, 331
Rolled Pumpkin Cheesecake, 391-
  392
Romantic Chicken Marsala, 332
Rouladen, 350

salad,
  German potato, 362
  Italian potato, 189
  party potato, 191
  wild rice and vegetable, 197
salads, 102-124, 279-289
  main-dish, 125, 129, 130-132,
    134, 139-141, 143-145, 148, 150,
    152
Salmon in a Horseradish Crust, 333
Salmon Pasta Salad, 148
salmon fillets, honey lime, 164
salmon steaks, broiled, 158
Salt-Free Homemade Mustard, 179
sandwich, marinated Mexican
  chicken, 299
saturated fat, 8-9 (table), 10
sausage,
  low-fat breakfast, 346
  low-fat Italian, 347
Savory Black Bean Casserole, 304
Savory Ham Balls, 351
scampi, seafood, 335
Seafood and Summer Vegetables,
  149
Seafood Scampi, 335
seafood entrées, 157-160, 162, 164-
  165, 167, 173, 324-325, 327,
  329-330, 333-336
seafood salad, easy, 134

seasoning blends for poultry of fish, 168-169

seasonings, selecting, 38-39

Sesame Coated Halibut, 334

Sharon B's Whole Wheat Apple Cake, 393

Shoe Peg Tuna Salad, 150

Shopper's Chili, 262

shopping, food, 27-29 (table), 31-41 (table)

Shrimp Casserole, 151

shrimp, barbecued, 157

Sinless Scalloped Corn, 192

Sirloin Barbecue, 180

Smoked Turkey on the Grill, 172

Smoky Bean Soup, 264

snacks, 48, 49-52 (table), 57

selecting, 41

snapper, kiwi orange, 165

soda, selecting, 41

sole, stuffed, 336

soufflé, sweet onion, 370

soup,

beefy mushroom and barley, 252

California blend cream, 253

chicken and rice, 254

cock-a-leekie, 256

fresh fruit, 377

fresh mushroom, 86

fresh tomato, 258

Irish potato, 257

Michigan bean, 259

pumpkin, 261

selecting, 40-41

smoky bean, 264

Sour Cream Banana Bread, 278

Southern Vegetable Medley, 196

Spicy Chicken Stew, 263

Spicy Orange Pork Loin, 352

Spinach and Bacon Crunch, 305-306

spinach croquettes, Popeye's, 248

spinach salad, overnight layered, 117

spinach with lemon and garlic, fresh, 186

Spring Parfait, 219

Spring Turkey Salad, 152

squash, Rhonda's stuffed, 368

Stand Up for Strawberry Pie, 220

stew, bayou fish, 127

stew, spicy chicken, 263

stir-fry,

basil or tarragon flavored oil for, 319

cumin or curry flavored oil for, 323

garlic or chili flavored oil for, 326

green bean and dilly, 187

Strawberries 'n Creme, 222

Strawberry Alaska, 221

strawberry crisp, rhubarb, 218

strawberry pie, 220

strawberry squares, creamy, 204

strawberry supreme, lemon, 210

Strawberry-Rhubarb Muffins, 101

stroganoff,

chicken, 322

Iowa beef, 344

Stuffed Sole, 336

Stuffed Tomatoes, 193

stuffing,

apple, 355

Christmas, 360

fruit, 361

sugar substitutes, selecting, 39

sugar, selecting, 39

Summer Baked Beans, 194-195

Summer Herb Buttermilk Bread, 102

Summer Vegetable Mold, 120

Summer's Here Fruit Punch, 92

Sweet and Sour Apple Coleslaw, 285

Sweet and Sour Cucumbers, 288

Sweet and Sour Tomatoes, 121

Sweet Onion Soufflé, 370

Swiss steak, old-fashioned, 349

Taco Casserole, 307

Tailgate Salad, 289

Tangy Cabbage and Dried Fruit Salad, 286

tapioca, fat-free, 376

Tarragon Flavored Oil for Stir-Fry, 319
Tarragon Turkey, 337
taste perceptions, 1-2
Terrific Tuna Melt, 324
tetrazzini, turkey and mushroom, 311
Tex-Mex Pork Loin, 353
Tex-Mex Slaw, 123
Three Pepper Beef Kabobs, 181
Three-Minute Bean Dip, 249
Tomato Pockets, 250
tomato Parmesan, eggplant and, 184
tomato soup, fresh, 258
tomatoes,
    fancy marinated, 110
    stuffed, 193
    sweet and sour, 121
Tortilla Cheeseburgers, 182
tortilla pizza, pork, 303
tortillas, 60-61
Tortoni Cafetta, 223
Traditional Pot Roast, 354
trans-fatty acids, 12-13
Tropical Fruit Upside Down Cake, 394
Tuna and Noodle Casserole, 308-309
Tuna Stuffed Manicotti, 310
tuna melt, terrific, 324
tuna salad, shoe peg corn, 150
tuna, broiled, 159
Turkey and Mushroom Tetrazzini, 311
Turkey Crepes, 312-313
Turkey Fillets Marinated Three Ways, 338-339
Turkey Roll-Ups, 153
Turkey Salad à l'Orange, 314
Turkey with Orange Raisin Sauce, 341
turkey on the grill, smoked, 172
turkey salad,
    Mexican, 143-144
    spring, 152
turkey,
    leftover, kabob style, 340
    tarragon, 337
Twenty Calorie Molded Salad, 122
Two Step Stuffed Peppers, 315

Vegetable Chowder with Bacon, 265
Vegetable Enchiladas, 316
vegetable kabobs, grilled, 188
vegetable medley,
    oven roasted fall, 367
    Southern, 196
vegetable mold, summer, 120
vegetable salad, wild rice and, 197
vegetables, 61-63
    cold sweet 'n sour, 280
    seafood and summer, 149
Veggie Baked Omelet for Brunch, 154
venison in the crockpot, roast, 331
vinaigrette, asparagus, 104
Vitality Punch for Brunch, 93

Waldorf salad, honey of a, 111
Want More Salad, 124
weight management, 17-24
Western Broil, 183
White Fish Creole, 173
white fish bake,
    quick Italian, 329
    quick Mexican, 330
Wild Rice and Vegetable Salad, 197
Wild Rice for Picnics, 198
wild rice, harvest casserole with, 297
Wrapped Carrots, 251

Zucchini Brownies, 224
Zucchini Lasagna Casserole, 155-156
zucchini, lemon, 190

More from M.J. Smith

Available from Chronimed Publishing

★ ★ ★

---

366 Low-Fat Brand-Name Recipes in Minutes

Here's more than a year's worth of the fastest family favorites using the country's most popular brand-name foods—from Minute Rice to Ore Ida, while reducing unwanted fat, calories, salt, and cholesterol. This timesaving book makes it easy to eat healthfully every day.   Paper, 368 pages, 1-56561-050-4, $12.95

60 Days of Low-Fat, Low-Cost Meals in Minutes

This indispensable book introduces more than 150 delicious, easy-to-make recipes that will help you save time and money while reducing your fat intake—most recipes take less than 30 minutes to prepare and use ingredients that cost less than $10 per meal. It features a 60-day menu plan that includes breakfasts, lunches, dinners, and snacks, shopping lists, and preparation tips; and is complete with nutrition information and exchanges.   Paper, 304 pages, 1-56561-010-5, $12.95

Around the World Low-Fat & No-Fat Meals in Minutes

Here's a sumptuous collection of traditional foods from Greece to Guam—without the traditional fat, calories, and time-consuming preparation. Whether it's Australian Carpetbag Steak or Greek Pasta Salad, here are the recipes for out-of-the-ordinary, quick, and irresistible appetizers, beverages, soups, salads, side dishes, breads, entrées, and desserts for any event—all low- or nonfat.   Paper, 425 pages, 1-56561-085-7, $12.95

Year-Round Low-Fat and No-Fat Holiday
Meals in Minutes
More Than 200 Delicious and Healthy Recipes
for Over 20 Holidays and Special Events

The definitive collection of the traditional holiday foods everyone loves—without the traditional fat, calories, and time-consuming preparation. This indispensable guide is complete with decorating ideas, summer grilling and leftover tips, and convenient ingredient substitutions. Paper, 304 pages, 1-56561-074-1, $12.95

Order by Mail
CHRONIMED PUBLISHING
P.O. BOX 59032
MINNEAPOLIS, MN 55459-9686

Place a checkmark next to the book(s) you would like sent. Enclosed is $_____. (Please add $3.00 to this order to cover postage and handling. Minnesota residents add 6.5% sales tax.) Send check or money order—no cash or C.O.D.S. Prices and availability are subject to change without notice.

Name _____

Address _____

City _____ State _____ ZIP _____

— or —

Order by phone—1-800-848-2793
Please have your credit card ready.

Allow 4 to 6 weeks for delivery.
Quantity discounts available upon request.
Prices and availability subject to change without notice.

Source code: TAA